SERENITY

SERENITY
A Boxing Memoir

RALPH WILEY

HENRY HOLT AND COMPANY / NEW YORK

Published by Henry Holt and Company, Inc.,
115 West 18th Street, New York, New York 10011.
Published in Canada by Fitzhenry & Whiteside Limited,
195 Allstate Parkway, Markham, Ontario L3R 4T8.

Library of Congress Cataloging-in-Publication Data
Wiley, Ralph.
Serenity : a boxing memoir / Ralph Wiley.—1st ed.
p.   cm.
ISBN 0-8050-0670-2
1. Boxing—United States.   2. Wiley, Ralph.   3. Sportswriters—
United States—Biography.   I. Title.
GV1125.W55   1989
070.4'49796'0924—dc 19   88-27282
[B]   CIP

Henry Holt books are available at special discounts
for bulk purchases for sales promotions, premiums,
fund-raising, or educational use. Special editions
or book excerpts can also be created to specification.

For details contact:

Special Sales Director
Henry Holt and Company, Inc.
115 West 18th Street
New York, New York 10011

First Edition

Designed by Katy Riegel
Printed in the United States of America
1   3   5   7   9   10   8   6   4   2

FOR COLEN AND SEAN

Contents

SERENITY

Prologue

I have always considered serenity to be an admirable state of existence. I have pursued serenity and found it elusive. So I have pursued the company of those I thought possessed it in greatest supply; they understand the futilities of worry and strife. The first person I met who had this serenity was my Uncle Charles, who was once a prizefighter. I was only a child, so with childish logic I assumed all prizefighters were serene.

I was right. In spite of their circumstances fighters indeed have serenity to a greater degree than ordinary people. Whether fighters gain their serenity because they face down life and death or because the sense to worry has been knocked clean out of their heads, I don't know. They might lose many things by the time they stop fighting, but they remain serene. So, *Serenity* is a book about fighters—who they are, why they fight, and how it feels to be one.

★

Oakland *Tribune*, November 10, 1977

Expressing a desire to know what it's like to be hit by the world's heavyweight champion brings only mumbled words like "masochist" and the old one-eyebrow-up look. Explaining that one doesn't want to be hit by a champ, one just wants to know how it feels brings hurled epithets like "Imbecile!" and looks usually reserved for residents of a home for the imbalanced. But it is not a bad thing, to want to know.

True, one is answered haughtily, but to want to be on the receiving end of a special delivery right from Ali, Louis, or the Rock isn't drinking from the fount of information. If anything, one may lose the small collection of marbles one has now.

Not bound by the same constraints of ethics and imagination as those that drove George Plimpton to actually raise his hands in defiance to Archie Moore and lose a half-pint of blood in consequence, I found Lou Nova and simply asked him. Yes, Lou Nova, of the Cosmic Punch and the two knockouts over Max Baer. Nova was in the Bay Area to boost the campaign of San Francisco supervisor George Medina and would also serve my own selfish purposes. After all, Nova fought Joe Louis and knows what it's like to be hit by the Brown Bomber, of all people. For six rounds, no less.

"Hiya!" The ex–heavyweight contender smiled up from a booth at Two Jacks Restaurant in downtown Oakland. "Encompass" is a mild word for what his hand did to mine at the moment of formality.

No time for mincing, Lou. I came here for one purpose and for one purpose only. To find out what it's like to be hit by . . . Well, if you'd like to discuss what you're doing these days . . . (One is not anxious to offend even a sixty-two-year-old ex–heavyweight contender. One merely wants to know.)

"I'm living in Hollywood," Nova said while adjusting the ring around his ascot. "I'm traveling, about to hit the college speaking circuit. Kids are into nostalgia these days, you know. They like to hear what it was like in the good old days. I still have an act that I perform at organizational functions and get-togethers. Basically, I do comedy. I played with Shirley MacLaine, you know. And in Carnegie Hall, I had a poetry recital once."

I see. But about being hit by the champ . . .

"Speaking of champs, I could make one out of George Foreman. He just doesn't know how to box. He's like Max Baer. Probably the two most perfectly built athletes I've ever seen. Which probably explains why they never bothered to learn to box. For a hundred thousand dollars, I could show Foreman how to box. I'd show him my Cosmic Punch"— vaguely explained recently as a combination uppercut–sneaky right . . . "and I guarantee he'd be champ."

Ahem. Without stepping on any toes here, Lou, what's it like to be hit on the button by Louis?

"Louis? Why, Louis didn't hit me near as hard as Baer did. Not even close."

Fine, fine. Baer was champ once. How did it feel?

"Well, I'll tell ya. My nervous system was on hold. For weeks after the fight, I was afraid to move my head for fear my neck was broken."

. . . Oh.

★

1
Heavy Socks

My grandmother, bless her heart, landed the first punch against me. She threw a crisply launched short right, but she was not intending real harm; she was most interested in setting my priorities straight. I was distracting at the age of ten, to myself and others, and the weaponry my grandmother had used against me in the past—threatening tones of voice, scowls, peach-tree switches—had failed her. So on an early summer morning in 1962 when I was ten, she hit me with her fist. It was inevitable, I suppose.

I didn't "have my belongings together," and my grandmother didn't want to be late for her first trip in an airplane. A jet, no less. We lived not more than ten minutes by car from the airport on the outskirts of Memphis. The plane was not scheduled to leave for three more hours. I pointed out this time discrepancy to my grandmother, who didn't want to hear it. She was around seventy at the time, so a missed appointment, wasted time, was much more important to her than to me. And she may have been a little fearful. I knew something was wrong. She had never hit me bare-knuckled before. She could have hurt me worse, but she pulled her punch. I realize all this now.

"Stop lollygagging! If you don't straighten up and fly right, I'm going to give a full report on you to your Uncle Charles once we get to California." I came to attention immediately, because any young boy with the brains he was born with deeply respects the distant uncle who was once a prizefighter. On the other hand, my grandmother, Elizabeth Ophelia Taylor, also knew that Charles was the most unassuming and imperturbable of her four sons, the most comfortable uncle for a boy to be around. He was, as far as I had been able to discern on Thanksgivings, the slowest to anger and the quickest to laugh, no matter what the circumstances. He had found the secret of serenity in spite of all the horrors of being an adult.

When my grandmother's children returned to the house they grew up in for Thanksgivings, the girls—my mother, Dorothy, and Aunt Helen, Aunt Minnie Blanche, Aunt Elizabeth, and Aunt Barbara—would trade gales of laughter before commiserating on their troubles, which, as bad as they might have been, were never so grave as those of the turkey, which they prepared and trimmed in a carefully learned fashion. My grandmother's boys—Uncle William (who was called Junior), Uncle Flowers (who was called Brother, or Tank), Uncle Herman, and Uncle Charles were all there on the best Thanksgivings—would sit around telling jokes which became funnier in proportion to the amount of whiskey they consumed, and they emptied fifths at what a reasonable doctor would call an alarming rate. Three uncles were gentlemen, outright dandies if need be. They wore razor cuts and sculpted mustaches. Herman was a mortician in Chicago. Tank was a bon vivant and raconteur on the South Side of the big town. He turned his alcoholism into a career as a rehabilitationist. Junior was perhaps the most efficient maître d' in the history of the Rivermont Hotel in downtown Memphis.

Uncle Charles, whom they all lovingly referred to as Charlie Boy, had a different sort of life, probably as unfathomable to his brothers and sisters as it was enviable to me. At Thanks-

5

giving, he might be dressed in slouchy khaki trousers, with the folds in his white socks lapping down over his brogans like melted candlewax. But his shoulders, which rolled like a champion boxer's, and his belly protested the confinement of a sports jacket. When his brothers and sisters teased him, or asked him to do his hound-dog howl imitation, he would smile good-naturedly and, if necessary, comply. If nothing else, doing the hound-dog howl allowed him to take off his coat.

Once, while mesmerized by this whirl of personalities at Thanksgiving, I had asked Uncle Charles why he suffered this abuse. He laughed loudly, the crow's-feet appearing like cracks in leather in the corners of his shaven face. He nodded toward his brothers and whispered to me, "Ask them who fought their battles for them." Then he laughed again.

This was his idea of a joke. In my youthful mind, I had long since placed Uncle Charles in the same league with Ulysses, D'Artagnan, Superman, and Bruce Benedict, halfback. For my grandmother to threaten to deliver me into the hands of this avenger, though, was precisely what I had in mind. I had business with Charlie Boy. I needed to know the secrets of fighting, the secrets I knew Charlie Boy Taylor possessed. I had begun to have a little trouble at Mt. Pisgah C.M.E. Church.

I could not simply stop going to Mt. Pisgah. Oh, no. My grandfather had been a pastor and presiding elder in Dyersburg, and his widow, Elizabeth, was a pillar of strength for Stewardess Board No. 1 for the remaining twenty-six years of her life. The church stood two blocks from our house. I found out much later that the initials C.M.E. originally stood for Colored Methodist Episcopalians. Whatever a Colored Methodist Episcopalian has at the unknown center of his soul, I have in mine, because I was raised in that environment. But I did try to work around it by the age of nine, when I was known to take walks between the Sunday school and the morning worship and, if possible, finagle an early exit.

It was during one of these walks that a neighborhood boy, one whom I knew already hung around on the corners, had challenged me. "I'll kick your ass," he said. He was a couple of years older but no bigger than I was. He put his hand in his jacket pocket as he spoke, as if something besides his hand might be there. I had no idea of how to respond. There was nothing but air in my jacket pocket. I had no time to consider what motivated him, so I showed him my heels. "Hey!" he yelled. Turned out he was a sociable bully. "I was just playin', but you better learn how to fight soon. One of these days, you'll be going to junior high school," he said.

I considered this while my Sunday school classmate and fellow truant Aubrey Pruitt laughed uproariously. Okay for you, Aubrey, I thought. After I spend two weeks this summer with the great Charlie Boy, we'll see if you can laugh through a busted lip. Then we went back into the church in time to hear the choir sing "In the Land Where We'll Never Grow Old."

So I had this business with my Uncle Charles. My grandmother, my cousins Bucky and Julius, and I rode the silver jet uneventfully to Los Angeles, where Uncle Charles and his wife, Izetta, greeted us with buckets of smiles. Bucky was fourteen then, four years older than Julius and me. He had the budding physique of a football tight end or fullback. I suppose this makes it seem as if I had overlooked my most available boxing instructor. But I was already employed as Bucky's sparring partner, work I neither understood nor enjoyed. Once, when I was eight, Bucky had been my matchmaker. We were picking up our copies of the *Memphis Press-Scimitar* for delivery along our route, which stretched in a distant eight-block radius from our house. A match was suddenly sanctioned by Bucky and his friends between me and a boy not much older than I was. I survived him, but couldn't land any sort of effective punch. Luckily, neither could he.

I felt sure this visit to Uncle Charles would remedy my

7

lack of punching power. We went to their small apartment. My grandmother grabbed a straight-backed dinette chair, sat down, crossed her legs at the ankle, threw her hands in her lap, and began regaling Izetta with stories of Charles's young life, while Charlie Boy reddened, chafed, and finally smiled. My grandmother loved her children, and they loved her, and they all loved hard, so every summer it would be a different clime for us: Chicago; Detroit; Los Angeles; Washington, D.C. Wherever her children settled, she felt, was home. She wouldn't think of not going to see Charlie Boy, even though she had never been in a jet before—or west of St. Louis, for that matter—and even though Uncle Charles's living conditions were always an unknown variable.

In California, I learned to shoot pool left-handed in a neighbor's garage and slaked my thirst with Joe Louis Milk while I figured on ways of getting the key information from Uncle Charles, who was so gregarious and regular that I would forget for hours on end that he once had been a prizefighter. On the Saturday before we left, I was awakened in the wee hours of the morning by a furtive knock on the front door. I saw good kind Uncle Charles answer the door dressed in his skivvies and an undershirt, revealing the scope of his back and the muscle structure beneath his shoulders. In the dim light, he seemed to be made of lead. In one of his great ham fists he held a Stanley claw hammer. He was wiggling it as I might have wiggled a plastic toy. The man said, "Sorry, mister. Wrong house."

The next day I asked Uncle Charles about fighting.

"Uncle Charles," I said, not looking him in the eye. "I . . . uh . . . don't want to get on your nerves . . . I just need to know how to fight."

Charles pulled his head back with the muscles in his neck without bothering to move the rest of his upper torso. He seemed amused by this. "What, boy?" he said.

"Ineedtoknowhowtofight . . . sorta."

"You mean you want to learn to box?"

"Yes sir."

"And you think your Uncle Charles knows how, eh?"

"Yes sir."

"How do you know?"

I had never seen him box. I didn't want him to think anybody had been telling stories behind his back, although they had been and I knew them all.

"Well, Butcher Boy, you already know how to fight. You've got Taylor blood. Besides, everybody knows how to fight, somewhere in 'em. Fightin', that's one thing. Boxin's another. You want to know how to box, you say so." His face moved closer to mine. "Boxin's harder to do," he said. He seemed to contract his vulnerable parts, what few of them there might have been, expanded his arms and shoulders, and bent forward from the waist. He put up his hands. I could see his eyes between his fists. His feet were slightly scissored apart. He rose on the ball of his right foot and lowered himself onto the heel of his left. At the center of this poised mass, his eyes shone most dangerously of all. This was not my Uncle Charles anymore. This was Charlie Boy Taylor, middleweight.

"Were you scared, boy?"

He had broken the trance.

"No sir."

I was an unconvincing liar. Uncle Charles had a good laugh on me before saying, "You got it then, Butch. Boxin's mostly watching the other man. Remember that. What you can see can't hurt you. Now, you shoot your punch like this." He snapped out his right, rolling the hand over with a muscular jerk that was audible in the still air. "Turn your fist. Throw it from behind the shoulder, with the legs, if you can. Then snap it." He threw four or five punches with each hand, stopping each one within a whisker of my immobile nose.

"Tell you what else. Cut the grass twice a week. Cut it good and close. Cut it in the morning, when the dew's down."

Then he let the subject drop. Was that it? I had expected him to turn me into a human buzz saw, but tall grass was not the opponent I had expected. I tried a back-door strategy.

"Who was the greatest boxer, Uncle Charles?"

"Ezzard Charles," he said, launching into a description of the former light-heavyweight champion. "Among the bigger people. I couldn't put nobody ahead of Sugar in the middles. Nobody could. But Ezzard Charles was a master boxer, too." His eyes lit up.

What about Ezzard was so great? Joe Louis was the champion in my grandmother's house. On my trips to the barber shops, I had found that Sugar Ray Robinson was the champion there. You couldn't argue with barbers even if you were of a mind to do so, because if they disagreed with you they could always cut your hair wrong. So the Sugar was the greatest boxer in the barber shop.

Uncle Charles then told me about Jack Johnson. "Li'l Arthur, boy," he said solemnly, referring to the former Galveston stevedore and heavyweight champion. "Li'l Arthur was a great boxer who didn't need to box. Once he hit you, you knew he could kill you if you didn't handle yourself right. Jack never killed nobody in the ring, which showed how great of a boxer he was. He could have."

Charlie Boy's father had told him all about Jack Johnson, and had also been his boxing instructor. Before becoming a minister in west Tennessee, Charlie Boy's father had been one to put up his hands at a smoker here and there. William Harrison Taylor was my grandfather's name. He eventually found Christ and favor in the eye of Elizabeth Flowers, but old Willum never forgot how. My mother had been the first-born, the first of William and Elizabeth's children to survive. They would have eleven more. Most had a tale or two of their father's great temper. He had no truck with insubor-

10

dination. When Uncle Herman jauntily informed my grandfather that he would not be going to college to study the liberal arts, but instead was thinking of getting married and going to mortician's school, Grandpa's reply was a looping overhand right, which missed, largely because Uncle Herman had jumped nearly out of the house to avoid the punch. When my grandfather found out that my Aunt Helen planned to board a truck bound for the endless cotton fields outside Memphis early one morning, he grabbed her arm and said, "I'll be goddamned if one of mine go." My grandfather had once told my mother to sweep off the front porch of the house he had built with his own hands before she ran off to do some personal errands. In her grumblings about this, Ma began sweeping dust over her father's shoes. He was wearing them at the time. "He just gave me this little backhand lick," Ma said. "And I thought the world had ended. I swept carefully after that."

My Aunt Elizabeth was the child who most resembled her father, with saffron skin and green-gray eyes. And even she felt the rod from her father after she and Uncle Flowers had come home past midnight after a supposed afternoon at the movies. Uncle Tank had left her at the Airways Theater with strict orders to stay there until he returned, whereupon he left for some dubious activities on Beale Street. Lappa was thirteen at the time. When they returned, after midnight, they took their whippings. "When he hit me, I saw that it broke his heart," said Aunt Elizabeth. "Then he told me, 'Your sympathy for others will be your downfall.' "

My mother said Charlie Boy was always the fighter. "They always knew when Charles Taylor was coming," she once told me. As a group, the Taylors were considered genteel folk, as I have gathered—genteel in the context of the environment of the Orange Mound neighborhood in Memphis in the 1930s and '40s. There was something to strive for, somewhere far off into the future, and they lived accordingly. They lived to

11

live another day. All except Charlie Boy. He would do a day's worth of hard chores and get a nickel in return. He would consider this coin in his palm, then walk down the street until he was out of sight and fire the nickel away, not even bothering to look and see where it landed. My grandfather had shown Charles the rudiments of fistfighting, and Charles took these lessons to heart. One day he came home from Hamilton High School after losing a schoolyard fight. He had been hit in the gut to decide it. W. H. Taylor looked at his boy's dusty face and said, "Well, you'll be in shape next time, won't you?" Charles looked at his father and said, "It'll be a long time before I lose another one." So it was all laid down and done for him from there.

Uncle Charles never cared a lick for schooling, Sunday or the weekday variety. Then his father became sick. There was little money, so Charles left home at the age of fifteen and joined the U.S. Army to box and send money home.

Uncle Charles was sent to Japan with Special Services. He fought as a middleweight in '48 and '49. He settled in Detroit after his first tour of duty, and fought professionally. He had five fights, went 3–2. Got $10 a round, fought no longer than ten rounds. Aunt Helen had married and moved to Detroit, where she worked at the post office. She and her family harbored Uncle Charles during this time. She counseled him as he waited for his fights and while he fell into a relationship with a woman who bore him a daughter. Maybe it was the high life he preferred to the regimen of training, or maybe he wasn't all that good, but Charlie Boy Taylor never did set the citizenry of Detroit on its collective ear. In Detroit, if a fighter didn't have the look of a Louis or a Robinson, he didn't stand out.

Aunt Helen saw Charlie Boy fight his last fight in the ring, in Windsor, Ontario. "Charles had put on this little gut and this man hit him in that gut after a few rounds. Charles went down to one knee and just couldn't get up. He didn't look hurt, he looked like he wanted to get up and just couldn't. And for some reason, he smiled."

A friend of his sister steered Charlie Boy to a custodial job. He never cared for the much more profitable automobile assembly lines. "Detroit," Aunt Helen said, "is where Charles learned to run the buffer." Charles reenlisted in the Army in 1951 and served with the field artillery in Korea. In 1961, or thereabouts, he moved to Los Angeles, where he ran the buffer in the halls of public and private schools, the very places he had done his best to avoid. During our summer visits to Los Angeles, he wore gray uniforms. He had married Izetta, who was from Louisiana. Theirs was a wonderfully stormy relationship which has held their mutual interest for the last twenty-odd years.

So I began junior high school unaware of the secret openings he had provided me on boxing matters. I suppose my father could not have done a better job of it, but Bucky, Julius, and I were separated from our fathers, early on. Thereafter, we three boys were known as Butchie Daytime (me), Bucky Evening, and Julius Knight, so dubbed by Uncle Charles. Bucky was four grades farther along than Julius and I, so through my eighth-grade year, Julius and I were known in the neighborhood and at Melrose High School as "Bucky's brothers." We were regarded as untouchables. Bucky had broken a blocking sled with his forearm, in broad daylight, with plenty of witnesses, at Melrose Stadium. After Bucky left college and joined the Navy, the honor of defense for Julius and myself fell into my hands. Julius was known as "Ralph Wiley's brother," and was eminently touchable now. Where Julius was concerned, I had no choice but to fight. I am four months older than my cousin Julius. From the very beginning we had a keen, childlike competition in our little boys' games, races, and wars. But a turning point came. Julius and I were four years old, five, I do not know. A raging fever came over us. I can vaguely recall the hot slice through my brain and the feel of the cool compresses placed soothingly against my flesh. Then I stood in the doorway of our small bedroom, watching my grandmother and her daughters attending to Julius. His fever had simply lasted longer than mine.

From then on, Julius stayed in our childhood. His mind moved forward reluctantly, two years to the ordinary five. He had been like me, slightly better at some things, slightly worse at others. But the fever stopped him, leaving him as if beaten like a prizefighter for many years. I continued to grow and to make friends and mistakes and to have classwork come to me with relative ease. I would come home with all the tales of junior and senior high school, while Julius would come home from his corner of the school in which he had been placed with the rest of the lost causes. He would laugh vibrantly at my smallest jokes. I felt so bad about what had happened to his life that I blocked it out of my mind. But I felt responsible for him.

One day during my freshman year in high school, Julius found me between classes. I saw a fearful look on his face, and then a look of relief at seeing me. He stood in front of me, his chest heaving with exertion. "Who is it?" I asked.

A boy came sauntering down the hall, pointing at Julius, with two other boys laughing and following. I knew this boy was not of the neighborhood. He was a transfer student from another part of town. His name was McKinney. I walked over to him and stood at what I imagined was good hitting distance. Without thinking, I put up my hands.

"Leave him alone. Or fight me."

McKinney launched into a tirade. I noticed that he was backing up. "I'll kick both your asses," he said.

"No you won't. See if you can kick my ass, but leave him alone. Don't say anything else to him."

McKinney walked away ranting. Feeling angry and foolish, I put my hands down. I don't know if he bothered Julius again. I didn't know how to handle the role of avenger.

There were eight boys and twenty-three girls in my original homeroom class of 8-4, the gifted and talented section of the eighth grade. The other seven boys would become my closest friends in high school, and some would stay that way after. One of the boys was named James Leroy Fitzpatrick. We all called him Roy. Roy had an obvious itch to confront me, and I had one to fight him almost from the very moment we laid eyes on each other. "Hey, pigeon toes!" were his first words to me. Roy was a leader, and I supposed he sensed a potential rival in me. Little did he know. If leadership was a personality trait of mine, I was determined to kill it off as soon as possible. Later, Roy would be my college roommate, my lifelong friend. We became acquainted by playing lick-for-lick in the chest in the boys' lavatory.

Maurice Taylor was another one of my original seven male classmates in 8-4. He was a short boy, all of five-five. He could be belligerent at times, but his was a smiling, joshing belligerence, designed to head off problems before they decided to rest on him. It was a good strategy, too. We called him Bull. He liked that name. By the ninth grade, Bull and I were fast friends. One day he came to me and said, "I hear Radio's looking for you." Bull was smiling. When it was said that some fellow was "looking for you" in this context, it meant that prospects were good for a fight. I didn't think that Bull was making this up, as he had already proved himself to be something of a seer. Most everybody likes to watch fights, especially those in which they are not participants, so Bull was smiling. I knew I had done nothing to this Radio, whose Christian name was Peter Joyner. Peter was seventeen; an aberration in an idyllic time, one of those fellows who made you wonder how he got in the vicinity of ninth grade when it was obvious that he had just been discharged, dishonorably, from an eventful career in the Army, or, more likely, the penal farm. Why on earth was he looking for me? For the hell of it, no doubt. This drew two emotions from me: fear, because Peter Joyner was much older, and anger, because it was useful. The school classes were taken to the Crosstown Theater to see *Gone with the Wind*. My eternal debt to Peter is that he kept my mind off the movie. In the crowded lobby, he had made a big show, saying, "I'll get you, smart man!" His lips were pulled back, accentuating a terrible, beveled scar that nearly encircled his right eye. The result of a childhood heater burn—or maybe the result of meeting the wrong end of a broken bottle. I looked into his eyes just as Uncle Charles had suggested. I missed nothing. In fact, rarely has anyone been watched as closely as I watched Peter Joyner for the next several days. Nothing ever happened. He never advanced on me. Later, I found Joyner to be a streetcorner philosopher and budding alcoholic who was not particularly dangerous to me or anyone else unless we stood between him and a pint of wine. Alphonzo Wilson, another one of my homeroom classmates, congratulated me on exposing Peter Joyner. Later, Alphonzo would hit me with a sucker punch while my back was turned in the cloakroom on a rainy day because we were sharing the innocent affections of the same girl. I laughed at him, surprised at my ability to take his best punch, and let him in on the fact that if he wanted to spring on everybody who shared the affections of this particular coquette, he would be fighting all day. Perhaps, I suggested to my old friend Alphonzo, he should start off with the Geech.

The first name on the roll of the accelerated class was Robert Aldridge. Everyone called him Geech or Geechie, so I followed suit. I didn't know this name was insulting. Geech might have been bestowed on Robert with that intention. Robert turned the tables and took the name to heart. He was the second fighter I met, the first I had a chance to study as a peer, in action and in everyday conversation. He was, in two words, my friend.

As far as I knew, Robert had no stable home. He spent

some nights at the home of one of his sisters, he said, but there were nights when he slept on the streets. He was an orphan of life, a street urchin who had been born at the edge of our neighborhood, across Lamar Avenue, on the other side of the shopping center, at the entranceway of the next neighborhood, Castalia, in a misbegotten row of shanties called Rats' Alley, which squatted hopelessly in the shadow of the giant Wayne Feeds grain storage tower.

Robert was short, eventually growing to about five-eight, with long, ropy arms and monstrously large hands, and a weight of about 165 pounds. He was the color of mocha. He had a short brow and a small head. He was smart. He might even have been brilliant. I always suspected as much. Rats' Alley's own Robert Aldridge was the very first name called on our roll of high-toned college preppers every day for five years, from the eighth grade until we graduated. Robert Aldridge and his shoes of holes and no heels. Robert Aldridge, who would disappear into the night after football or track practice. The Geechie, who could knock your ass out if he felt like it.

Robert and I got to be close because he would amend or create interesting classroom games. Capitals. Largest Cities. When something would strike Robert as being funny, he would laugh an infectious laughter—laugh until he ran out of breath. His face would twist into a writhing mask, tears would roll down his cheeks until at last he would draw another rasping breath. I imagine Robert must have appreciated the small joys in life much more than the rest of us. He invented other games. Desktop Golf. Desktop Football. Desktop Baseball. But the game at which Robert was most proficient was not a game at all. His best game, by far, was fighting.

There was a bully named Bishop at our grade level, an older, bigger boy who had developed early physically. He liked to come to gym class to pick out his victims. One day

Bishop came to the gym and picked little Maurice Taylor. Robert didn't like this. Bishop had Maurice by a good fifty pounds and six inches. Mismatch. Robert suggested that Bishop stop taunting Bull and leave him alone. Bishop turned to take Robert's measure. He looked Robert up and down, then said, "You the little ugly punk called Geechie?"

Robert's reply was eloquent. He hit Bishop with a right so quick, so thunderous, so perfect it made a sound like a paddle on a backside. There was no need for a second punch. Bishop reeled backward onto the bleacher seats, his jaw swelling by the time he landed flat on the boards. We celebrated wildly, and Robert laughed his wild, infectious laugh. To put Robert's KO in perspective, Bishop was later known as a "good-sized juvenile" down at the jailhouse, where it took three policemen to subdue him one unfortunate night in his future.

Outside of football practice, the most violent act I witnessed in these years occurred in the summer before our senior year, sitting in the bleachers of the Hanley recreation center, as football heroes watching the less prestigious game of basketball. Suddenly, Robert saw Johnny Watkins. Johnny was older. Twenty, perhaps, and Robert's size. Johnny was considered a proficient street fighter, and when the look I knew well came over Robert's face, I could not believe it.

"You! Johnny Watkins!" Robert jumped down from out of the stands. For some insane reason, he took off his shoes. Now he would be helpless on the slick gymnasium floor.

"Geech! No!" I said.

"I donwanafightya, Geechie! It didn' mean nothin'," said Johnny, his eyes dancing in a panic toward potential avenues of retreat. Robert threw the right, but his depth perception was way off. Johnny only felt the breeze from that right, but his eyes got bigger.

"Idonwanafightya, Geechie!" Johnny and Robert and the remainder of the kids inside the center moved outside. Everyone behind me was abuzz with this unexpected match of the century. They followed the fighters as if compelled by pipers. Robert pulled a comb from his back pocket, presenting it like a rapier. Then Johnny pulled a comb from his back pocket, and we all began to laugh. Perhaps it was just another one of Robert's jokes. But then Robert dropped the comb and advanced quickly on Johnny, who ran away, looking down at the ground as he zigzagged off. Geech wanted to fight. Johnny wanted to survive. In flight, Johnny spied a soda bottle, scooped it up, broke it on a tree, and turned back to ward off Robert with it. Robert sprang to the side—but not backward. That was his undoing. He bounced into another tree and back into the bottle. He took the jagged circle of glass full on his left arm. Blood spouted, sprinkling my shirt with red drops.

"No, Geech!"

Robert tried to run away, but he didn't make it far. He was bleeding heavily. He sat down hard under a tree and breathed deeply. I used my hands as an ineffective tourniquet, and we waited there together, saying nothing.

Robert was delirious from loss of blood by the time we were in the ambulance. He was in danger of bleeding to death, and there I was, helpless, representing his only available family. His eyelids fluttering, Robert repeated one question again and again as we sped through the streets.

"Did I win? Did I?"

Leroy Riddles and I talked later. We couldn't figure Robert out. After all, we were all seniors. There was much to look forward to, too much at risk for the drop-of-the-hat fighting in which Robert indulged himself so haphazardly. Leroy and I made it through senior year without a bad word passed between us, no small accomplishment. Around us, boys were periodically jacking, bugging, thumping, twirling, and jumping on one another. If I have given the impression that my childhood consisted of the threat of one fight after another, let me correct myself. It just seemed that way every now and then.

So, to keep in tune, there were sessions that were called "friendlies," which were box-offs between brothers or cousins or bosom buddies or acquaintances. These didn't carry the weight of real fights but hurt nearly the same. Being adept at friendlies warded off real trouble—they were exhibitions of skill or the lack thereof. By our senior year, I was six feet tall and had played football for four years. People knew that the Golden Wildcats did not mess around on the football field. Football was a good teacher of self-defense, and Melrose was a traditional prep football power. Like boxing, it is the next thing to war, as Jim Brown would later say. I learned how to deliver a blow, accept a blow, and do both stoically. Football and boxing were similar, but it was in football that I learned that to limit oneself to fists in the act of physical offense and defense was the height of folly. I developed some of the ballplayer's arrogance even though I played football more than I was a football player.

As it turned out, Leroy and I had a friendly on that matchmaker's delight known as the last day of school. Somehow, while killing time and reminiscing, standing out in front of the Golden Sundry, Leroy, who was called Egg Fu, and I began sparring playfully. Before we knew it, we were surrounded by the denizens of the corner, Frank Baker, George Cook, Nazareth Finley, and Ronald Clayborn. Even our own were there—Bull Taylor, Roy Fitzpatrick, and, of course, Robert Aldridge. They were a vocal audience.

"Get 'im, Fu!"

"Whatcha got, Wiley?"

"Y'all show us somepfin!"

"Anybody jumps in, I'm kicking his ass."

"Anybody jumps out, we kicking his ass."

"*Yeahhhh!*"

"Fu'll whip 'im."

"Damn straight."

"Ahdun-know-ow."

"Crush 'im, Fu!"

"You gon' *need* some Merthiolate!"

Leroy and I had a bond of friendship and communication that often went unspoken. We knew we were in mounting trouble even as we boxed. Our minds whirled as we threw out our punches, landing our blows on each other's shoulders and chest and sometimes high on the head. We both kept our chins down. The crowd around us grew bigger. We couldn't just put our hands down and have that be the end of it unless we put them down at the same instant. If we didn't, the one who put his hands down first might have to fight with another boy with a hidden grudge, or one who just believed he saw a weakness he could exploit for the good of his own reputation. We were trapped in the circle.

Leroy and I were inspired at the same time. Without a spoken word, we wheeled around and stood poised, squaring off against a full circle of boys, against everybody else, with our own backs touching. We would go down together, if necessary. We were the ones smiling now. The circle broke up immediately, and everyone laughed. Someone said, "Y'all are something else." Those who could stomach it went off to buy cheap wine. Leroy and I chose not to join up. Certainly not just then. We were already drunk with power. We had won, and our friendship was cemented for life, then and there.

A month later, we all met one more time at the corner, to attend en masse the opening of the Mid-South Fair at the Fairgrounds. This would be the last time I would see many of my friends and rivals. Fitz and I would soon catch the bus to Knoxville, on our way to play football as much as to go to college. As all the boys stood together one last time, dressed in our best goods, looking as boys do when they think they are at their best, I heard an argument behind me, at the doorway of the Golden Sundry. It was Levi, a bully from Castalia.

Fairly big, thick-armed, he was threatening one of our crowd. Frozelle Jamerson. A barber's son. Then Levi turned and stared at me.

"What the hell you lookin' at?"

This action by Levi sent me spinning beyond mad into calm—the hitting zone where fire must meet fire. Dressed to the nines, I squared Levi off with great anticipation. I think he spun on me because he felt I was the weakest. I hated him for picking me. I hated myself for being picked. So Levi would have to pay. I understood Geech now. There were no other consequences to consider but that he must go down. I knew I could take him.

"C'mon, punk."

Levi snorted, squared off, looked around, then sprinted off in the general direction of Castalia. Frozelle came up to me and said, "Man, you are crazy. Look at you, dressed all up. You woulda messed it all up." He shook his head.

Thus I made it through childhood. The best punch I had taken had been thrown by Alphonzo Wilson, and I could honestly tell him that he hit no harder than my grandmother. I thought that was the end of it. I would be a spectator from now on. How foolish, how naive, how happy I was then.

2

Dues

I took the long way to the New Oakland Boxing Club in Oakland, California, most likely because I had no idea I was heading there all along. Once there, I scratched in my notebook, studied the effect of the jab, the cross, the feint, all the intricacies involved in one three-minute round after another, after another . . .

When I left Memphis on a Greyhound bus with my friend Roy Fitz, I had not chosen writing—it chose me, or at least was holding me up to the light for closer observation. At Knoxville College, I was oblivious to the specifics of real life, for I began there as a football player. I remained so in both mind and body until my left knee was made unstable by an awkward landing in a long-jump pit, by a jolting leg tackle, and, finally, by doctors-in-waiting at the University of Tennessee Medical Center. After I awakened from surgery, I couldn't feel my toes, although the pain was intense up and down my left leg. I told the attending doctor that the cast was too tight. He told me it was postoperative pain. Morphine would ease it. Wouldn't I like some morphine? This was my first experience with a person in authority who found it nearly impossible to believe that someone not in authority might know something too. No, I wouldn't like some morphine, and you can keep the phenobarbital, too, thank you.

Ma was at my bedside, appearing calm but wringing her hands in her lap and thinking heaven knew what. When she was pregnant with me, she was also attending graduate school at Northwestern, getting a master's degree in English supervision and curriculum. She was a pianist, a choir director, whatever she chose to be, basically, and she had seen to it that I was exposed to most of her strengths, though the arts had been like restraining straps to a child like me. But there in the hospital, my physical training proved its worth. While my genteel mother listened, horrified, I promised the doctor in no uncertain terms that I would rip the cast off with my bare hands if necessary. He acquiesced to the hopelessness of my ignorant superstitions with a great, pitying sigh. An orderly clucked too before sawing the cast off. Blood rushed to my toes and I felt so much joy for the blessings of circulation that the post-op pain was all but a laughing matter. It is possible I might have lost my leg, had that cast not come off. That night, the lures of football and writing traded places on my short list of priorities.

What happened to me was fairly routine at large universities—but I was at a college. I was more than a statistic. I slowly joined the regular student body and went to the School of Business. Dr. Evelyn Stewart, the head of the Communications Department, gave me *The Elements of Style* and told me to study it. I thumbed through it two or three times, always putting it down for cram sessions of business law, econ, or accounting.

These years melted away. I continued to play football, because I was expected to play, and I still enjoyed outwitting defenders and catching passes. But my great preoccupation with the game was gone. The School of Business and the social life of the campus kept me occupied. Out of curiosity, I took a class entitled Afro-American Literature. The instructor—the standard bearded male—was impressed to redundancy with Langston Hughes, Countee Cullen, and Richard Wright. I had immersed myself in these poets and authors, and my heroes were in the process of changing from Superman, D'Artagnan, Cassius Clay, and Ulysses to Paul Robeson, Alexandre Dumas, Rod Serling, and Ida B. Wells.

I got my first newspaper job with the *Knox County News* by going to see Dr. William McArthur, the head of the Mathematics Department, a man who had saved in a miserly fashion for years, then decided on the advice of a fat man named Fields from out of town to splurge by buying a weekly newspaper in the city (the *Knox County News*). The *News* soon was publishing a second edition called the *Keyana Spectrum*, which later became the *Knoxville Spectrum*. This second edition was to appeal to the darker folk of Knox County, a beautiful region of mountains aproned by mist and sweet river valleys, where dogwood and azalea and lilac grew like common weeds. The Gateway to the Smokies. Also the gateway to poverty and its ugly handmaiden, racism. I asked Dr. McArthur for a job—to write a column about sports. For more than a year, I wrote terrible stories and worse columns. The *Spectrum* folded soon after I had graduated and left Knoxville for good. Losing me was not part of the paper's demise. Upon graduation, I went directly to Chicago, and Chicago was not so very unkind to me. But it was unkind enough. After three months I left for California—I had heard there were at least six daily newspapers in the San Francisco Bay Area. California turned out to be the best thing to happen to me since I came out from under anesthesia at the UT Medical Center.

I applied for a job as a reporter at the Oakland *Tribune*, which was housed in a green-roofed old building with a spiral tower at the corner of 13th and Franklin streets in downtown Oakland. The New Oakland Boxing Club was catercorner from the newspaper building. I didn't notice it at first. I was worrying about my interview. I mentioned I had been a football player who had ended up writing stories for Dr. Mc-Arthur's weekly. Danny Norman hired me as an editorial assistant—copyboy, as I found out when I reported for work and took up my most important reading material: the instructions to the coffee machine.

The Tribune was owned by the Knowlands, a conservative family which had begun publishing with the idea of rivaling the Hearsts across the Bay in San Francisco. Oakland was the real melting pot, the sister with the great personality, populated by what seemed like all mixtures of continental origins. The names on the "copyperson" call sheet reminded me of this every day. It was a good place to be at the time. There wasn't enough room or time to discriminate, and no one seemed to be in the mood for it anyway. The weather was too nice. The Knowlands seemed blind to the multiethnic character of the city, while leaving the growing outer areas primed to be swept off their feet by the suburban papers, whose circulations had exploded.

I worked as a copyboy for just about a year. By work I mean I worked nearly every shift the clock had to offer. I did not spare the grumblings while doing my work, and my work was all the work the titled employees would rather have none of. I learned what was considered news and what was not, and that most of the stories lay somewhere in the middle.

The computer keyboard quickly became a close acquaintance. Things got so that when a new electronic creation came out, I heard about it. "Ralph, we got a new machine here. Teleram. Got a cassette in it. Cassette. Hell if I know for what. You figure it out. Take some time to get the idea, then show the courthouse reporter how to use it." By "take some time," my boss meant "take some lunch time." As experience goes, this position was invaluable. What appeared to be a treadmill was in fact a fine education in the newspaper game. But the treadmill part was most clear to me at the time.

The most crucial chore for a copyperson at *The Tribune* was answering the call of the light board, a metal contraption of fifty numbered lights, any one of which a reporter or editor or other miscreant at a desk station could turn on with a flick of the wrist. The light board hung overhead, like a gray guillotine, above the most traveled hallway on the fourth floor. It was best seen from the coffee machine. This monster's lights emitted a low, almost imperceptible buzz. At times, ten or more lights would go on at the same time. It was a sobering sight.

But after the final deadlines were met and makeup for the later editions prepared, even a copyboy might learn something from the histories of the faces on the copy desk and of how the newspaper business was one great, cannibalistic, incestuous, wonderful old bitch.

After the year's apprenticeship, I seized an opportunity when the National Basketball Association and the American Basketball Association merged. The sports department was in need of a story on Julius Erving for its special pro basketball supplement. No one in the sports department knew that much about Erving. I stifled my incredulity and asked if I could see what I could come up with on Doctor J. I was given the go-ahead by George Ross, the outgoing sports editor, and John Porter, who was the editor of the supplement. The story was well received, and I was hired as a prep sports writer and soon became the prep sports editor. I ran the pictures big and let my fellow tyros write to their hearts' content. I had good space to work with so I used it.

After a brief stint cityside covering retirement dinners, grand openings, the cophouse, autistic children, etc., I was transferred to the sports department. *The Tribune* sports department was worthy of note. Among the many characters of the diverse staff was Paul McCarthy, the boxing writer. He smoked an endless chain of cigarettes and spoke in an impressive bass. Paul never did come to terms with the fact that George Foreman had been beaten by Muhammad Ali in

Kinshasa, Zaire, on October 30, 1974. Foreman lived in and boxed out of Oakland, and Paul, as all beat writers tend to do, had grown close to his subject matter. Like many others, he had come to the conclusion that George Foreman was unbeatable, at least by Ali. After Ali's incredible victory, Paul backed off the beat a little. He had been so sure of George, and of himself, and now he just didn't know anymore. Besides, he had been in the business for a long time. It was Paul who first encouraged me to muster myself on over to the New Oakland Boxing Club to see what I could come up with.

The New Oakland Boxing Club was just off Franklin Street, on 12th Street. Over the next five years I would meet many old boxers who came through downtown Oakland like prodigal sons: Earl Turner, Lou Nova, Jimmy Lester, Lew Jenkins, Johnny Gonsalves. A few of them had been on cards with Jack Dempsey or Max Baer, who was from Livermore, across the first set of Eastbay hills. The very name of Baer, or even of a Baby Arezmendi, a functional multiweight of the '40s and '50s, could send an older *Tribune* staffer into half-hour tales.

Bob Valli, the sports editor, gave me boxing as my first beat. I think the scars around my eyes impressed him. He didn't know they came from football. I would have other beats, easier to know the general histories of, predict results in, and, usually, do a reasonable job covering, as daily newspapers cover sports. Which is to say, like a blanket. There were the baseball teams, the San Francisco Giants and the Oakland A's; the football teams, the Oakland Raiders, the San Francisco 49ers, the Stanford Cardinals, and the Cal Bears; and the basketball teams, the San Francisco Dons, and the Golden State Warriors of the NBA. They were all somehow familiar. I could tell by body type the position an athlete played in his sport. I could guess heights to within the half-inch. I could watch a quarterback throw and move his feet under a heavy pass rush and know how good he might become, or how bad. I could watch the way a left-handed hitter reacted to a left-hander's curve ball and have more than a glimmer of how that hitter might do in that at-bat. I understood the footwork of men trying to defend the basket. I knew a shooter when I saw one. But in boxing, I had to learn from scratch. I made no assumptions.

Billy Conn, the former light-heavyweight champion, once said that a boxer striking a layman was "like hitting a girl." The professional boxer was as competent at his science as a mathematician, as committed to his art as a musician.

The bottom rungs of the ladder of boxing knowledge for me, were up a wide, creaking staircase littered with empty liquor bottles and smelling of old urine—the stairs that led up to the New Oakland Boxing Club.

A life-size poster of Ali stood silent sentry outside. One flight up, the club was really a dingy ballroom with a high ceiling. The room stank with a stink that was somehow inoffensive. The musk of sweat hung in the air and on the canvases. The boxing ring's ropes had been stretched by the weight of many men's backs. An office had been partitioned off near the entrance. Hopes and dreams were filed there, near the older men with cigars who were waiting for their meal ticket to come walking through the door.

Posters of past champions were plastered on the high walls. Out of reach. The room was always busy with the sound of rope skipping, the flutter of the three-speed bags being punched, and the unique sound of leathered fists striking skin-covered muscle and bone. A few men and boys were always around. None of them were very far up the ladder themselves, yet, compared to the man on the street, they were superior at the art and science of self-defense. And this is what they had come to the club for. Some of them—picked-on teenagers, Police Athletic League charges, bullies who had been convinced, one way or another, to try to turn their aggressiveness into a dollar—were there for specific reasons. And then, for others, the club became a way of life—as it was for Erwin Williams.

When I met Erwin in December 1977, he was a twenty-three-year-old professional fighter who could still afford to be called up-and-coming. He had a record of 14–0 and was preparing for his first big fight, for the middleweight championship of California against George Cooper. George was thirty-two and rarely seen in any gym anymore. Erwin was tall and not overly muscular, but he did have a fast pair of hands and pretty good legs. He had been taught the basic sequence of punches by a number of street fighters in West Oakland, and, later, by the old heads around the club.

Dick Sadler stood out among the old heads. He was a brown leather thumb of a man with deep eyes and a peppering of small moles on the skin beneath them. He hadn't gotten over Foreman losing to Ali either. Sadler had been George's trainer, and it was he who gave me lessons on the sequence.

"There's up and down and there's in and out, and there's what follows what and what counters what," he said. "Every punch that get thrown leave the opening you must see. You must see it, now. But there ain't no real way to explain it. You have to see for yourself." He gestured to the ring as if it were a daughter he wanted to give away soon. "Well, young man. Inside or out?"

"Out," I said, quite confidently, with no trace of disappointment or embarrassment. Dick looked me up and down. "That's prob'ly best," he clucked.

There were younger men working with charges of the club as well, like Jerry Blueford, a thirty-four-year-old cop who represented the Police Athletic League and his own Oakland Youth Boxing Club. "Boxing breeds respect," he told me. "For the other man. I don't care if any of these kids ever become pros, or even good amateurs for that matter. I'm trying to get them into something they can work at. Off the streets. If they leave here in a couple of years and rob a bank, at least they didn't rob it while they were here."

Sadler was more succinct. "This ain't church," he said, "but it'll do."

Boxing was on the one hand barbaric, unconscionable, out of place in modern society. But then, so are war, racism, poverty, and pro football. Men died boxing, yet there was nobility in defending oneself. Men like Sadler and tedious observance by rote showed me that the opening of the boxer's sequence was basic, like the opening moves of a backgammon player. Six-one. Five-three. Four-two. Each additional roll of the dice—each additional feint, punch, or countermove—factored the sequence upward. And that was only the first round, the first three minutes. Meanwhile, the boxer who must react instinctively to each offering of the sequence was being subjected to mayhem of the highest order.

The better the boxer, the earlier he knows when something is wrong in the procedure. This knowledge is called skill. It's a mixture of speed, acuity, experience, instinct, rough math, and a kind of genius or insanity, take your pick. Will has nothing to do with skill.

In the classic sequence of boxing, especially among the lighter weights, the plan works off the jab, the straight thrust of the left hand if you're right-handed. Everything begins there for the professional, unless he is a hard puncher for his weight and, consequently, more fighter than boxer. There are three options for the opponent when offered the jab. He can attempt to slip to either side or move back. He can counter the jab with another jab, hook over or under the jab, or absorb the jab, helping nothing but an abstract and more distant strategy. The spice is this: The initiator does not necessarily have to throw the jab to find out what the opponent's reaction will be. He can feint the jab, then judge the opponent's reaction. Other than the damaging punch, the feint is the most telling action of a fight. For every move there is a counter, and the feint draws out the counter for study. Without a feint, there should be no damaging punch unless a man is outclassed.

A boxer can be outclassed by speed, by weight, by ability to punch hard, or by ability to take the sequence further. On rare occasions, a boxer can be outclassed by sheer will alone.

In fact, more often than not, will determines the most interesting fight, because the lure of the promoter to the public is
to make the most even—and most attractive—match between
fighters on class criteria. It's like a human cockfight. All things
being equal, who will win?—the man with the most will to
win the fight. The man with less to lose outside the ring usually
has the most to gain inside it.

Erwin had will for fighting, but not enough of it. As it
turned out, he probably had a glass jaw. His 14–0 record had
been gained in six-rounders against young men like himself,
but Erwin was quicker than they were. George Cooper was
miles beyond anyone Erwin had ever faced. The fight was to
be held outdoors, at a futuristic structure called the Concord
Pavilion, across the hills from the Bay in the smoothly rolling
plain of Contra Costa County. Erwin was a brakeman for the
railroad. He told me he came to the club for the money. His
manager, Bill Sanford, felt Erwin was about to go off like a
Roman candle on Cooper and the sky was the limit after that.

"Erwin's too fast for an old man like Cooper," Sanford
said.

"Yeah," said Erwin.

"If he tries to slug, we're ready," said Sanford.

Erwin was equivocal about this. "I don't think I'll have to
slug it out with him," he said. "I'll just box him."

"Erwin don't even like him," said Sanford.

"No, I don't," said Erwin.

Whether or not Erwin liked Cooper turned out to be im-
material.

★

Oakland *Tribune*, April 27, 1978

CONCORD—Oakland middleweight George Cooper taught
Erwin Williams a boxing lesson, spurred a controversy, and

held on to his California state title in the bargain last night at the Concord Pavilion.

Before 2,867 boisterous fans evenly divided in their loyalty, Cooper waded through Williams's backpedaling defense to score a smashing technical knockout at 3:00, the end of the fifth round. That's where the controversy erupted. "Right now, it's going into the books as a TKO," said state athletic commissioner Ray Tennyson. "But errors were made, and I don't know what the Commission's final say will be." Tennyson also said Williams may have grounds for protest of some sort. The noisy crowd prevented referee Jack Scheberies from hearing the bell at the end of round five. Timekeeper Hank Lewis sounded the bell during Scheberies's count over the prone Williams. Tennyson said Lewis should not have sounded the bell until Williams got up. The round was over when the TKO was scored, according to Tennyson, who then, as confused as anybody, said he would recommend the fight be called no contest. He was certainly right about that.

Cooper butted Williams early in the second round and was twice warned for hitting in the clinches, the second time near the end of the fifth. Scheberies, later intervening, chastised Cooper while Williams wobbled around the ring, looking for the impossible escape.

When the action resumed, Cooper planted a three-punch combination on Williams's jaw and temple and the younger man went down. He was up at the count of nine, but out on his feet. "The damn bell rang then," said Williams's manager, Bill Sanford. "My fighter was up after the bell rang. The ref didn't know what to do. He just waved Cooper back in. We will protest this."

"He couldn't have gone another round anyway," said Cooper's manager, Henry Winston. "We would have been glad to continue, but then Erwin might have died."

Scheberies ended the fight with no time officially being

kept and with Cooper flailing away at the defenseless Williams. George celebrated victory by going over to Williams's corner and giving love taps to Sanford. "He hit me," said Sanford. "It was a dirty fight from the start to the finish, even after it was over. Cooper came over and slugged me."

Cooper, calm after the rout, offered this: "It was Erwin's mistake by getting involved with those handlers of his. They're no good. They made this a personal thing between me and Erwin, and had him believing it. Erwin was bumping into me all week, giving me dirty looks in the gym, that kind of stuff. I'm not that kind of guy, but he made me very angry."

Cooper, 46–6–1, seemed to have a bee in his bonnet from the beginning of the fight, leading the fight instead of adopting his usual, counterpunching style. The first telling blow was not a punch. The fighters' heads clashed in round two and Williams emerged stunned, with a deep gash over his left eye. Erwin became tentative after that, sacrificing his offense to try and protect his gushing brow.

Williams's corner did a good job with the cut between rounds, but neglected to suggest to Williams that he throw punches. Especially rights. Cooper, ogling the cut eyebrow, repeatedly dropped his left. Williams (14–1) landed only three or four stiff punches—all rights, all on the back end of combinations, all early, all fruitless.

Erwin had gone from up-and-coming to his comeuppance in nineteen minutes, by the clock. After this hard, fast fall, he went back to the New Oakland Boxing Club, heeding only his wounds and the words of Sanford, who told him that his loss was a fluke and that he, Erwin Williams, could one day be champion of at least California and get some real dough, not the chicken feed the railroad threw his way.

I would see Erwin from time to time after that. He usually looked as though someone were following him. The loss had been no fluke. Cooper hit Erwin with everything but his mother's pots and pans. From ringside, I was amazed by Cooper's ability to land his forearms, elbows, and the crowns of his shoulders into Erwin's befuddled, bleeding face, time and again. So boxers weren't limited to using their hands after all. Cooper shot a right past Erwin's ear, looking as if he'd missed a punch but actually rubbing the ear raw with the glove laces on the underside of his wrist. Cooper smashed a right hand on the gash on Williams's forehead. The blood came at me in slow motion. I leaned back and the droplets fell across the legal pad that bore my frantically scribbled notes. (None got on me.)

I never did another story on Erwin. A few years later, after I had moved away from Oakland, I came back to town on a visit and found, to my utter surprise, that Erwin Williams was scheduled to fight some old pug from Los Angeles that night at the Oakland Auditorium. I took a friend, one of the eight original boys from my high school homeroom, Larry Mallory. He had played for three or four years with the NFL's New York Giants. I thought he might appreciate this.

Erwin was in fine form. He wore purple trunks and me-ticulously arranged white socks with purple piping above white boxing shoes. For three or four rounds, Erwin danced around the bent and battered-looking old pug from L.A. Erwin shot out his left hand, scoring with the jab, setting himself to throw a right every now and then. The older fighter, who had not even bothered to comb his hair beforehand, was not returning punches. He looked to be in his forties with a body that seemed unbothered by training of any sort. The only actions he seemed ready for were getting paid and going home. But there was something about the way he avoided Erwin's right. . . .

"This is a joke. The old guy's had it," said Mallory.

Knowing Erwin's history and getting my first feeling of boxing *déjà vu*, I said, "I don't know. If Erwin just runs in there behind that jab, he might run into—"

This was not quite out of my mouth when Erwin, sensing

he had the older man in trouble, ran in behind a right he had landed. He never saw the delayed counter right the older man threw. The pug had turned away from Erwin behind his left shoulder, effectively hiding the bunching of muscles in his back, beneath his right shoulder. Then he landed the only purposeful punch he would throw all night. He put everything he knew into it. If it landed, he would get paid and go home. If it missed, he would get paid and go home. It landed. Erwin went out like a broken light bulb. A mournful "ooooowwww" rolled through the house. One woman screamed to be allowed to go to her Erwin, who lay as if in state.

"Love!" she screamed. "He needs love!"

"Air," I said to Mallory. "He needs air."

Later in that year, 1978, when George Cooper defended the California state middleweight title against Erwin Williams, my grandmother died. I had known my grandmother as a taskmaster and an avenging angel whose deadly glances in church could turn a restless boy into stone. Or she could undo her hair and comb it so gently there was no sound other than a whisk-whisk that could have been the rustling of wings. She sang hymns in a lush vibrato. And she could offer up gems: "You think the world owes you something? I owe you something. I owe you a kick in the ass, and I'd give it to you if there wasn't a callous under my foot." But after her second set of boys departed, there was no need for her to stay. She left this mortal coil a clear clean winner by unanimous decision.

My grandmother, Uncle Charles, and Robert had been the ones who awakened my interest in fighters. My grandmother's life had been completed, as far as she was concerned, well before she died. She smiled perpetually in the last years of her life, pleased to be free from modern times. Two of her sisters died not long before her, and a third sister died not long after her. With her beloved William dead for some twenty-seven years, there was, frankly, no one with whom she wished to relate in this new world, with its "Al Lewcindors" as she might say. There was also the seaminess which had begun to creep into her part of Orange Mound. Six liquor stores within one block was bad enough, but the block parallel to Saratoga Avenue, which had just been Brooklyn Avenue in her day, was now known as the dope street, where the people from downtown made their drop-offs. She pretended not to see. There were no new things under the sun to her, and if there were, there was no one with whom she cared to discuss them, other than my Aunt Elizabeth, her lap baby.

"You're going to forget your old grandma," she had said to me on that June day in 1970 when I left for college.

"No, ma'am, no I won't," I said. She knew better.

At her funeral, a photographer took a family portrait as we stood around her burnished coffin. We wore varying looks of acceptance, misery, denial, and grief on our faces. Uncle Charles's usually serene countenance was smitten by a look of pain that no punch had ever caused him. At this somber meeting, I began a tradition of posing for a picture with Uncle Charles, his great ham fist under the point of my chin and me with my collection of knuckles and bailing wire cocked alongside his jaw. Charlie Boy mugged magnificently for the camera, rolling his eyes up and letting his jaw go slack while I smiled like the devil. This was the only moment of levity in the entire week for him.

The family said its goodbyes, and I went back to Oakland and the boxing beat. Shortly after my return, a well-mannered young man from Nigeria in a cheap suit a size too small came up to me in the boxing club and introduced himself. Bashiru, a student at the University of California at Berkeley, said he wanted to become a boxer because he wanted to make money. This was where he could learn to box, was it not?

"Have you ever boxed amateur?" I asked.

"I have never boxed at all," said Bashiru. "But I have wrestled all over Nigeria."

Wrestlers feel superior to boxers. Perhaps they should, since a wrestler's body may be stronger than a boxer's, overall, and wrestlers are allowed more avenues by which to incapacitate a foe. Bashiru looked every bit the wrestler when he strode from the dressing room in tattered boxing trunks. I couldn't help but smile. Wrestlers feel they can more than hold their own with boxers until their hands are encased in gloves. Then everything changes.

Bashiru did not exercise to build up a sweat. He did not attempt to hit the heavy bag. I thought he didn't want to embarrass himself. He climbed into the ring, stone cold. A partner had been geared up, and gloves were placed on Bashiru's hands. His education had begun. He was smacked about the ring, but never so hard that he seemed to wish to cease hostilities. He threw punches like a pitcher throwing fastballs. They floated harmlessly through the stuffy air. Bashiru fought like a drowning man. After three three-minute rounds of this, he climbed out of the ring chastened more by his inability to land a punch than by the many blows his foe had crash-landed on Bashiru's thick body.

Wrestling, Bashiru told me, was an honorable way to exert oneself for fun, recognition, and profit in Nigeria. Wrestlers in Nigeria traveled throughout the country and were treated as heroes. "Here in America, my new home, I will box for honor and money."

Of professional wrestling, Bashiru said, "I tried that. I went to wrestle as a professional. I met the promoters. I was given a name I did not like. I'd rather not remember it. I was given togs and told I was to wrestle Moon Dog Mane. I was told that I should be mean and act African. I said that I was African. I did not have to act. I asked if I defeated Moon Dog Mane, who would I wrestle next, and how much would I be paid."

I imagined the look on the promoter's face.

"I was told that under no circumstances was I to win or try to pin my opponent. I was to practice routines with him. It was to be a trick. I said I could not lose on purpose. I was told no one expected me to win. So I came here."

Over the next few years, not only would Bashiru learn to box well enough to gain something of a reputation, he would eventually fight Carlos DeLeon for the WBC cruiserweight championship of the world. Bashiru would learn the art of self-defense and the art of self-promotion. Before fights, he proclaimed that he had to win so that he could afford to bring all three of his wives to America. That got noticed. Eventually, Bashiru Ali became the North American Boxing Federation cruiserweight champion of the world. He fought for eight years, until he was knocked out in 1984 by Henry Tillman, an Olympic gold medalist, at 1:25 of the first round of their fight for the NABF title. Bashiru hadn't done badly for a fellow who never figured out how to throw a knockout punch. He had become the United States Boxing Federation cruiser- weight champion, with a record of 17–2, before I left Oakland. He was 27–10 when he finished. His biggest payday— $5,000—came when he fought Mike Clark, a former card dealer at a South Lake Tahoe casino.

One of the reasons Bashiru lasted was a fight for which he wasn't paid much, a loss in which he was shown how much he had to learn by a stoic from Stockton named Alvaro "In- dian Yaqui" Lopez.

Yaqui Lopez was the finest fighter in northern California at this time, which said as much for the fighters of northern California as it did for Yaqui. He held no world champion- ships, but he had fought for the light-heavyweight champi- onship four times. He always lost these fights, but he always made a good fight of it. Although I met Yaqui many times, I never heard him say much. It was yes, no, maybe not. His brother-in-law, whom I began to call Yaqui also, did the talking before the Indian's fights. He insisted Yaqui had been jobbed out of the title against Victor Galindez in Rome on

September 17, 1977. He also lost a decision to Galindez on May 6, 1976. From what I saw of the films of both fights, Yaqui had a point. He could easily have been declared the winner both times. But Yaqui had never seemed bitter about that, or anything else. In fact, his visage was uncluttered by emotion of any sort. He seemed to be the most contented man I had met in California.

Yaqui had fought fifty-three times by the book when I met him but looked as though he'd been in many more than that. He no longer had the speed and vitality of his youth, but he had so much experience that nothing could make him seem nervous or confused in the ring. He always threw the proper counterpunch. He led when he had to, rarely bothering with feints anymore. Fighting Yaqui was like fighting a mirror. When you punched, he punched you in the spot you left unprotected. But now he was fighting younger, stronger men. Lopez was sometimes beaten until his head could not right itself. But after they revived him, the blank look was still there. He always wore it. Lopez's mind stayed calmer than any fighter's I had met. He was my first consummate boxer.

Indian Yaqui Lopez was never known as a champion, but he was a maker of champions. If you could not beat him, you could not become a world champion. If you could beat him, perhaps you already were one. In 1979, Yaqui fought Michael Spinks, who was coming up slowly through the light-heavyweight ranks. His brother, Leon, was the fighter of the moment, having beaten Muhammad Ali in just his fourteenth pro fight. (Of course, Ali was no longer Ali when that happened.) Michael Spinks beat Indian Yaqui Lopez and learned tricks he would later use on Larry Holmes to become the first world light-heavyweight champ to beat a world heavyweight champion. Yaqui Lopez, who had been called a bum in his time, had been ahead on points over Michael Spinks in their fight before age, lack of punching power, and speed betrayed him. "I had to knock him out or I would have lost,"

Michael said later. "I want no more of that Indian. Not at these prices."

Later in 1979, Yaqui was beaten up by a bald convict at Rahway State Prison in Rahway, New Jersey. Yaqui would go anywhere to fight for money. Since Saturday-afternoon fare was hard for television to come by at certain times of the year, the cameras followed Yaqui into the prison, where James Scott knocked him out with a terrible vengeance.

By December of 1979, I had become one of two sports columnists at the Oakland *Tribune*. Robert Maynard had come in as editor-in-chief at the *Tribune*, which by this time was owned by the Gannett Corporation. In Oakland, the competition for readers came from larger papers like the *San Francisco Chronicle*, the San Francisco *Examiner*, and the *San Jose Mercury News*. The Gannett company fathers wanted to show that they could actively compete in a highly competitive market, and so began to spend considerable money to make the *Tribune* a better paper, publishing a morning edition called *Eastbay Today*. This was a limited test case for the company's more ambitious project, a national newspaper to be called *USA Today*. At the time, the national paper was on the drawing board, so Gannett threw some of its profits at us instead.

On December 14, 1979, the day before covering the Cal Bears in the Garden State Bowl in East Rutherford, New Jersey, I went to Rahway State Penitentiary to interview James Scott, a two-time loser on robbery convictions serving thirty to forty years, who was also a contender for the world light-heavyweight title. Rahway ruined my day. It was as if the world had dropped the sum of its sores into one of New Jersey's gritty smokestacks, then chose not to watch as the results of the experiment filtered into this place. From its forbidding rotunda on down, it was a loser.

Within the prison, Scott, inmate 57735, insisted that he could not lose. His record at the time was 18–0–1. He felt he could be champion of the world, if only the world would allow him to prove it. But there was really no hurry. James Scott had nothing but time to kill. At thirty-one, he had been in and out of penal institutions since he was thirteen. He grew up hard, fast, and poor in Newark and took several minor falls before two robbery convictions pinned him as a habitual criminal. The convictions proved one point—James Scott could box better than he could steal. But there was another point to consider. Could boxing be a rehabilitative tool? Scott hoped to convince the right people that it could.

The horrors of prison cannot be adequately described except by a James Scott. Listening to him talk was like a tramp through the lock-up. "Jails are just what they aren't supposed to be—breeding grounds for crime," he said while watching himself batter Yaqui on videotape. "When you take all hope away, then there is no reason for rules anymore. Take a man's hope away and he will say, 'What the hell am I toeing the line for?' The Rahway State Boxing Association is a first. Some people hope it fails.

"I learned to box in jail. Out of necessity. I got my head beat in a lot. I first went to jail at thirteen. For truancy. Truancy! In there with rapists and murderers and stick-up men—these were the examples of manhood I had."

The emotional appeal is a great one—the man has a chance to be a champion among men. But I must cast aside emotion and rule within . . . the law. Scott's past social behavior outweighs what he has accomplished in prison. I don't think Mr. Scott has had an easy life. I don't think there's any question that Mr. Scott has devoted himself to being a boxer . . . yet I am faced with his disciplinary record.

—New Jersey state judge Nicholas Scalera, stating his reason for denying Scott bail, pending appeal of his 1976 parole violation.

"I was placed in the hospital for the criminally insane after con fights in this prison," said Scott. "Fifteen months I was there, in protective custody, they said. In those fights, it was life and death. Do you understand me? Chaos. There were stabbings. I defended myself. I wanted to live. I lived. This is exactly my point. Now, in this same prison, guys are settling their differences with the gloves instead of shivs."

Scott was picked up for parole violation in 1975 after leaving the state of Florida. Also, a car belonging to Scott was used in a robbery. Scott, with witness corroboration, says he didn't have the car on the night in question. Still, with his record, his case was deemed open-and-shut.

Scott had someone in the Jersey state government working to prepare an argument on his behalf for the state's minimum custody board. Minimum custody prisoners are allowed work furloughs. On such a furlough, Scott saw himself beating Marvin Johnson and becoming the uncrowned light-heavyweight champion of the world—uncrowned, because neither the World Boxing Council nor the World Boxing Association was going to let the title sleep in a prison, though the people involved with either group had no reason to be sanctimonious about it.

"I'm paying to be in jail now," Scott said. "I've made a little money from the TV fight. I've been able to hire an attorney. I took my parents off federal assistance, and ten percent of what I win goes to an organization which benefits the victims of violent crimes. I pay two thousand dollars for my living quarters here, per year. I pay one hundred and six dollars a month to eat. It's only eighty-five dollars if I don't eat eggs. I'm supposed to be here for rehabilitation, right? Boxing is the only thing that can do that for me in this place. Look around you. There's nothing else here. Nothing but grief. There is the TV. The marijuana floats around, with the pills and the homos. The law libraries and reading rooms aren't crowded anymore.

"Some of the guards hate the ground the inmates walk on.

If you react, you're headed for the Vroom Building"—wherein the offender was given "the treatment." "I don't have the answers. But the men who have 'Corrections Officer' on their badges—that isn't what they do."

One exception was Steve Scherer, the recreation officer who helped form the Rahway Prison Boxing Association. He was college-educated and had been at Rahway for four long years—two facts which separated him from most of his more sullen counterparts. When I met him, Scherer's eye was blackened from being sucker-punched by a new prisoner. That prisoner became a temporary resident of the Vroom Building. His actions made Scherer's viewpoint more convincing.

"If they stop James now, something bad will happen, and not just in this place," Scherer said. "My view is different from what ninety percent of the guards here think. This kind of program can work, despite the fact that there's no money and no staff. But I don't think the people in power want the title in prison. And if James fought for the title, he would win. I don't know what's going to happen. If I leave, the whole thing will probably go down the tubes. You have to be a little crazy to work in a prison."

As I left the prison, I asked myself, Then what must you be to live in one? James Scott got out of Rahway. He was eventually transferred to Trenton State Penitentiary. His fights are no longer televised.

In July 1981, back in Concord in Contra Costa County, I met a man who might have been tougher than James Scott. Elmer Verlin Jenkins. They called him Lew.

"Cain't do nothing no more," the old man said, wheezing ruefully. He smiled a little bit anyway, a little leer of a smile that spread his flat nose and beaten eye sockets out nearly to his ears. "Just got out of the horspital last Friday. Sixteen days in there. Fluid, stuff in my lungs. The pacemaker they put over my heart in February . . ."

His wife broke in. "The darn thing just hasn't worked too well."

He corrected her. "It ain't that, you know it ain't that, Lupie."

She sighed in admission. "His heart's giving out. That's what it amounts to."

His eyes looked out over uncharted vistas. "No more," he said. "No nothing. I cain't even walk from here to there. The horspital told me all this. No more. I'm through . . . well, ain't I? Ain't I? You know, I *hate* this. I've been active all my life."

Indeed. Some may not know of Lew Jenkins. Some may have heard of him. But some recall him very well. In 1980, at a Boxing Hall of Fame dinner in Anaheim, a partially paralyzed and senile Joe Louis was wheeled toward a trio of aging fighters—Lou Ambers, Henry Armstrong, and Lew Jenkins.

"Joe's face lit up when he saw me, jest lit right on up," Jenkins said, savoring this last encounter of old, hard men. "They said he couldn't recognize nobody. He recognized me. He started moving and trying to wave and making his noises." Maybe Joe Louis was trying to ask Lew Jenkins the question he had laughingly asked back in the old days, back when they were champions:

"Hey Lew, how you throw that right hand?"

Lew Jenkins first threw that right hand at cotton stalks sagging in the shimmering summer heat of Sweetwater, Texas. He was born in 1916. He shared his adolescence with seven siblings and the Great Depression. He weighed 129 pounds as a teenager and would be roughly the same weight all his life—a lightweight. If Jenkins hadn't been, in his words, "my own stupid man," he likely would have done better than merely a nineteen-month reign as the lightweight champion of the world during 1940–41. But it was under the sun of Sweetwater that fifteen-year-old Lew realized why the cotton stalks fell so easily. "I just had that right hand, natcheral," he says, his Texas drawl still in place. "I didn't even have to draw it back. I'd throw it from here, straight, a shot. I was skinny, but boy, I had that right."

Jenkins's natural right landed him a job with T. J. Tidwell's carnival for two years, fighting all comers. "I've fought three rounds for a quarter," he said. "Five dollars was a big purse then." He joined the Army at age nineteen, won the Fort Bliss post title, then got a sixty-day furlough and went to Dallas, where a husband-and-wife promotional team by the name of Griffin gave him a shot and a name: Lew.

"They said, 'Lookit him, he's starving. Give him a fight.' I had nine straight KOs. I went back and bought my way out of the Army for a hundred dollars."

In '38 and '39, he fought thirty-five times for the Griffins. "In '39, I went to Mexico City to fight," he said. "Rough, boy. You didn't know if you'd get your money—or your bullet. I had four fights. I knocked 'em all out, one in eleven seconds. They had to count ten over him, you know. They went berserk. They weren't gonna let me go. They were crazy to see me fight. I had to get out of there." There was only one place left to go. "I got right off in New York. I won ten straight. Seven KOs. And I had the town. Joe Namath was a baby compared to what I did in New York. See, the crowds, they like that right hand. They like that. You can win a certain way and nobody cares, you won't go anywhere. But I was a hot rod. I had what they wanted. That right hand."

Jenkins was a crowd-pleaser. The crowd never stopped roaring during his knock-down drag-outs, and he had the tapes to prove it. The tapes are re-creations, but he didn't know it. Or maybe he did know it and it just didn't matter. He remembered the crowds just that way. And the crowds knew Lew—"the Living Death, the Medical Freak, the Sweet Swatter from Sweetwater"—was never out of a fight as long as he could cock his right.

In May of 1940, he fought Lou Ambers for the lightweight title. Ambers began fighting in 1932 as a professional. By

1940 he had a record of eighty-eight wins, six losses, and six draws and had never been knocked out. He had beaten the great Henry Armstrong. He had killed a fighter named Tony Scarpati in the ring with his fists. Jenkins knocked out Ambers in the third round. A year later, Jenkins knocked out Ambers in the seventh. It was a matter of styles. Ambers was obviously a superb lightweight. Ambers beat Armstrong, Jenkins took Ambers, Armstrong took Jenkins. But what a trio to have at one time in history.

"Duran? Duran couldn't stay with people like this," said Jenkins of the premier lightweight of this era. "I see nothing. I *know* he couldn'a stayed with Armstrong. Who was the best I ever fought? Only one man I can say. Armstrong.

"I tell you something. I used to be real bad on the race question," Lew said, smiling at me. "See, I had never met a better man than me, any color. Then I met Armstrong. Halfway through the fight, it dawned on me. I could never beat him. So I stopped being thataway right then. Right in the middle of a fight. And I've been a happier man ever since.

"They didn't stop fights then like they do now, either. It was fight until you couldn't fight no more." That was the premise under which Jenkins went about his grisly work. He was an utterly ruthless fighter who would elbow, choke, and butt. He'd hit you on the break. He'd hit you while you were down. He'd hit you until it was over. The other side was that he had no qualms about being hit. He required forty-one stitches after his July 1940 fight against Armstrong. He needed forty-three more after a December match that year against Fritzie Zivic. Jenkins nearly lost his eyes. But in between the Ambers fights, Lew was the toast of New York.

He poured his title down the drain. One night he was listening to Peggy Lee sing a song dedicated to him in the Meadowbrook Ballroom in New Jersey on a September night in 1941. Wahooing, three sheets to the wind—"Peggy Lee, boy. Peggy Lee!"—he lit out on his motorbike and ended up in the hospital with his back broken. He finished fighting in 1950 with a record of 66–38–5.

Jenkins had cared nothing for training for fights—just for winning them. He smoked a pack and a half of Camels a day and drank his fill of Seagram's V.O. during his brief rule in New York. He drank before fights, during fights. One night he ran a motorcycle into a Little Ferry, New Jersey, traffic circle at eighty miles an hour. He cracked three vertebrae and was never the same again.

"I threw it all away," he said evenly. "Would I have changed it? Lord God, would I have changed it, oh yes! I was an idiot. But they couldn't slow me down. Nothing could be done. I was so foolish I don't even like to look back on those days."

It was 1946 when he met his second wife, Lupie, in California. Jenkins was walking along at Camp Stoneman in Pittsburg (CA) when "I nearly ran over him in my car," said Lupie. "He shook his fist at me, then he smiled. I was so scared I gave him my right name." They were married on their second date. "You either do or you don't," said Jenkins.

They did, for thirty-five years, all spent in Contra Costa County or flying around the country. Lew, ever spry, jumped into rings for prefight introductions, the big hands clasped overhead. People don't forget a hitter.

Jenkins had a heart attack in 1974, and things slowed down a bit. They lived in a low, quiet condominium not too far away from their son, Lew Jr., his wife, Linda, and their children, John, Jim, and Stephanie. Much had been made then of the sons of boxers, like Marvis Frazier, son of Joe, and Ray "Boom Boom" Mancini, son of Lenny. The sons were fighters, too. Lew Jenkins, Jr., was in the business of computers.

"Who's better off?" cackled Jenkins the Elder. He was as proud of his son as a man can be, as proud as the other two old fighters were of their sons, and possibly more so, for Lew knew what kind of toll his kind of life could exact.

Evening came gently to Concord. The feeble old man with fluid in his lungs, a pacemaker over his heart, and ten thousand punches etched in his brow and memory, slowly assembled himself to let his company out. He slid-walked a few halting steps before Lupie called out to him, "Don't go too far now, Lew." Lew stood at the door and held out his skinny right arm. He steadied his frailness and opened the big, gnarled right for a parting handshake. I took it.

It was like a rock.

> My eyes fell on a little bird
> with a beautiful yellow bill
> I beckoned him to come and light
> upon my window sill
> I smiled at him with happiness
> gave him a crust of bread
> then quickly closed the window
> and *smashed his fucking head*
> —Lew Jenkins

3
Vegas

You could've struck a match on Eddie Mustafa Muhammad's eyebrows. The rest of his face seemed to be even harder. He could never get his body in that kind of tune, but visage-wise, Yaqui, Scott, and Lew Jenkins had nothing on Eddie from Brownsville in Brooklyn. I met him when he came to Oakland to fight an exhibition at the auditorium for the Clara Muhammad School for Girls of the American Muslim Mission in the fall of 1980, during his short reign as the WBA light-heavyweight champion. About three hundred people showed up, many of them because they believed the promotional rumor that Muhammad Ali might be there. Ali's name was still magic. On the other hand, Eddie Mustafa had a good chin, a decent right, and no charisma. Charisma is like a great knockout punch—some of us have it, some of us don't. No accounting for it.

Mustafa fought a listless four-round exhibition. According to the Lew Jenkins Theory, boxing fans don't like exhibitions. They pay to see a man knocked out. The three hundred people showed up anyway. Maybe the Clara Muhammad School for Girls would get a couple hundred dollars out of it. Some little girls, wearing pressed green dresses, were in attendance at the exhibition that night. They were the only ones that mattered—I gave Eddie Mustafa credit for knowing this—and they were the only ones smiling when the exhibition was over.

I remember Mustafa most for something he said on that night back in 1980: "Now I'm ready for Vegas."

Vegas took time to prepare for, and to get used to. I had been going to Vegas to cover fights for two years by the time 1980 rolled around and had begun to get the feel of the place. From 1978 through 1982, I went eagerly and left more eagerly. On the whole, the Vegas cards were headlined by great or near-great fighters, but often, fighters with a claim to greatness would not fight each other. When they did, the results were spectacular. It was a Golden Age of Boxing, and Vegas was the fighter's ultimate stage.

I could not join them in their feelings. My impression was that Las Vegas was a place built on, and in the anticipation of, the misfortune of people. Its existence is based on the assumption that the seven deadly sins are a heavy favorite to at least show, and that vice needs a place to call home—a place where it can name its own price, and get it. Joy was an unsubstantiated rumor I only heard mentioned once in Vegas, and that was in passing. For all its opulence and grandeur, Vegas was next to nowhere. But for fighters, or gamblers, or those related to them, Vegas was the most exciting trip to hell imaginable.

The first sound I heard when I disembarked at McCarran Airport for the first time was the rapid clanging of a long series of heavy coins striking metal. Someone had hit a small jackpot on one of the many slot machines which proliferated in the airport. The pots of the slots were designed to announce a small strike loudly, to turn the sound of money dropping into the sound of bells ringing deep in your brain. People looked at the woman who had just hit with such envy you'd have thought she'd found the fountain of youth. In response, she filtered more coins into the slot. I would learn this sound and these looks well. Even small scores were well publicized in Vegas. The clanging of coins was incessant indoors.

For visitors like me, Las Vegas consisted of one wide boulevard—the Strip. The Strip was engulfed in light. The neon configurations gave the impression that Vegas was exciting, that something wonderfully enticing was going on somewhere. The best thing I could say about the place was that Hoover Dam must have worked. Electricity was never a problem. The marquees of the gambling mansions were mesmerizing light shows. Inside the hotels you were bathed in more muted light which didn't chase the darkness very far. Sunlight was not allowed past the foyers. Well inside the gaming halls, you couldn't tell if it was day or night. Needless to say, this architectural phenomenon was not accidental. Time stood still in Vegas.

I nearly always stayed at Caesar's Palace. It beckoned like a siren for hire. It was a structure right out of some Greco-Egyptian inspiration and the Romans' follow-through, offset by the trappings of a twentieth-century hedonist. The entrance to the hotel and casino sat a hundred yards off the Strip behind a delicately manicured lawn that was encircled by a wide driveway. Marble and granite statues struck various emotional poses along the driveway. At night, the exterior of the hotel was illuminated by several bands of lights that gave off a soft green glow. The hotel was the color of dollars after darkness fell. Nothing had been left to chance.

Inside the hotel was the casino, dotted by a few restaurants and gift shops. The crap tables and roulette wheels and keno stations and blackjack bars and sports book and slot machines ran night and day. They overwhelmed the decor, which included the dealers, pit bosses, and patrons, who stood and sat and moved like cats on catnip over the lush carpeting. The air was usually heavy with tobacco smoke, curses, and the occasional giddy cheer of relief. I rarely heard genuine laugh-

ter in Vegas. Nothing was taken in total good humor. Everything had an angle. Even winning. You won to make up for
your losses.

People flocked to Vegas like moths to a flame, especially
during championship fight time. The high rollers came in, and
no doubt Caesar's could have filled my room with fatter calves
than I. Some of the rooms of the hotel were outlandish, with
octagonal tubs and mirrors on the ceilings and round beds. I
felt like a sucker, even though I lost a total of only $30 there
in my lifetime.

In Las Vegas, I first talked with Muhammad Ali. In Vegas
I saw him beaten to within an inch of his life. In Vegas I met
Sugar Ray Leonard, Marvelous Marvin Hagler, Kenny Nor-
ton, Larry Holmes, Thomas Hearns, Wilfred Benitez, Vito
Antuofermo, Alexis Arguello, Mike Weaver, Roberto Duran.
I was more than happy to meet them there, for they were the
saving grace of the Strip.

The first boxer I met in Vegas stood in the North Tower
of Caesar's—a statue of Joe Louis in boxing gear, thrice life-
size, ominously squared off and turned at an angle to defend
a bank of elevators. When I met the real Joe Louis later that
day, I was shocked. Crippled by strokes, old Joe was in a
wheelchair, pushed by a smiling man in a sleeveless T-shirt.
The wheelchair pusher's biceps undulated like rats under a
quilt as Louis's head tilted this way and that, according to
the guide's navigation. Louis was resigned to the wheelchair,
so he had to be pushed to the fore, where high rollers, celebrities, fighters, fight people, and journalists could pay homage
or simply ogle and say, "That's Joe Louis!" Many of these
people wanted to talk to Joe. Some simply stared. People
touched his hands as he passed. Louis was still the main
attraction. A woman said, "He looks so happy." I doubted
it. First of all, he was in a wheelchair. Second, he was in Las
Vegas.

In those days, the biggest fights in boxing were held in a

prefabricated outhouse behind Caesar's called the Sports Pavilion (instead of at Yankee Stadium or in Madison Square Garden). Louis ended up as an official greeter for this brilliantly lit place of darkness. The heavyweight champion of the world in those days was a seemingly well-intentioned man named Larry Holmes, who was defending his title in April of 1981 against a man named Trevor Berbick.

The preliminary fights that day in the outhouse were macabre tarantellas performed by men who could not fight or even dance very well. One prelim stood out, billed as a "Return Grudge Match." Return Grudge Match, eh? What was Louis–Schmeling the second time around? This return grudge match was a North American Boxing Federation super lightweight title bout between Irish Leroy Haley of Las Vegas and Willie Rodriguez of Allentown, Pennsylvania. The NABF? Super lightweight? It seemed they'd make up anything as long as someone could be champion of it.

Willie Rodriguez had fought many times before he met Irish Leroy Haley. You could see it in his eyes. He had beaten Irish Leroy Haley before, and if his life depended on it, he could probably do it again. But his life didn't depend on it. He would get $2,000 or so, maybe, win or lose. After expenses. Before taxes. Willie didn't want to look too good. He didn't want to fight many more times. Fighting hurt. He was tired of it.

Irish Leroy Haley was the color of damp mahogany. He looked like Joe Frazier scrunched down to a jack-in-the-box. Haley wore high white ring shoes and knee socks. His trunks were white with black stripes down the sides. A bright green shamrock was stitched on the right leg. Rodriguez didn't notice the splendor.

The fight was an atoll of classicism in a sea of iniquity. Rodriguez bent from side to side from the waist, firing straight right hands west and east off Haley's head. Irish Leroy snorted. He knew pain. He expected its company. He was looking for . . . *this*! His left hook smashed into Rodriguez's head. But Rodriguez had been in this room before. He tied up Haley's stubby arms and they began again.

By round twelve, Irish Leroy was no longer immaculate. His right eye had been butchered by twisting jabs and crosses. The pressure on Haley's feet from the chase and retreat, the give and take, had buckled the outside seam of the shoe soles. They were cheap to begin with. His white trunks dropped below his belt and turned pink with blood. Mucus hurled from the mouths and noses during the in-fighting had turned the shamrock blue. Sweat was thick on Haley's back, and a small brown spot tainted the remaining white portion of his trunks. Rodriguez's face was bloody, too. His sides were flaming red. And he was backing up. Irish Leroy had found something to fight for, while Rodriguez had not.

The bell sounded. Irish Leroy threw up his hands. Rodriguez's eyes narrowed. His sneer was soft. He could have won the fight just as well. The judges awarded the fight to Irish Leroy Haley, the new NABF super lightweight champion of the world. Haley did a full somersault, nearly missing his feet. He steadied himself, grabbed the ring mike from the announcer, and yelled, "Ladies and gentlemen, I showed up tonight. I am the champ!"

Someone brought out a belt, a red piece of plastic adorned with a cheap-looking medallion. Haley donned the belt, then stumbled while leaving the ring. People laughed at him. Haley stayed in full ring regalia while the Holmes–Berbick bout was announced and contested. Haley answered when people called out, "Hey, Champ!"

Joe Louis had been forgotten in the action. They wheeled him away from all of it, and the next morning he died. He died just before the April 15 income tax deadline. He lay in state later in the prefabricated outhouse of Caesar's Palace. Nothing stopped. Not the roulette wheels, the misery, the lies, the return grudge matches, or anything else Louis had greeted while bound to his wheelchair in Las Vegas. It was business as usual in the counting house while Joe, the dead hero, greeted gawkers in the outhouse. He had fought longer than he should have because he had to pay off back income taxes. He didn't manage his money well. Other people didn't manage his money well either. They just spent it. Louis fought many exhibitions to give a lift to Army troops during the Second World War. He didn't want or expect a dime for that. That had been his duty. And that was fair, wasn't it?

He could have been buried not far away from the prefabricated outhouse, in the Nevada desert, but somewhere a decision was made to take his remains to Arlington National Cemetery, where the rest of the dead heroes lay. Dead heroes are apparently civilization's most favored kind. Finally, when it doesn't much matter, somebody was wise enough to care for Joe Louis properly. But that decision was made after the April 15 deadline. We were a little late. It was after midnight. We were delinquent on our taxes to Joe Louis. Isn't that right, Joe? Maybe he'll greet us again someday, friends.

I saw another great fighter nearly die in Las Vegas when my old hero, Muhammad Ali, now thirty-eight, went into the ring with his old sparring partner, Larry Holmes. It was difficult for me to believe that Ali had any business in the ring with Holmes. Time beats everybody. Holmes was a competent champion who had sparred upward of a hundred rounds with Ali himself. At thirty, Holmes was near his peak. The champion. The best. I prepared for the worst.

Don King made the formal announcement on Friday, September 5, 1980, at the Fairmont Hotel in San Francisco, a quick jaunt over the Bay Bridge. I had met King before and would again later at the first Duran–Leonard fight in Montreal in June of 1980. King had been part of the promotional package because of his working relationship with Duran, with whom he wildly celebrated and danced a jig at the end of the fifteenth round. King was a self-made man and a self-made caricature. I would meet him many more times, but in the lobby of the Fairmont on a brilliant summer afternoon was one of the times I remembered best. Don King, ex–numbers runner (before numbers became legal and known as the lottery) and convict, swept as regally as King Solomon across the carpeting toward the main conference room, flicking the ashes from his Havana cigar into a small silver tray he carried in his right hand.

"Don King, have you got a minute?"

"For paragons of the fourth estate? I have a lifetime," King said.

Then he began to crow. King's laughter was designed to carry and turn heads. Why was this man laughing? I have heard many people join King in laughter, whether they intended to or not. King gave me my few minutes, then threw his latest pitch to the assembly of media. When King would later have his problems with the Internal Revenue Service, I would look back on that Friday in the Fairmont and wonder how he couldn't have seen it coming. At one time in his notorious past, King would have been escorted from the halls of the Fairmont with all due haste. He would have made the house detectives drool.

As silver rattled on china, King explained in his bombastic way how he, and not rival promoter Bob Arum, had come to be a part of Ali–Holmes. He spoke of Arum and Egyptians and of making this fight happen and of Ali's exhortations to "get them millions."

King explained that he was but a part of the promotional team. The Caesar's Palace banner behind the podium was much larger than that of Don King Productions. King explained that there was money to be made. Big money. The people listening in the Fairmont understood the concept of big money well enough. But as King warmed to his favorite subject, members of the Fairmont audience fidgeted. As King's voice grew louder, discomfiture turned to chagrin. As the millions mounted, chagrin became outraged wonder.

"Muhammad Ali is going to get eight million," King said. "Larry Holmes is guaranteed three million. Taxes? This is a great nation, but it can't be a great nation unless we pay our taxes. The fight business is predicated on lies. Managers are lying to other managers, saying, 'This ain't nothing but a payday, my guy doesn't have a chance.' When all the time they're believing their guy can knock the other guy out and move on to a bigger payday. When I first started promoting in the '60s, fighters were getting the same thing they got in 1952 to fight a four-rounder in Madison Square Garden. One hundred and fifty dollars. The first fight of magnitude I promoted was Ali–Foreman. Both fighters got five million. Before that, the biggest purse had been two and a half million apiece for the first Ali–Frazier fight. The Ali–Holmes production, all told, may gross fifty million."

That brought forth a murmur and at least one unsuppressed hoot. How much of this is your cut? What's your end, smart guy?

"I will enjoy whatever compensation that I receive for my services," King said. And that was that. Those who had been made uneasy by the sight of Don King at the Fairmont now knew with certainty that they did not like him. As King had insisted, boxing was full of lies and liars. But there are no lies in the ring. Muhammad Ali was thirty-eight years old. That was no lie. It was no lie that he had only the faintest of chances against Holmes. So why would Ali risk his grace? Because money talked and King was the living proof.

Muhammad Ali had chosen Vegas as the place of his final rite of passage in the ring. The wheel of fortune seemed like a good bet to play. Even Bundini Brown, Ali's old sycophant and good luck charm, showed up, in blissful concentration at the chance to be personally responsible for yet another Ali miracle. "Larry," Bundini cried at Holmes while the latter finished his fight-week workouts. "Larry, Larry. I used to love you. But you have crossed the line, Larry. You're fightin' more than a man, Larry."

Holmes stared at Brown with disgust. "Stop embarrassin' yourself," he said.

Holmes was a well-respected champion among the boxing rank and file at the time. No one had a bad word to say about him—other than that he couldn't punch and hadn't really fought anybody. Couldn't punch compared to whom? Any man who weighed 212 pounds, sans fat, and was trained to deliver punches as a means of survival for as many years as Holmes had could definitely punch, as far as I could see. He was not a one-punch knockout guy, not a Lew Jenkins Theory guy, so the punch was a rap against him. When he disproved that rap by knocking out contender after contender, he would be presented with other raps. He was to become to raps what iron filings are to magnets, and all because he was not in the image of Muhammad Ali. Holmes didn't measure up.

When Holmes won the WBC heavyweight title from Kenny Norton in Vegas on June 9, 1978, he had done it with a torrid application of hammer-and-tongs punching in the fifteenth round. It had also been a fine hour for Kenny Norton. Norton was strong and could be a crushing puncher. Yet Holmes had fought him without caution and traded sweeping hooks and battering straight right hands with Norton. It was Holmes who won the ring center in the fifteenth round and the title he was to keep for seven years.

Before the Holmes–Ali fight, Norton showed up, a splendiferous model and part-time actor who had an enviable gift of gab. Norton had never truly liked fighting. He had done what he had to do. He didn't like getting hit. He left the ring with his senses intact, although a final loss to cripple-shooting Gerry Cooney counted for something against him. Later, in 1986, Norton, driving a classic European car, would swerve off a freeway ramp in Los Angeles and wind up in a tree with a broken jaw, a fractured skull, a broken leg, and an unrecognizable face. If he had been a lesser man, physically, his neck would have been snapped like a twig. The brain injury impaired his motor ability and speech, and he ended up like Muhammad Ali anyway. Destiny is destiny.

But Norton had tried to avoid it, and he didn't want to see it happen to anyone else. Before the Holmes–Ali bout, I asked Norton who he thought would win. Norton said, "I just want to see a good clean fight. I can't make predictions, other than the fact that I don't want to see Ali get hurt." Norton was that kind of man.

Ali had little chance, if any, against Holmes. But there was always the memory of 1975, and the night nobody saw in Zaire against the unbeatable (sic) George Foreman. No film of this fight has ever been offered for mass public consumption in America. I saw a few still photos and heard descriptions and interpretations from people who were there. Ali had won when there was no way he could win that night. This was five years later, but you could never trust a legend to die quietly, and that was what sold tickets to what turned out to be a mismatch.

Even Angelo Dundee was unsure. I met him outside Café Roma, a Caesar's Palace restaurant and melting pot for the fight crowd. "Thanks for meeting me, Ang."

"Anytime."

"Hope Ali looks as fit as you do."

"Oh yeah, my guy looks great. . . ."

Ang was great. Ali was working harder than usual. Ali looked quick, quicker than he'd looked in years. Ali was, in short, Ali. Angelo's exit line was one that always stayed with me, over the years. "I'm through being amazed by Muhammad Ali," he said. Angelo said this with a wave and a shake of his head. If Ali were to knock out Larry Holmes, then read from *Othello* and dance in the ring with the beautiful Veronica

Ali immediately after the bout, Angelo would not be surprised. I had a different interpretation of the line. Ali had no chance.

"So am I, Ang. So am I. See ya."

Ali must have known. There was no way for the mind of a master boxer to deceive itself on these matters once in the ring. I also knew there would be no chance for me, not for any exclusive interviews with the great champion in the week prior to the fight. I tried, though. I tailed him and his retinue on the Wednesday before the fight, after a press conference, ending up in his suite at Caesar's. The room was full. Threading my way through the layers of people, I found him in repose on a huge sofa, a pillow resting behind his large head. It was nearly twenty years since he first "shook up the world." His mouth was open in mock anger, and he held up both hands with the fingers extended save the left thumb curled into his palm. "Nine!" he said, signifying his prediction for a ninth-round knockout, giving the photographers and reporters the vintage Ali they wanted.

The youthful vigor I had known from film and videotape and imagination had metamorphosed into something different. When the picture-taking was done, Ali settled farther into the couch, his face wearing the serene look of an elder of immense knowledge. In terms of boxing expertise, he was better than ever. But physically, he was done. He had no way to exhibit what he knew. Briefly, I wondered who had first said that youth is wasted on the young. Still, here he was. Muhammad Ali. One of the five most famous people in the history of civilization. A man who had changed things.

Such men take risks amounting to life and death. When I looked at Muhammad Ali, I saw men, his contemporaries, who were shot down and killed at the same time that I was a boy, admiring them all very much. Martin Luther King, Jr. John Kennedy. Robert Kennedy. Medgar Evers. Malcolm X. To do battle with ignorance requires fearless men. Change terrifies the ignorant. The ignorant lash out when confused.

The ignorant ease their confusion by thinking of change as a threat to life as they know it. They kill what they do not understand, for it threatens them. It may make them better, but, they feel, it is better to be safe than sorry. So survival keys these ordinary men who end up becoming generals more quickly than the likes of Muhammad Ali, the kind of men who send themselves into battle first.

It was Malcolm X's philosophy of self-defense and determination that Muhammad Ali personified, and in so doing, changed nearly everything for nearly everybody. Before Ali, there was no such thing as a truly independent black heavyweight champion of the world, one who chose who made money off him, and certainly none with the gall to be outspoken, not to mention well-spoken. Ali was portrayed in the nearly all-white media with disquiet when he began his twenty-year run as that most magnificent of master boxers, a bigger Sugar Ray Robinson. A Robinson that never deferred to whites. Convention, at that time, meant subservience on the part of black men. Muhammad Ali simply said, "I am the greatest," and in so saying, spoke volumes. To me, at least.

Athletically old at thirty-eight and comfortably reclined on that couch in Vegas, Ali awed me. He predicted he would win the heavyweight title by stopping the feared Sonny Liston in 1964, then did it by *backing Sonny up* with hard, lashing combinations, at the same time smoothly avoiding Sonny's tremendous but by comparison ponderous blows. *Wham-wham-wham- wham. Oops. Oops. No-you-can't-hit-me-Sonny. Wham-wham-wham- wham. You can't stop me.* After, Ali said, "I shook up the world! I am the greatest of all times."

I, for one, believed him. Ten years later, as a copyboy at the *Tribune* on the red-eye shift, I killed time between runs by typing RALPH WILEY IS THE GREATEST SPORTSWRITER IN THE WORLD, BAR NONE, again and again and again on assorted IBM Selectric typewriters. I always carefully ripped the evidence to shreds. I did this with no conscious reference to what Ali said. But where had I found such indomitable dreams? Where else did I gain the temerity to think it?

Some time after Ali had beaten Liston a second time, circa 1965, *Sports Illustrated* interviewed Floyd Patterson and helped him explain "Why I Can't Let a Muslim Be Champion." When Ali beat Patterson on November 22, 1965, punishing him vindictively in the process on the same day Jack Kennedy had been shot two years earlier, Ali was vilified, but left an even stronger image in my mind. What in the world did religion have to do with boxing? Nothing. Not even the worship of Ali. The eventual reality for Ali—the self-proclaimed greatest of all time—would not be a draft board of the federal government or even legend status, but Larry Holmes, his old sparring partner. There could not be a greatest of all time, just the greatest in a moment in time. A moment was to be remembered and evaluated against other moments, when the eye of the beholder and the skill of the participants had changed. And everything changed, like it or not. Life was a series of moments, of perceptions. Most people accept the way they choose to remember things as fact. What choice do we have? Such is the power of public relations, the power of an article in *Sports Illustrated*, the power of Muhammad Ali.

I distinctly remember one television interviewer from when Ali was a young, flashy contender. Flabbergasted by Ali's nonstop proclamations, the interviewer finally said, "Just let me see you close your mouth for ten seconds." Ali said, "That's impossible. That's impossible. I'm knocking out all bums and if you're not careful I'll knock you out." I was a boy and remember being happy that he had not shut up. Somehow, it didn't seem right that he should.

When Malcolm X was asked by yet another flabbergasted interviewer some time before the first Liston fight in Miami, "Do you consider yourself militant?" he answered, "I consider myself Malcolm." Ali learned from this man who had not said yes or no to whether he considered himself a condition. He considered himself alive, existing, with all the inherent possibilities of being himself. And, through Muhammad Ali, this is what he gave to me. Ali himself said it best later. Less than a year before the Liston fight, Ali was Cassius Clay and saying fearfully, "I want no part of Sonny Liston. He's a bad man!" But Malcolm X taught him that self-defense was a human right and obligation: "The man has crippled you. He has clipped your wings. Broken your legs. And then he puts you on the race track and condemns you because you can't keep up with the other runners."

Ali remembered it this way: "One day I met Malcolm X in New York. We got on the airplane and all the white people were saying, 'There's Malcolm X!' Everybody was so afraid. He had no guns, he didn't bother nobody. Bulletin in Miami— Malcolm X has just got in town. Keep a good watch out. News. Hello, everybody. CBS News. We understand that Malcolm X just landed. He got in a cab. We don't know where he is going.

"That made me feel good. I said, Hey, man, I ain't never saw a black man get so much respect. He's got the white folks scared? I said, I wanna be like him. Everywhere he'd go, white people got his autograph. They respected him. And I'm getting ready to fight Sonny Liston. They all came to get Malcolm X's autograph. I said, this man does nothing but stand up for truth, speaks bold, he's bigger than a boxer!"

But that had been sixteen years ago.

"Champ," I said, in an effort to wedge my questions past the cry of all the others. Several of my fellow journalists looked at me with distaste. They had been calling him Muhammad. "You know more about what to do in the ring than any man alive."

Ali held up an index finger. "Of all times," he said, his voice beginning to rasp. He had talked a lot that day and was getting tired.

64

"How does it feel, not being able to do the things you once could do in there?"

He didn't answer right away. His eyes left the room. My attention was riveted to him. When he finally did answer, he was speaking more to himself than he was speaking to me.

"I can still do things," he said slowly. "I raised Larry. Raised him up. He meets his teacher in me."

Ali had his final moment of magnificence in the ring just before the fight, taunting and grimacing, exhorting the crowd. Once the fight began, it was all Larry Holmes. The dissection was workmanlike. Ali could not offer his jab to the quicker Holmes, who beat him time and again to that punch and the following right. It was sacrilegious to me, watching Muhammad Ali being outquicked. After that night, I knew that in this life, anything can happen, given time.

It was the seventh round, on Friday, October 3, 1980, when Muhammad Ali, the last of the great heavyweight champions, reached down into what was once his limitless reserve and found that Time had drunk him dry. Three rounds later, he sat drooping on his stool as his minions argued and Time, for once, stood still. The ringside doctors, manager Jabir Muhammad, and trainer Angelo Dundee wanted the world title bout stopped. And they were right.

The record book reads: Larry Holmes retained his WBC heavyweight title on an eleventh-round TKO when Muhammad Ali failed to answer the bell for round twelve. The mercenary exercise was over, and so was the era. Ali's eyes were blackened and closed as he was whisked away from the cheers, taunts, boos, and tears, up into the counting house, where he began to salve his wounds with the thought of the multi-million-dollar payday. The King was dead. Long live the King. Holmes said, "I beat a human being. I did pull back one whole round because I was hitting him at will. . . ."

I didn't know what compelled Holmes to spare Ali in the seventh round, but I had an idea. Holmes was on his way to winning every round on every card. He had landed a square left hook into Ali's right side, and the great champion doubled over in pain. Holmes had already made it obvious he was younger, stronger, quicker, and talented enough to make all that count, to do as he pleased with Ali. Now Ali, in tortured bedevilment, turned away from Holmes, leaving his temple and jawline exposed for Holmes's straight right. For years to come, Holmes's straight right would be the most devastating and least appreciated punch in the heavyweight division. At that moment, it was likely at the height of its power.

The survival instinct always shows up; in the ignorant, it shows up early. In great, champion fighters, it shows up only when they are near death. No matter how courageous a fighter might be, after enough pain, enough blows with no hope of meaningful retaliation, the body takes over the mind and says, "Go, old friend." Joe Frazier turned away—unconsciously— while under the hands of George Foreman in Jamaica years before this. I would see the survival instinct more often in less determined fighters, but every fighter, every human, has it. Now Ali turned away, and Holmes stood over him, his right cocked. He looked like a man holding a mug of beer. And Holmes just backed off. I never had any problem respecting him after that.

Marvelous Marvin Hagler was to fight Vito Antuofermo for the middleweight title behind Caesar's, on November 30, 1979, on the same day that Sugar Ray Leonard met Wilfred Benitez for the welterweight crown. Hagler occupied the undercard. He was not considered a headliner then, even though he was fighting Vito for the undisputed world middleweight championship. It was still Ray Leonard's card.

Leonard had charisma. Marvin, on the other hand, didn't have a pulse as far as the world was concerned at the time. He was a journeyman with an impressive knockout record. He was fighting in a time of several famous and great midweight fighters—Leonard, Hearns, and Duran. Hagler thought that this was his bad luck. Far from it. Of the four, Marvin was the inferior boxer. But he was bigger than they, big enough to have his own class.

Back in 1979, Hagler had been avoided like the plague by middleweights. He wore his head shaved. He was a good-natured man, but a dangerous, hard fighter. Hagler considered himself to be one of the better fighters alive. And he was right. But few knew enough about him then to agree. Hagler would be borne out over time, but even back then he considered himself the uncrowned champion—much, I suppose, as he still does. Who among us does not, I thought as I first saw Hagler walking among the crowd in the press tent. He was passing out white plastic flyswatters emblazoned with typed script. He gave me one and smiled a winning smile. The fly-swatter said: "VITO THE MOSQUITO, I'LL SWAT HIM LIKE A FLY—Marvelous Marvin Hagler."

"Remember, it's Marvelous Marvin," he said.

"Okay, Marvelous."

The Muhammad Ali School of Self-Promotion attracted many students. Middleweight fighters always seemed to be more like ordinary folk than the larger-than-life heavyweights. The lighter-weight fighters were like physically gifted elves and brownies. Middleweights just seemed regular. Hagler accepted all this with a degree of misunderstanding. He worked hard and suffered greatly as only a fighter in training does, to be seen as larger than life or magical and to have paydays commensurate with these traits and abilities. Instead, he was largely ignored. All he knew was that somehow this was costing him money. He felt he could beat anyone his weight. There ought to be a market. So he talked in long, rambling sentences designed to captivate the listener. He wasn't evasive during an interview, or inside the ring, either, as it turned out. Healed cuts sliced through his eyebrows. He seemed formidable enough, and he felt he had something to prove.

Two days later, Antuofermo and Hagler fought for fifteen

bloody rounds, bashing and bouncing off each other like toy trucks in the hands of incorrigible boys. Antuofermo was a tank on short legs who threw wide punches. Hagler took the shots and answered them. The draw which was declared seemed eminently fair. It was not Sugar Ray Robinson vs. Jake LaMotta, but it wasn't 1947, either.

I underestimated the implications of the Hagler–Antuofermo fight. In a later battle, Hagler would stop Vito, but on cuts, and eventually Marvin would prove to be, for a while, peerless at his weight, 160 pounds. But meanwhile, the welterweights, Leonard, Hearns, and Duran, provided a higher level of boxing skill, and much more intriguing personalities for me. They were, in a word, better boxers, even though Hagler would later beat Duran and Hearns. But then, Duran would beat Leonard, and Hearns would beat Duran, and Hagler would lose to Leonard. Marvelous should have been proud to be included in such fighting company and to have the chance to become rich, to boot. But that was not to be. Hagler left the ring a psychologically beaten man. He was between Sugar Ray Leonard and history. So he had to go.

I thought about the time I saw Joe Louis at the end of November in 1979. I had approached the wheelchair during a brief parting of well-wishers and curiosity seekers and given Joe the OK sign with my right hand. I didn't smile. Louis's eyes were wide open, cognizant, but his jaw was slack. I started to speak but held myself back because I could not think of what might be the right thing to say, and I wanted to say the right thing or nothing at all. I wanted to tell him that he would always be the champion in some houses. But I had become an inquisitor by trade. I was best at offering questions, not answers, and I was shy with strangers by nature. So I had nothing to say to Joe Louis, because he couldn't reply. I was not up to the situation.

I stepped back and studied his hands. They were broad, with thick fingers that were curled inward. He seemed as if he couldn't make a fist. I stared at the right. Imagine reaching out your hand and touching a flame. The speed at which you bring your hand back is the speed at which Louis once punched out with his right.

I remember his eyes standing open and going blank while a small, dapper fellow in a tuxedo stooped so that his eyes would be level with the old man's. The small fellow winked and smiled, as if he and Joe Louis shared some private joke. The small man's name was Sugar Ray Charles Leonard, the great welterweight as consummate entertainer. Boxing, Vegas . . . it was all his show now.

4
Leonard

"I'm only as good as the guy on the stool."

That was one of Angelo Dundee's favorite sayings. As a trainer, Angelo was excellent. When Angelo said "My guy will win," everyone knew who he was talking about. Angelo had been in the corner with hundreds of fighters in his time. But when he said "My guy," everyone knew he was talking about either Ali or Leonard. Angelo was only as good as they were. When Ali fought Henry Cooper on June 18, 1963, Angelo had pointed out to the referee that Ali's glove was slit. Angelo made this assertion after Ali had been dazed by a Cooper left hook. Some noticed Angelo had scissors. But the fact remained that Ali, in getting his glove repaired, had extra minutes to regain his senses. He went on to stop Cooper on cuts. But Ali was gone. It was Leonard's time now.

In Leonard's case, when Ray fought Thomas Hearns in the greatest fight I ever saw live, Angelo leaned over between the twelfth and thirteenth rounds and said, "You're blowin' it, kid!" Leonard likely knew the status of the bout. After all, he was in it. But Angelo did what he could do. The greatest of champions didn't need advice. A trainer was employed to map out some kind of physical training regimen and make sure it was adhered to. There might be a suggestion during the fight. Whether or not it would be noticed over the hundreds of other suggestions that are screamed during a championship bout was another matter. But I believed the fighter blocked most of the noise out. A champion knew what he wanted to do in the ring, even if he couldn't do it. The trainers took out the fighters' mouthpieces, offered water, helped clean up cuts, and argued points later. The fighters fought.

The better trainers also provided excellent public relations for their fighters, and so it was with Angelo. Leonard had won the Olympic gold medal in 1976, and by November 30, 1979, he was 25–0, without having had what people called "a real test." At this point he was not up to his fullest proportions as a welterweight. His chest was not deep. His shoulders were narrow. His boxing abilities were by far his most impressive physical traits in the ring. He could throw a wide variety of punches—the whole ball of wax: hooks, jabs, leads, crosses, uppercuts, multiple combinations of all these, new applications of some. He could throw these punches with either hand, and he had power in both hands. He had the full ticket.

I asked Angelo if he might introduce me to Leonard, so that Ray might feel more comfortable talking. "My guy'll talk," Angelo said. "But he can't tell you how good he is because even I don't know that."

Leonard was physically unimposing. He was small in his clothes. Most fighters have an uninspired handshake, but Leonard took this to another level. His was like boiled spaghetti. His hands had already pounded on many heads. He was a headhunter, like Ali, so his hands were already tender. We were in one of the ballrooms at Caesar's for an informal soirée which attempted to mingle the members of the press

71

and a few celebrities with the fighters who could stand this company with less than disastrous results. Leonard was smiling, pleasant, but not at all talkative. He was completely confident that he had Wilfred Benitez's number. I saw no reason to dispute him.

"Are you looking for a knockout, Ray?"

A wink. A smile.

"What about Duran?"

"I can beat Duran. But I'm fighting Benitez."

"What about Tommy Hearns?"

"Awesome. That's what Thomas Hearns is."

"You beat Tommy in amateurs."

A wink and a smile. "I'm hoping everybody forgets. I'm hoping Tommy forgets."

Leonard then became distracted by the whirl of personalities around him. Back then he was so full of himself. He was always confident, but I never saw him quite as confident as he was on that evening. He could win the world title and beat Benitez on pure skill alone, and he knew it. "He's the best at the weight since Sugar Ray Robinson," Dundee had confided. Since Leonard was the one now employing Dundee, Dundee added, "My guy might be as good as Robinson."

Benitez was a fighter who matured early. He won the world junior welterweight title when he was eighteen, and at twenty-one he was at home in the ring. He was a very young Yaqui Lopez. Benitez counterpunched, and if he happened to be stronger and quicker than his opponent, he would win, as he had done thirty-eight times without a loss going into the Leonard fight. Benitez was too proud of his looks to be a counterpuncher for as long as Yaqui had been, however. The advent of the Leonards and Hearnses signaled a long demise for the young counterpuncher. Leonard defeated Benitez on a fifteenth-round TKO, splitting open his forehead in the process.

. . .

I had gotten to know the sportswriters from the Bay Area. Since we worked and often traveled together and had the same problems, miseries, and brief exultations, a camaraderie developed. But covering boxing was more of a lone-wolf operation for me. The competition among writers covering a fight was less keen than on the football, baseball, and basketball beats. For the biggest fights, it was news by formula. The press conferences were arranged, and we were given fact sheets, the "tale of the tape," and mass interviews. I got most of my information by hanging around coffee shops, looking suspicious. I also knocked on a hotel door or two. Sometimes I got in. Sometimes I didn't. I became accustomed to judging fighters on my own instinct and the opinions of the people actually involved, preferably the fighters themselves. Only rarely would I consult with another writer or even offer a prediction out of print. Covering a fight was different.

I knew hardly a soul for my next meeting with Leonard, which came in Montreal in June 1980. Here I met Red Smith, the columnist for *The New York Times*. He was old and looked tired, a magician bored with magic while still spinning straw into gold three days a week.

I had predicted in print that Leonard would defeat Roberto Duran for the undisputed welterweight championship, so the first question I wanted to ask Smith was who he thought would win the fight. We were at the weigh-in. Smith brightened up when I said hello, and soon I was convinced he was the most agreeable man I'd ever met in the business. "Hi, howareya," he said. "Beautiful day, isn't it?" Then he smiled and said, "You know, I like Duran in this." He'd already written that Duran would show Leonard another side of fighting, the side of will, a deeper depth than Leonard was accustomed to, a depth he might initially fear and could not presently cope with. Smith was right on the money. I was not, even though it was not because I wasn't impressed with Duran. I was.

The stories say that Roberto Duran knocked a horse onto the cobblestones of Chorillo, Panama, when he was fifteen years old, 125 pounds, and not at all angry. He was just a muchacho trying to make change for a sweet or the favor of a girl by showing off. The men of the streets had promised him coins for the feat, the same coins he received when he danced for *touristas* or when he took on contracts against the faces of unlucky peers. Now, at twenty-nine, Duran weighed 147 pounds, having trimmed down from 165. Leonard weighed considerably less than a horse. However, horses didn't hit back. The point was not to question Duran's punch as a welterweight, even though he was a natural lightweight.

There were several things to take into account about Duran. He was a finisher. He may have had the most accurate, the most agile, the greatest right hand in the business. Also, Duran didn't get the credit he deserved as a boxer. He was a master boxer, a term that may be accurately applied to no more than a hundred men in the entire twentieth century. He was 69–1 at the time, not only because of his Hands of Stone, *manos de piedra*, for which he was famous and feared, but because of his consummate ring generalship. He was always in balance and could punch with both hands *and* was a great defensive fighter, able to avoid all but the best-conceived punches. He cut off the ring or expanded it to his liking. Duran hadn't gone past third grade, but as a fighter, he was a willful genius.

It had been seven years since Leonard had lost a fight. Duran had not lost in eight. They were both highly skilled in the science, but Leonard had not yet become a master, for he hadn't developed his will completely. And after talking with Red Smith, I felt if the fight lasted long, it would come down to a test of wills. I didn't know at the time that the most devastating quality of Duran was not his boxing skill but his resolute will. For him, the fight was never over. Hostilities merely ceased for a while. To Duran, being hit was something to remember, something to avenge. It is sobering to face a man like this.

On June 20, at Olympic Stadium, before 46,317 people, the largest crowd I'd ever seen at a fight, a light-heavyweight named Cleveland Denny took some heavy punches to the head thrown by Gaetean Hart, a bullish man from the eastern provinces of Canada, in the second preliminary to the Leonard–Duran bout. Denny's hands had come down before the final blows. He couldn't defend himself. Denny was removed from the ring, limp. I watched this without cognizance and later was told that Denny might never wake up, and he didn't. He died. It was only a rumor then, but the information quickly made the rounds at dark and dank Stade Olympique. Denny was dead? Later, I was told that when Hart received the news he sank to his knees. He attended the funeral and begged the forgiveness of Denny's widow. I never heard Hart's name again after that.

No warning had come that Denny was being beaten to death. No red light. No loud noise. But Denny was dead. I noted it passively and chose to consider it one of life's many grim jokes. It had been Denny's time. That was all. But this was what Leonard confronted as he entered the ring to face Duran.

Leonard's followers brayed, stomped, and cheered as he entered the ring. Aretha Franklin was there. I remember her eyes glistening. Leonard held his arms aloft, bent at the elbows. He was unconvincing. His face betrayed his doubts. He was fighting Roberto Duran, and for the first time, he really didn't know what might happen. Duran, on the other hand, seemed all business, jangling his arms to the sound of blood-stirring, amplified drumbeats.

They fought a bruising fight. This was the night when Leonard proved to himself that he could face anything in the ring. Duran, the lightweight champion, buckled Leonard's legs with an overhand right in the second round. Leonard, happy to be alive in the same spot where Cleveland Denny had just died, eventually saw that he was all right and began to fight back. The two feinted and exchanged in blurs, toe to toe, never sacrificing their defense, for fifteen rounds. It was a great little fight. There was really no doubt that Duran was the victor. Also, there was really no doubt that he could probably never beat Leonard again.

"Esto!" Duran screamed loudly afterward, slapping at his chest. *"Esto! Esto!"* This! This! He spoke of his heart. His heart had done it, he was saying. Leonard was brought into the interview area, already wiser. "This was the toughest fight of my life," he said. "People questioned whether I could take a big punch. They got their answer tonight."

Leonard had received his own answer. From then until he quit the ring, he would rule the middleweights with a quick, iron hand. No matter how talented or strong or skillful or willful they might be, Leonard took care of them somehow. First Duran in their rematch in New Orleans. Then Tommy Hearns. Finally, in another age, 1987, Leonard would make a fool out of Hagler, who had once fought on his undercard. And all the while, Leonard would keep that smiling image worthy of display. Like Ray Robinson before him, he would make it look easier than it was.

Yet, Duran was more fascinating to me because of his psyche. He had half-stolen Leonard's heart before the Montreal fight with his supreme confidence, not to mention the insults. Twice he called Leonard a *maricón*—a homosexual, the ultimate Latin fighter's insult. This is a common enough practice among all ring opponents, but Leonard had never heard it directed at him from the sneering mouth of a would-be legend. Duran verbally abused Leonard's wife, Juanita, in a language Leonard didn't understand. Duran was coldly, instinctively obsessed. Duran was a raven riding on the back of a wolf running across snow and ice. See, stalk, hunt, kill—live to hunt again.

At the weigh-in before the Montreal fight, Duran had inspired chaos and reveled in it. The announcers spoke English and French, but not Spanish, so when announcements were made, the Spanish-speaking followers of Duran would look at each other and then back at the podium, demanding some kind of explanation. None was forthcoming. As Duran entered the room, his crowd of followers surged forward. "Ladies and gentlemen, please," the English-speaking announcer implored. "Would you people back away. You're not doing anything for Roberto with this. Back away. *Back away.* You people, get down from there. Please, please, stay back! You're hurting your man!"

Duran was smiling. Nothing was hurting him. His face was a mask of stony detachment, framed by a stickly beard, with irises that contained no light. His hair was swept back and he appeared to be smiling in contempt—of what, I could not say. Duran's natural weight, the weight of his bone structure and punching power, was lightweight, the 135-pound limit. He had been a legend at that weight. Now, at 147 pounds, he had won the welterweight title. He would eventually fight at 154 pounds, even at 160. He would last fifteen rounds in losing a decision to the befuddled Hagler, who was out of his boxing class against these folk. But Duran had no answer at 154 pounds for Hearns, who knocked him out quicker than you can say ten. Duran's weight would go even higher than this when he wasn't training, and he didn't look good with weight. He was meant to be thin. Gaunt. Hungry. He resembled Portofino the Fat and not Roberto Duran whenever he added the excess poundage. Even his eyes became softer. They sat farther back in his face.

Leonard and Duran fought six months after their Montreal

meeting, this time in New Orleans. Leonard had now paid the piper on the question of heart, the matter of will. Duran no longer chilled that hidden part of him. He had confronted it, and from then on was a changed fighter. Now it was a question of skill again, of ring sense, of execution. This time Leonard's superior lateral movement and hand speed would come into play, and he would box Duran from a distance. Duran had no answer for this. Leonard dropped down on his heels only to counter hard punches with hard punches of his own. But even while losing, Duran was the central figure.

In New Orleans, two days before the second Leonard fight, Duran came through the lobby of the Hyatt Regency hotel next to the Superdome, where the fight would be contested. It was late at night. Duran was in shape, but not as trim as he had been in Montreal. I came alongside him and his friend, who apparently was named Luis. Or perhaps that's just what Duran called him. Luis didn't argue. Happily for me, Luis was friendly and somewhat bilingual. I spoke to Duran with a nod of respect. He returned the nod more coolly.

"Would you ask Roberto if he'd mind answering a few questions? *Hay preguntas,*" I said to Luis, adding my laughable Spanish in hopes of a better entry.

"What kind of questions?" Luis asked.

I produced a notebook and pen and tried to appear all business, since the informal approach didn't appear to have disarmed Duran. He rocked from his heels to his toes, his hands clasped behind him, as he waited for an elevator. He looked like a dictator.

"Does Roberto expect the fight to go fifteen rounds?"

Luis translated. Duran broke his silence.

"One round, if he knows Leonard," Luis said, smiling. "Are you a fan of Leonard?"

"I am a journalist. A fan of all fighters, and no fighters."

Luis translated for Duran, who looked at me and then spoke again and pointed to my notebook. I cursed my slow recognition of his rapid tongue. "Duran says you should write that Leonard is not in his class as a fighter, that Leonard is a baby who should be afraid that Roberto will kill him this time and make his trembling wife a widow."

And, boy, did I write that down. "Will this be in the newspaper tomorrow?"

I said that it would, leaving out which one. I exited the elevator with Duran and Luis, although it was not my floor. Duran seemed even more put off by what had become an imposition. He spoke again, more gruffly.

Luis was apologetic. "The interview is over."

"Just one more question. Roberto has never been knocked out. Would he feel it's time to quit if Leonard knocked him out this time? Or would he come back?"

Almost fearfully, Luis translated for Duran, who was striding purposefully now, eager to arrive at his destination, where he could shut the door in my face and Luis's too, if the chattering fool continued to disobey his wishes. He whirled and spoke contemptuously.

"He says no one can knock him out, especially not that girl, that Leonard. He says he is Duran. Do you understand?"

I walked away scribbling furiously while Duran slammed the door to the room.

Three nights later Duran would be defeated on a sixth-round TKO, waving off Leonard with the words *"No más, no más."* Though Leonard had claimed the universal welterweight title by fighting a smarter fight—from outside in—Duran remained the most talked-about fighter at the time. Only then, it was said that Duran's name lived in infamy. He had quit. People had plunked down their good, hard-earned dollars to watch a great fight and Duran had quit cold. Abject cowardice from Roberto Duran—it was impossible, but true.

In the post-fight press conference, Duran's words were translated as meaning that he said he had a stomachache. Many examinations were made of his diet in the hours prior to the fight. What Duran might have meant—what I believed he meant—was that his stomach hurt, but not from inside out. Leonard had landed shattering left hooks to Duran's body in the fourth and fifth rounds, powerful blows struck as quickly as snakebites. Duran's arms were involuntarily slowed down by this underpublicized body attack. When a posturing Leonard windmilled his right hand and landed a left jab in Duran's face, Duran dropped his hands in dismay. He could not counter. He saw it, but he could not throw it. His right was frozen by a battered right side that overrode the reflex to punch. Leonard began to edge in closer after that, dropping down in anticipation of landing heavier punches.

Duran, in his fighter's heart, knew that he would be beaten badly in his current shape, even made to look foolish. So he waved the fight off. At the time, he had no thought of the "shame" that might go along with this act. It was a prudent act, and Duran, for all his fearsome fighting ways, was a prudent boxer. Muhammad Ali had fought with a broken jaw for some ten rounds against Ken Norton in March 1973, and lost anyway. This kind of courage is recognized only by eulogists and sportswriters. Duran's was another kind. He knew when he was beaten, and he would prolong that feeling for nothing and no one. He would live to fight again, but he would not suffer the indignity of being pummeled while slowly becoming defenseless. At times, there is nothing noble in surviving but survival itself. Duran understood who he was and what he was doing better than any other prizefighter I would encounter. But Leonard would join Duran in this deep knowledge of himself, eventually.

It soon became obvious that a Leonard versus Thomas Hearns fight would have an epic feel, especially after Hearns won the WBA version of the welterweight title by crushing Pipino Cuevas in two rounds in Detroit. I had met Hearns before that, before Leonard met Duran, in February 1980. He had knocked out Fighting Jim Richards in Vegas while Leonard sat at ringside. Nineteen months after Hearns had toyed with Fighting Jim, the Hit Man met Leonard at Caesar's Palace. They were by then the WBA and WBC welterweight champions, respectively. Leonard had fought Duran twice and after some good, bruising exchanges completely overwhelmed Ayub Kalule, a strong and, at the time, undefeated junior middleweight from Nigeria. Leonard had vaulted up in class physically since the Benitez fight. His body had developed to its welterweight peak efficiency. His calves and shoulder muscles ridged out far past the bone. He looked like he was sheathed in elastic. He was more like a cobra than Hearns, who liked to be called the Motor City Cobra better than Hit Man, his original, more arresting nickname.

Soon people would be calling Hearns the Get-Hit Man, derisively—too derisively for a man who won four world titles and lost a grand total of three fights in ten years. But he was fighting people's feelings. He was fighting Leonard, whose boxing world it had come to be. Hearns had captured the public notice by nearly decapitating poor Cuevas at Joe Louis Arena in his hometown of Detroit. There I saw what a monumental problem Hearns would be for any 147-pound opponent. He was six-one, with a triangular torso that was wide with muscle but not really deep anywhere. His punching power—the right—was deadening. He had what people wanted to see. The hot rod. The Lew Jenkins Theory, the KO punch. Hearns hit Cuevas with the straight right hand and Cuevas nearly did a somersault. Then he convulsed. Hearns hit him again with the right and Lupe Sanchez, Cuevas's manager, fired a white towel into the ring while Pipino, by now safely facedown, hugged the canvas, literally for dear life. The sound of Hearns's right landing flush was a frightening sound, like a bat striking a softball. "Eet eesn't fair," Sanchez would say later. "He ees too beeg."

By now I was writing four columns a week for the *Tribune*, and pissing people off all over the place. If one of my column days happened to fall on a day which also required a news story, I did both. Deadlines measured my life. I had, out of necessity, developed a typing style which was not pretty to look at but could make the keyboard of an average word processor scat like Ella Fitzgerald. My left hand typed fluidly, just as it had been taught in class long ago. My right hand only used the index finger and was more assertive, punching with a harder strike. The right hand thought while the left reacted. I made typos with the left. Never the right. I typed like a boxer. Like Ali.

The Leonard–Hearns fight was to be held on September 17, 1981. The next day was a column day, so it would be double duty for me. I felt I understood how good each fighter could be, their histories, their strengths. I was as ready to see how it would come out as anybody. Leonard was twenty-five, Hearns was twenty-three. There was no question that Leonard was the more mature fighter of the two. There was also no question that Hearns could punch with the right as if he were holding a steel bar in his fist. There should be plenty to write about and not much time to do it. This was much better than having plenty of time to write about nothing.

Anticipation ran high everywhere, and Leonard was the lead actor, for better or worse. Next to the *Tribune* building was Eddie Butler's Ringside Bar. The newsfolk made a beeline here after work and left in less straight trajectories for home later. Eddie Butler, who had been a fighter once, stopped polishing his beer glasses one day and looked up. There I was. "Ralph, you going down to Vegas?"

"Sure, Eddie."

"Hey, I think that Leonard's got a little geek in 'im, don't you, Ralph?"

"I doubt it, Eddie. No more than your average welter-weight."

"Waal . . . I like the puncha. Gimme the puncha every time. Leonard's a tricky little sneak, though. Give him that."

"It won't be easy either way."

Bill Eaton and I were discussing the many possibilities of Leonard versus Hearns one day shortly before I was to leave for Vegas. I offered that in his own way and time, Leonard could prove he was the Sugar Ray Robinson of his generation if he won this fight.

What did I want to go and say that for? inquired a cartoonist who happened to be passing by. He had never gotten in the way of a good opinion before that I knew of. But I had struck a nerve. "Nobody," he bellowed, "is as good as Robinson. Never was. Never will be. You got any idea of how many times Sugar Ray Robinson fought?"

"Some," I sniffed. "Two hundred."

"Two hundred and one."

I didn't like to be wrong.

"And Leonard?"

More my speed.

"Thirty-one. I think."

"There y'are. No comparison."

I knew a lost cause when I saw one. "I suppose. We'll watch it. Then we'll talk."

The Leonard–Hearns fight turned out to be a timeless piece of boxing. There have been hundreds of great fights in history. The young, ubiquitous Ali against the fearsome Liston. The old, masterful Ali against the ultimate puncher, Foreman. Rocky Marciano in maniacal desperation against a master boxer, Ezzard Charles. Pep and Sadler. Zale and Graziano. Jack Johnson, driving through Stanley Ketchel's mandible after the middleweight had knocked Jack down and embarrassed him in Colma, outside San Francisco. Robinson, hooking, hooking, hooking. Louis on a bombing run against a dozen men, against Conn. Some people even preferred the memory of Ron Lyle versus Foreman, or Yvon Durelle and Archie Moore knocking each other down. But I never saw a better fight than Leonard versus Hearns, because I saw it live.

Hearns came in stupefyingly confident, while Leonard was wary and evasive. They would fight the same way at first. The hunter and the hunted. Leonard had avoided Hearns's eyes at the weigh-in. Thomas was 146½ pounds, and at six-one he looked like a suit of armor from the front. A side view revealed his lack of depth. His only buffer was his right fist. So far, that had been plenty. Leonard was 147 on the button and looked just as fit, but more natural. Deeper.

It was a warm night, bordering on hot, when referee Davey Pearl called them together. Everyone who meant something to boxing was there. They were outnumbered by celebrities two to one, and the celebrities were outnumbered by ordinary people ten to one. All eyes were reserved for the two men under the lights.

Hearns half-lidded his eyes and stared at Leonard in the center of the ring. Hearns was completely fearless—and a fearless man can be a fool sometimes. This was the small window Leonard had to come through against Hearns. Again he avoided Hearns's eyes. They turned their backs on each other to wait for the bell. As I scanned the crowd, I heard a difference in the humming and buzzing of the voices that precede a championship fight. This sound was loud, heated, like a chant. This was not the sound of ten thousand idle conversations. People were making noise, some of them without knowing it. The tribe was preparing for the ritual of survival.

The bell rang and—oh, what feints! What speed! Between the first and second rounds, I noticed the studious eyes of Ali. He had the same look on his face a law professor might wear while sitting in the back of mock court as his protégés argued cases brilliantly. Ali was satisfied.

On September 17, 1981, Sugar Ray Leonard, the twenty-five-year-old fighter with the little-boy looks and laser-beam hands, became the undisputed welterweight champion of the world with a fourteenth-round KO over Thomas Hearns. A

firestorm of left and right hooks to the body and head—all
following a devastating right to the jaw—relieved Hearns of
his senses and ability to fight back at 1:45 of the fourteenth.
The end had come with Leonard so far behind on all official
cards that he needed the knockout to win the fight. Battered,
Hearns, a warrior, ended the fight on his feet.

"Maybe one-half to three-quarters of my sight was gone,"
said Leonard, who went to 31–1 with twenty-two knockouts
despite Hearns's wicked assault on Leonard's left eye.

Mike Trainer, Leonard's top adviser, was upset after the
fight. "I think the powers that be in boxing don't like Ray
Leonard," he said. The reason for his mood was the scoring
of the fight. Judge Chuck Minker had it 125–121, Hearns,
going into the fourteenth. Judge Duane Ford had it 124–122,
Hearns. Judge Lou Tobat had it 125–122, Hearns. Unless
Leonard had won both final rounds by two points each, he
could not have won the fight. I had scored the fight 125–124,
Hearns, going into the fourteenth. So by winning the last
two rounds, by whatever edge, Leonard would have won
the fight. The scoring of the fight seemed right in line to me.
The greatness of it was Leonard's climb through that small
window.

The pivotal moment of the fight came in the sixth round.
The power was obvious then. There would be brief exchanges
of punches, thrown and countered like lightning, and then
separation. In the first six rounds, there was no clinching, just
Leonard moving deftly, Hearns stalking him nearly as deftly,
Hearns being Leonard's equal (!) in punching speed, and having superior arm length, while Leonard was the superior tactician. Leonard knew that one mistake, either way, and the
fight would be decided. Hearns was not as aware of this, and
it ultimately undid him.

"He's throwing bombs already!" Leonard hotly confided
to Dundee at the end of the first round. This is the level at
which they confronted each other. They were both so abom-

inably quick. They both had the power punch. Once either one was hurt, the deadly sequence would begin against him. Neither could safely face the other at less than full strength, with other than complete faculties, so for the better part of three rounds, Leonard feinted, and answered feints with feinted counters. Then, after the sixth round, Hearns was hurt, first by an unseen, well-hidden half uppercut, half left hook to the point of his chin. After the sixth, it was Hearns's turn to try and survive—to box. In what was the most amazing display of the science of boxing I had ever witnessed, they switched roles in midfight and kept their level of proficiency. Hearns became the master boxer, Leonard the irresistible puncher.

In the first two rounds, when Leonard chose to circle and evade, Hearns confidently held the ring center, comforted by his superior punch. Faced with Hearns's long, stinging jab— and the prospect of the dreaded right—Leonard could not win rounds from the perimeter, and he lost those two. Leonard was waiting, picking his spot, looking for that mistake in reaction. Hearns made it in the sixth round after winning four of the first five rounds on my card. He became overconfident. As Leonard stepped inside and bobbed low and away (he had done this in the previous round, to gauge Hearns's reaction to the tactic), Hearns stood above him, throwing hooking punches that whistled over Ray's head. Leonard bobbed once, twice, and on the second bob he came up with that low-angled left. It was almost impossible to see without a slow-motion replay to help. It wasn't the most powerful punch, but Hearns never saw it. It knocked his chin backward. Leonard followed with a strong right. Now Hearns was dazed. Leonard confronted him, and after about twenty seconds of stalking and setting up, ripped off a gunshot of a left hook, digging it cleanly into Hearns's right side, in effect taking that vaunted punch from him. Leonard had paralyzed Hearns's weapon.

Now Hearns was in the Room. The Room is a term borrowed from Muhammad Ali, who in his book *The Greatest: My Own Story* compared being knocked into a state of hurt and altered consciousness to being in a dark room with—and I am mixing Ali's descriptions here—bats blowing saxophones. From this Room, Hearns proved his mettle. Here is where Duran, the cold survivalist, had said *"No más."* Here is where Hearns, the hot rod, the man who goes for all or nothing, was knocked into the ropes, legs buckling, his mind unaware. He fought through the smoke. He came back to hurt Leonard. To take his eye and come back to lead on points. But the real point had been made. Hearns stayed, but he was changed. He didn't like the Room. No one does. No air there.

From the seventh round until the fourteenth, Leonard claimed and stalked the center ring. Hearns proved in those seven rounds that he could box, feint, move, and survive. But he was fighting from his toes now, and he was not that kind of fighter. Now he had to try to be sweet, like Sugar. He had lost his power. Meanwhile, Leonard's left hook was whittling away at Hearns's body, while Hearns chiseled away at Leonard's left eye. The only question was whether Leonard could catch up with him before time ran out.

By the twelfth round, the mutual respect was obvious. Hearns won the tenth, eleventh, and twelfth rounds, somehow. Angelo had his say about the kid blowing it. Then Leonard showed that part of him that allowed him to be a fighter. The part beyond skill.

In the thirteenth, Leonard's face became a horrible mask of swollen eyes and rage. It was a simple one-two that did it. Left-right, and Hearns was his. The killer instinct flowed through Leonard as Hearns's hands came down. Leonard pounded him through the ropes. Hearns got up, shaking his head, saying no, that doesn't hurt, but Leonard, knowing better, furiously drove him back down again. And again, Hearns rose from the dead. What did it take to stop this man?

In the fourteenth, Leonard found the spot, flush along the

jaw with a sweeping right, accompanied by more or less gratuitous blows. Hearns was locked in the Room to stay. He didn't go down, but he was out.

Leonard didn't want to ponder rematches with Hearns the night after the fight. And who could blame him? He had just canceled Doomsday. He had buried the undertaker, and there was no need to resurrect him. After that, as Leonard reigned, I always saw Hearns as king of the undead, the Nosferatu. "I take my hat off to Mr. Hearns," said Leonard. "I don't have much to say regarding a rematch. I have just proven—to myself—that I am the greatest welterweight in the world. But I say in my book we both are still champions."

You could take that to the Room, and the bank. Eddie Butler was inconsolable, but no more untoward remarks about Ray Leonard were made in the Ringside Bar. He had turned out not to be a geek. Later, Emanuel Steward, Hearns's trainer-manager, said, "There was an entire history of boxing in that fight." Leonard won and became the Sugar of his time. As I grow older, his performance in the Nevada desert will only grow greater in my mind until one day when some magnificent new welterweight comes along so I can say to his aficionados that he couldn't have carried Leonard's mouthpiece to the water bucket. I can start my own barber shop now.

Four and a half months later, the following February 1, it would be Sugar Ray Leonard who would commandeer the halls of a great San Francisco hotel. Dressed in a brown leather artilleryman's shirt cinched at the waist by a wide belt which connoted no championships, Leonard was the focus of a press conference held at the top of the St. Francis. He had been named *Sports Illustrated*'s Sportsman of the Year and was about to make what had been considered his final fight against Bruce Finch in Reno. Leonard had beaten Benitez, Duran,

Kalule, and Hearns—fighters with a combined record of 177–1–1 when he fought them—in succession. And he had stopped them all. None went the distance with the little man from Palmer Park, Maryland. Later, of course, Leonard would come back, retire, then come back again to face history and Marvelous Marvin Hagler, retire, then come back again, this time saying, "I'm not retiring again until they start hitting me more than I hit them." The Hagler fight years later, as it turned out, was a walk in the park compared to Leonard's fight with Hearns. All Leonard had needed against Hagler was his speed and a little pizzazz. Hearns had required more. Much more. Again and always, it was a matter of two styles mixing.

Even though Finch was 30–3–1, he was the nearest thing to a tomato can that Leonard had seen in years. Finch was the No. 4 welterweight contender. Such was Leonard's mastery, fighting the No. 4 contender was like a weekend in Bermuda. But Leonard's eye had been traumatized by Hearns; although it had been made tender in his pre-Hearns training sessions, it was Hearns who took it. Already, people wanted Leonard to fight Hagler. It wouldn't happen for five years. Leonard wasn't so sure at the time. When he had taken Kalule's junior middleweight title, he had said, "I don't like how I feel at [154 pounds]. It was just an experiment. I am a welterweight." Leonard believed, correctly, that Hagler would not drop down to 154, the happy ground between his 160 and Leonard's 147 pounds. "I can't go up to one-sixty," Leonard said.

From the lectern in the St. Francis ballroom, Leonard picked Gerry Cooney to beat Larry Holmes that summer. Holmes and Cooney were scheduled to fight in June of 1982. The master boxer's mind is not so easily fooled on these matters. Cooney was an unfinished fighter, a bully fighter, with only the nebulous, unreal "puncher's chance" to beat Holmes, who by then had defended the title eleven times. Cooney, on the other hand, had never even been hit hard.

Leonard mentioned "hunger" and "wanting it" as Cooney's skills. I asked Leonard if some of his suspicions about the Cooney–Holmes fight didn't stem from his knowledge that Holmes had been upset with Davey Pearl for stopping the Hearns–Leonard fight. Leonard looked out of the tall windows atop the St. Francis and said, "I think you or anyone would squawk if they had lost a great deal of money on that fight."

Aha. If you weren't with Ray, you were against him. It seemed that this was how he had begun—been forced?—to view the world. Pleasing all the people all the time was as tough as they said it was. It had begun to wear on Leonard, and his growing wariness about people was not totally unjustified. There was only so much of himself that he had to give. He would fight Finch in Reno, where Jack Johnson had fought Jim Jeffries many years ago, setting off racial violence all over the country, even though Johnson—multilingual, an automobile mechanic, an avid reader of Hugo and Dumas— had maintained that he too was fighting only for himself and no one else. But people latch on to champions for any number of reasons, whether the champions or the people like it or not. Leonard avoided the subject of Johnson, which I tried to bring up in some innocuous context. On the other hand, Holmes's handlers called him Jack in their heated encouragements between and during rounds of Holmes's fights.

For all his ability in the ring, Leonard, the ultimate ruler of Las Vegas during these times, had trouble making everybody respect him. All champions are going to be hated by some, envied by others, seen as a threat to still more. So Sugar Ray Leonard, the brilliant, delicate warrior, had become very careful with his image, as far as he could control it. Being allowed to fight—and to be paid—was the only fairness a fighter could expect.

Seven years later, after Leonard had retired and returned three times, after he had shaken up the world, albeit not quite so jarringly as Ali had, by beating Hagler, he would still be only thirty-two years old, preparing to fight one Donny LaLonde, a Canadian light-heavyweight. Leonard reveled in his celebrity by now. He was an institution. That would do. He stood backstage at a music concert at Constitution Hall in Washington, D.C., in the late summer of 1988, looking not a day older than twenty-five, having his picture taken with a young band whose members were his juniors by a decade. The band members treated Ray like royalty.

By 1989, the drums were beating for Leonard to face Thomas Hearns again in the ring. But much had happened to both between 1981 and 1989. Many fights. Many doubts. Back in 1982, Bruce Finch and anybody who came with him could not beat Sugar Ray Leonard, not in a million rounds. Finch knew it, Leonard knew it, I knew it, and the next day's readers of the Oakland *Tribune* would know it shortly.

It was a bright winter's day over San Francisco Bay, in February of my thirtieth year, 1982, when I left Ray Leonard in San Francisco. The setting sun shone a beguiling light through the girders of the Bay Bridge as I drove back to face the VDT keyboard and the next deadline. I had a job to do, and it involved doing what I liked and what I did well. There were no accidents on the Bay Bridge that day, so, as far as I was concerned, all was right with the world.

5
Workmen's Compensation

Whatup, breeze and all you cools. Check how the deal went down. I was rollin' in the Bay Area, sixty a minute. Down for big fun and def at it. Bumping. Then I got rang by Peter Carry of *Sports Illustrated* magazine of the Time, Inc., group of the Yard, New York, that held up one whole side of the 'Hood. Peter ran it down and clicked. Setting standards either back or forward by light-years, I exed the Bay and did *Sports Illustrated*, effective March 11, 1982. There it is. Put in the pocket. Served. Knocked. Was I real or was I real, word? Real as sin in the garden. Yo.

I had become acclimated to the tempered sun of the San Francisco Bay. But I had no choice. I had to throw down hard, or else spend the rest of the big run asking myself, "What in the eight walls of hell is wrong with you?" A workman's compensation is more work. Working for the magazine. Yo. Magazine. A great-sounding word. I was rollin', cools. I've learned it's human nature to be rollin' at times like those—and even if it isn't human nature, you can charge it to that account and not worry until the bill comes due. Your conscience doesn't bother you when you're rollin'. So E-Go took me for a spin. Larry Holmes and I had that in common. I'll explain later. Right now it's my go.

Whatever professional sport I covered would mean fights anyway, or some version of them. I knew this after watching the teams and the personalities of the Bay Area for the previous six years. It's like, I had just missed the clubhouse bouts of the battlin' A's, the bad-tempered but world-championship-caliber baseball players in Oakland in the early and middle '70s. They were known to swing at each other nearly as often as they swung at the baseball. They didn't shave, either. They were definitely not bogus.

I was around for the arrival of Billy Martin, the Roberto Duran of the major leagues, as manager of the A's in 1981. Billy's reputation as a man who would fight at the drop of a wet bar napkin had preceded him. The first time I met Martin, during spring training, he had looked at me squarely and said, "I don't like that crap you wrote." I had written something about Billy not appreciating it when a Yankee outfielder named Mickey Rivers had used the Yankee clubhouse phone to see how his ponies were doing at the track. "Watch yourself," Martin said. So I checked. I heard Billy had a cute little left hook. I stayed on his right.

A few days later, after watching the A's new style under Martin, a running, daredevilish style led by the Hendu, Rickey Henderson, I wrote a column called "Billy Ball." The A's eventually turned that phrase into a marketing slogan which caught on somewhat. Every other sportswriter in America must have used those words or some derivative in the next five years, including Howard Cosell himself. Billy, for his part, got a book out of it. He never complained about that.

After I moved back East, the A's came into Yankee Stadium. Billy was still the A's manager. I went to the stadium to hang out. I saw Billy and told him I was having a hard time finding an apartment. He suggested I go to Woodbridge, New Jersey. So I went there and rented an apartment for a year and that is how Billy got his revenge.

At their preseason training camp in Santa Rosa, California, the members of the Oakland Raiders would often—like, every day—provide impromptu sparring sessions. The rookie offensive and defensive linemen would be tested by the likes of Art Shell and Gene Upshaw, or John Matuszak and Matt Millen. The coaches and the team's managing general partner, Al Davis, would make no attempt to halt these hostilities, preferring to move farther off to one side, smiling tight little smiles. This action was considered good for the club. Fighting was just another set of calisthenics to the Oakland Raiders. Pro football was a cold game, a game of physical reprisals, and they knew it better than anybody else at the time, save the Pittsburgh Steelers. As Millen liked to say, "This ain't a please-and-thank-you game." There were fights that they remembered, the way fight fans remember Marciano–Walcott or Louis–Schmeling. Horace Jones versus Art Thoms. George Atkinson versus Marv Hubbard. To the Raiders, these were the timeless boxing classics.

Millen, the thick linebacker, was a particularly sedate realist. We called him Spike. He liked that name. He would rage on the field like Attila himself, then come off the field and be as obliging as a shoe clerk who had five mouths to feed. Once he had to be dragged away by his teammates from some mounting on-field fray. He was in his fullest agitation and seemed ready to kill people dead, if necessary. He came to the sideline, where I stood anxious to meet him and make note of his dementia. "Hi, Ralph," Millen said with a smile. He had the sound and manner of Linus saying "Hi, Charlie Brown." He was not angry. He was in. The light was on upstairs. He had merely been going about his business on the field. No hard feelings.

In 1978, the Golden State Warriors of the NBA had a rookie on their roster named Wayne Cooper, a six-ten center from

New Orleans. Coop had narrow shoulders and hips and a soft, sweet jump shot. But he had no idea how violent the action under an NBA basket could get, and only a faint idea of how to handle the happenings once they did cut loose. Coop got his nose broken, and was surprised when he was told to get a mask and keep playing. Why, Jerry West had his nose broken fourteen or fifteen times, Coop was told. One broken nose was just warming up.

So Coop played in his mask to protect his beak for several weeks. Toward the end of this time, the Warriors played the Atlanta Hawks at the Omni. Coop was being pushed about too much for the taste of Al Attles, the Warriors' coach at that time. "Get tough, Coop!" Attles roared. Al was a native of Newark, New Jersey, like Marvelous Marvin Hagler. Al could be inspirational because he had been known as "the Destroyer" during his playing days with the Philadelphia and Golden State Warriors. Nobody messed with Al.

Inspired, Coop flung off his mask and went back in against Atlanta to wage war beneath the NBA backboards. After engaging the enemy for a few trips up and down the court, Coop ran by the bench and asked, "Can I have my mask back?"

I liked Coop. I liked Al. Attles was one of the best men I'd met. In his natural bass, he liked to joke that he and the Dipper, Wilt Chamberlain, had once scored 117 points in a game. His punch line: "Dipper only had a hundred." His laughter had the sound of a concrete mixer in low gear. Franklin Mieuli, the Warriors' owner, said that the gigantic Wilt had tendered physical respect to no one save Al Attles, whose stiff hand checks could and often did leave bruises on the hips of the players he guarded. Al could crack your jack and never look back on the real side.

I had taken the stories about Attles's temper and reputation as some phase he had gone through on the way to his current maturity and serenity until one day in Phoenix, where the

Warriors were playing and losing to the Phoenix Suns at the Veterans Memorial Coliseum. Some fan was ragging on Al, hard. This often occurs at NBA games, and I had always known the kindly Attles to overlook what I considered high insult. However, this fan, in the ardor of his newly found attentions, got personal.

Attles started up the stands. He was not moving very swiftly, but there was something about the way he moved that caused Clifford Ray and Nate Williams, two of the more grizzled Warrior veterans and the strongest players on the squad, to race up and grab Attles from behind. They barely slowed his pace. Fans sat stunned. Williams and Ray got a better grip, dug in their sneakered heels, and were able to achieve a stalemate with Attles, who seemed to be paying no attention to them at all. He was focused on the heckler. They stood there straining against each other until enough seconds had elapsed for the fire to cool in Attles's eyes. The heckler sat there, the color of eggplant. Later, I asked Ray if his intervention had really been necessary. Ray was amazed that I was so naive. "Hey, man," he said, "Al wasn't going up there to give that guy no autograph."

There was no reason to believe I wouldn't cover fights, one way or another. The fact that I would cover anything for *Sports Illustrated* was due at least in part to the recommendation of Ron Fimrite. Fimrite was a senior writer at the magazine, an author of seamless stories who had the common sense to make his home in San Francisco. I would go to the city to see him in the weeks before I left for New York, meeting him and imbibing at various watering holes, where I ended up zotzed while he stayed fresh as a daisy.

I arrived on the twentieth floor of the Time-Life Building in Manhattan figuring to go as hard as I could for as long as I could. I never stopped to figure out what I meant by that when I said it. It sounded like something Angelo would say to his guy. I went to see the boxing editor. I told him if he needed a fight covered, I was available.

The magazine had two writers, Pat Putnam and Bill Nack, covering the lion's share of good fights. There were always the dud fights. Those might be mine for the asking. Putnam had boxed in his younger days, a story written all over his puffy, scar-crossed face. Pat got into the mood for the fights he threw down on with remembrances of days past. He spoke almost lovingly of Inchon, almost as though he had vacationed there. I remembered that MacArthur supposedly had said that the Koreans were the finest fighters in the world. Pat didn't remember MacArthur saying any such thing. I asked Pat who was the best fighter he'd seen. He was quiet for a moment. Then he said, "Leonard."

I was assigned a fight between Salvador Sanchez and Rocky Garcia for the WBC featherweight championship in Dallas, in May 1982. Holmes would be fighting an exhibition there, hoping to stay toned for the Cooney fight, which had been rescheduled for later that summer. Holmes had defended the title eleven times by then, and defended it by knockout ten times. I had seen him defend the title six times, seen him floored by three different heavyweight contenders and watched him get up off the canvas and batter those contenders into submission. I couldn't remember another heavyweight champion who could do this with such detached regularity. The man was definitely not bogus.

It was being knocked down that signaled Holmes to start fighting seriously. I had watched him take it easy on the old Ali. I saw him feel sorry for Renaldo Snipes, get knocked down for his trouble, then get up and run Snipes out of the ring. I had seen him rocked and floored by Earnie Shavers and watched him rise up and knock Shavers out. Trevor Berbick, Mike Weaver, Lorenzo Zanon, Leroy Jones—these men were all like fresh angel food cake to Larry. By the time the Cooney fight came off, Holmes would have been the heavyweight champion for nearly four years. A workman's compensation was more work.

Leonard had been a better boxer, but Leonard, at his best,

weighed 147 pounds. Hagler's chin seemingly could survive a bolt of lightning, a Hearns right, but Hagler weighed 160 pounds at his fittest. Hearns had the hot rod, the Lew Jenkins, the right hand. The term "pound for pound," while a useful literary device, didn't really count when exacting flesh in the ring. Holmes was the superior fighter to Leonard. Why? Weight. Sugar Ray Robinson was a superior boxer to Joe Louis, as far as that went. Who was the superior fighter? There could be no question. The heavyweight. Who wins fights between Robinson and Louis, or Leonard and Holmes? The heavyweight. If you doubt this, ask your grandmother.

For Holmes, fighting was his end. But it was everything except fighting which distracted the world he battled to champion. His workman's compensation would eventually turn into bitter fruit. His muddy speech, his less than handsome face, his honesty, his stiff, relatively skinny legs which could not dance, the color of his skin, and, finally, his bitterness toward the world which refused to understand him were the reasons for his thin harvest of respect. Holmes could do nothing about these things. Put him in the ring in his prime and all he did not represent and could not do mattered very little. He could stay in the ring for only an hour at a time, but it was time well spent.

Snipes had knocked Holmes down in the seventh round of their fight in Pittsburgh in 1981, one of those Holmes defenses that I attended. Holmes had gotten up off the deck to do his number on Snipes. Holmes had been jab-sticking away at Snipes's eyes, examining those eyes after each flurry, a scientist in a laboratory. Holmes had pulled off and was just getting in some exercise when a looping right from the 200-pound Snipes crashed into Holmes's jaw. Holmes went down heavily. He got up smiling. Four rounds later, after hitting Snipes at will with the hard left jab, now applied in a more businesslike fashion, Holmes crossed Snipes's lower jaw with the right hand. Snipes's face contorted like clay. He was being beaten into a senseless heap by a cavalcade of those rights when the referee, Rudy Ortega, stepped in to stop it at 1:05 of the eleventh round.

Snipes had been upset with Ortega's decision. Snipes had gotten up twice after being knocked down by Gerrie Coetzee and won. However, Coetzee was not Larry Holmes. Ortega said, "There was no question. Snipes got hit by a tremendous shot by Holmes and was driven into the corner. Holmes was right on top of him. Snipes had lost control and Holmes continued to hit him with no response. People don't understand that it's not a popular decision, when a fight is stopped. It's one man's decision. If a fighter has no chance to win and is being punished, the fight should not go on."

Nevertheless, the crowd at the Pittsburgh Civic Arena booed Ortega lustily as Holmes settled in next to a ringside table to be interviewed by Howard Cosell.

As far as I had been able to tell, it was Holmes who helped turn Cosell against boxing, as much as anyone. Cosell was asking his biting, atypical questions and Holmes was saying "Yes, Howard" with more frequency than even Howard imagined possible. Then along came Gerry Cooney near the ringside seats. Holmes, well aware of his shortcomings as a speaker/self-promoter, thought about it for a second and then spun into emulation of his mentor, Ali. Holmes jumped up from his seat while Cooney was five feet away and approaching in the friendliest of all possible manners. Holmes, playing the only kind of charades he knew, told Cooney not to come any closer. Cooney took him at his word. In his gesticulations, Holmes inadvertently hit Cosell in the mouth. Cosell was prevented from being ringmaster for this potential circus, which quickly came unglued without his stewardship. A little blood was in Cosell's mouth. As for Cooney, his mouth resembled a sprung bear trap. His wary eyes asked, "Is this guy for real?" Cosell recovered like a pro and closed the broadcast.

Later, after Holmes disposed of Cooney in the ring, he

fought Randall Cobb and Cosell did the commentary. As Holmes battered Cobb, Cosell appeared to sign off from boxing for good. "This is a disgrace," he said. Holmes was too good, too quick for Cobb. Holmes jabbed and one-twoed at will. Cobb was happy to get the payday. He was a hardy sort. He never seemed in any danger of losing his life, or even of being knocked down. Holmes was kind that way. Rarely was he a cruel fighter. Cosell, his stentorian tones revealing his newfound disgust, had seen enough of both men and apparently of fights in general. There were no more Alis, no new worlds to chart and capture.

Cosell broadcast the Olympic boxing matches of 1984, but disavowed his loyalty to the sport and quoted scions of American medicine in the new knowledge that boxing was dangerous. The devil, you say. A man of Cosell's letters and experience had to have known that boxing was a risky occupation and possibly a social and physical abomination years ago, when he took his facile technique to the feet of Ali, helping that legend to grow, assisting the forming of his own legend as well. As Cosell himself might have said, the danger of boxing was no scoop.

When Carmen Basilio had prepared to meet Sugar Ray Robinson for the second time in March 1958 (Basilio had earlier scored a decision over the Sugar in September 1957), Cosell had no such qualms. There he was, laughing, having a good time, mike in hand as always.

Cosell: "Carmen, I've talked to ten sportswriters today and nine of them pick Sugar Ray Robinson to win this rematch. Your reply?"

Basilio: "Nine of 'em are wrong."

Cosell (smiling): "Thank you, Carmen."

When Ali had outclassed and taunted Floyd Patterson and Ernie Terrell, Cosell didn't react as he did when Holmes merely outclassed Cobb. But Cosell had been younger back in those days. I suppose people are allowed to grow.

"That was the moment, the Cobb fight," Cosell would say years later. "I respect every man who has ever fought for a living, but the tawdriness, the crookedness of the so-called sport and my own evolution as a man made me no longer able to countenance it. I don't want to see another man fight."

Did he ever speak with Ali about these feelings?

"Can't. Can't talk to him anymore."

The punches, of course.

"Of course."

Would boxing be outlawed?

"Yes, I think so."

I must admit I had not expected Cosell to be so naive on this last matter. Surely he didn't believe boxing would be outlawed just because he, as famous as he was, suddenly deemed it socially unacceptable.

Going back over it, I think Holmes's failings as a competent foil for Cosell made the champion nearly as fed up as Holmes's fists had made Cosell. The morning after the Snipes bout, back in Pittsburgh in 1981, Holmes had emerged from an elevator at the Pittsburgh Hyatt in an evil mood, ranting to Don King about what he would do to his trainer, Richie Giachetti. Holmes felt he was being spied upon and apparently believed Giachetti had something to do with people spying on him. King nodded, overly sympathetic. It was common knowledge by now that the promoter was being watched by the IRS and the FBI for crookedness, if not tawdriness. "I'll punch Richie's ass out," Holmes said, gnashing his teeth.

He strode to the front of the room which had been set up for his morning-after interview session. Pat Putnam and the late Dick Young were there. There might have been three or four other working journalists in the room. Remember charisma? And that Larry didn't have any? "No more letting anyone off the hook," Holmes said, not waiting for questions. "Snipes was awkward. Pretty good, but mostly awkward. He had more than I thought he did. Lucky I came in shape. He

101

wasn't bad, but I have to say that my mind wasn't a hundred percent on Snipes, either.

"Wasn't no tough fight. Look at me. My face isn't all busted up." Holmes's face rarely was after a fight in those days. "He hit me maybe five or six times. He used his head more than his hands. His style will confuse a lot of fighters. Not his ability. His style. Trevor Berbick and Snipes would be an interesting fight because they both can take a punch and neither one of them knows what he's doing.

"On a scale of one to ten, I'd rate my performance in this fight a six. I didn't use my jab enough. I was trying to get some work in on my left hook. What hurt me was Snipes's attitude after the fight."

This was a key admission by Holmes, as his career proved. People's attitudes could hurt him, and when he was hurt, he lashed out. He knew no other way to be. It was like he had been "jobbed by some chump. . . .

"I'm the champion. He didn't hit me like Earnie Shavers hit me. I wouldn't say the punch he knocked me down with was a lucky punch, but I've been hit harder. I had been feeling sorry for him, trying to keep from hitting him in the eyes anymore. But after he knocked me down I started thinkin', 'If he gets hurt, so what?' " Another key admission. Holmes didn't really like hurting people—at least, not anymore. "Then I didn't care." I had never heard a champion warm to his subject in this way before.

"I made the mistake of letting Shavers off the hook. I was beating him and his eyes was hanging out, almost. I said, 'Quit, man. Don't take no more of this.' I felt sorry for him. Then he knocked me down. So I got up and knocked him out. Last night, my brother Jake and Snipes's manager got into it. Snipes was callin' me a chump, sayin' I wasn't nothin'. So Jake calls his manager an asshole and the guy tried to put up his dukes or something. Jake wanted him after that. Now, I'm the champion and I wouldn't mess with Jake Holmes."

Dick Young said, "Larry, the guy said Jake called him a muddafucka."

"Well," said Holmes, "he was acting like one. I was tryin' to stay back but Snipes was comin' too so I had to show Snipes that I would take him if he got involved. But I understood how he felt. All us fighters are like that. We're out there fighting for that hundred-and-ninety-five-dollar belt. He thought he was gettin' cheated out of his chance. But he was hurt, and I was gonna do him a little worse than I did Leon Spinks."

Holmes had crushed Leon in three brutal rounds after what Holmes perceived was an insult directed at Diane Holmes, Larry's wife. I thought under the circumstances Snipes should have sent Rudy Ortega a dozen roses. "I thought the referee was good too," said Holmes. "He made us fight. He wouldn't let me clinch and work on something I wanted to work on, but he was a good referee. He even got hit pretty good in there once. He stepped in at the wrong time and . . . that ref can take a pretty good punch." Holmes laughed his uninfectious laughter.

At the time of the Snipes fight, the Cooney fight was scheduled for the following March. "Cooney in March," said Holmes. "That fight last night is goin' to make the Cooney fight more interestin' for people. They'll say, 'Lookit, Snipes knocked him down. What'll Cooney do to 'im?' Just remember, I've been knocked down three times and every time I get up to knock the other guy out. Out. Cooney will be made for me. He's not gonna be duckin' and weavin'. They'll play up the age factor. They'll want to push the fight back later in the year. Won't matter. I'll win that, then beat Weaver again, maybe Snipes, then close the books, retire."

It was not realistic for Holmes to think he wouldn't continue fighting until he was beaten.

"Well, that's right, you've heard all this before. You know I'll change my mind the next day. But I've been thinkin' about

103

Cooney since Cooney came up. I sleep Cooney. This is a fight I want and one fight I will not lose."

We closed our little spiral notebooks, and the meeting broke up with murmurs. Holmes fascinated me and I wanted to hear more, but he was hard to get. I caught him in the lobby.

"Why will you keep fighting after Cooney? That'll be thirteen title defenses. So it has to be for the money, right?"

I had the bad idea of answering the question for him. Holmes interrupted me with a wave of his hand. "I may sound arrogant or bitter, but I'm gonna tell you what it's all about. I'm rich already. Rich as I need to be. I don't fight for money. I fight to convince people that no one can beat me." The elevator arrived and whisked Holmes away.

The next time I saw him was in Dallas a couple of days before his exhibition and the Sanchez–Garcia title fight. By now the drumbeats of promotion had a racial undertone. It was the time of *Rocky II* at the movie theaters, and Sylvester Stallone was stirring up passions and making a killing at the box office. He and director John Avildsen were preying on what Robert Penn Warren called "that something inside," that confrontational self, through the audience's vicarious vanquishing of a threat to civilization named Mr. T. Avildsen and Stallone had cast a former bodyguard named Lawrence Tero as the opponent for Rocky, and Mr. T, with his million gold neck chains, loud manner, and lack of any discernible redeeming grace, filled the bill. Avildsen later insisted that this was "simple dramaturgy to help the audience identify." In other words, white and black starring as good and evil, respectively, was big box office. Clarity, above all else.

Stallone and Cooney would soon make the same cover of *Time* magazine. Ironically, if a fight expert had dropped down from Mars and looked at that cover, he or she or it would certainly have chosen the chiseled Stallone as the fighter and the doe-eyed, soft-shouldered Cooney as the actor. H. L.

Mencken said you'd never go broke underestimating the intelligence of the American public. Neither Avildsen, Stallone, Mr. T., Cooney, nor Holmes were going broke soon. They had a market.

It was the beginning of May 1982. Dallas enjoyed bright, clear weather in the days prior to the Sanchez–Garcia bout and the Holmes exhibition. Both were to be held in a new facility called the Reunion Arena. I could reacquaint myself with Holmes at my leisure. A species study. At the time Holmes employed a sparring partner named Jody Ballard, who was big enough to be a champion and undoubtedly would have been if he could have punched as quickly as he talked. But his boxing skills were limited to the bottom half of the top hundred working heavyweights in the world. He was agile for a big man, but his punch was slow and didn't pack a contender's wallop. Ballard was old enough to know that this situation was not likely to improve for him. Still, he was good enough to be a consummate braggart, and he was engaged in the presumption of his own greatness with a roomful of media on the day before Holmes's exhibition.

At first, Ballard seemed only to be making sure of the microphone's throwing power before his employer, Holmes, arrived. "Is this thing working?" Ballard said loudly into the mike. Ballard heard his own voice magnified, and a look of bemusement came over him which reminded me of George Benton, an ex-fighter from Philadelphia who serves as a trainer in the camp of Dan Duva. George had been interviewed in the ring after one of his fighters, Johnny Bumphus, had won on TV. Bumphus had won, but not sharply enough for Georgie, who said into the camera, "I don't know what the hell he was doing in there." Georgie looked shocked, then surprised, then pleased. Hey, he'd said "hell" on television and no one was taking him to jail. Ballard now had the same look on his face. He could get away with something here.

Ballard wore a ten-gallon cowboy hat that sat small on his

head. "Ladies and gentlemen, I am the greatest fighter in the world. *I will soon be the heavyweight champion of the world!*"

Holmes had just entered the room through double doors to the right of the makeshift stage. Timing. Holmes's jaw was firmly set, his small eyes narrowed and slanted inward in a deadly gaze as he approached the podium. Ballard backed away, watching Holmes for any show of force. Holmes's mouth twisted into a sneer. He held Ballard's eyes until he decided to turn to the audience. Put off, he snapped off answers to a few questions in forgettable monosyllables and left without so much as a backward glance.

Ballard was a good professional heavyweight boxer, but there was nothing he could do with Holmes, and he knew it. Later, Holmes cuffed about three different opponents during the exhibition, including the silent Ballard. I recalled Norman Mailer's exultation when he hit José Torres, the former light-heavyweight champion and Mailer's boxing instructor, with a right hand. I blamed Ernest Hemingway for that. No way in the world Norman Mailer hits José Torres with a right hand unless Torres is asleep or allows it to happen for the sake of Mailer's ego. If Torres wanted to continue to get paid to be Norman Mailer's boxing instructor, it was best he let him get one in.

Holmes was impregnable and fought the Dallas exhibition well within himself, despite Ballard. Holmes seemed removed, already up to the mark. He was as relaxed as I saw him all week during the Sanchez–Garcia fight, sitting ringside as Sanchez methodically outpointed the challenger.

In the minutes between rounds I tried to draw words from Holmes, who was in the near-trance many boxers fall into when watching other skilled fighters fight. Sanchez had been hit flush by a well-calculated Garcia right in the fifth round. Sanchez had acknowledged this at the end of the round by giving Garcia a respectful pat, while Garcia attempted to pull up the boxer underwear he wore beneath his trunks.

"You gotta enjoy the ones you take, just like the ones you give out," Holmes said. He seemed almost wistful.

I believed what Holmes meant was that you had to appreciate the skill it took to land meaningful punches against a person who was trained to fight through such punches or avoid them altogether—or that you had to appreciate the mistakes you made and appreciate how those mistakes led directly to a result, a negative payoff. Cause and effect. There was a theory, a progression, a calculation, and no one appreciated that more than the heavyweight champion, who knew you had to understand the ones you take just as you understand the ones you give out.

The Cooney fight went according to form at Caesar's Palace in Las Vegas. It was a mismatch, despite the odd scoring of the judges. Holmes gave Cooney ring respect, because a champion assumes professionalism in those he fights and because Cooney did have a good left hook. The sun could rise in the time he took to throw it, but it did have weight behind it. Cooney's best tactic in this fight was—surprise—a stiff left jab. However, a jabbing contest with Larry Holmes would not do, Victor Valle's frantic admonitions aside. Valle was Cooney's trainer, and between rounds his frantic advice ran to comments like "He's a shit. This is shit!" I began to have a deeper appreciation of Angelo Dundee, and of Eddie Futch, who was in Holmes's corner, making calm suggestions to Holmes. After fighting a workmanlike first round, Holmes set Cooney up for a basic one-two in the second. Nothing special, just the kind of crossing right that usually wore Holmes's opponents down before the fifteenth round. It was not Holmes's knockout cross. But Cooney, touched on the temple by this, the basic right hand of a champion, went down in a slow, backpedaling motion. Holmes was more shocked than Cooney.

The gentleman was already in the Room, but the festivities had barely begun. Holmes could have finished him then had he thrown caution to the winds. Instead he took Cooney deep into the fight, exhausting the younger man's abilities to such an extent that Cooney began to deliver low blows—heavy low blows. The fight was halted because Holmes shrank into a knock-kneed posture of pain after one such low blow. These were the high points for Cooney, tactically. Holmes kept up the jab and the one-two, and eventually, in the thirteenth round, Cooney fell of attrition and his own ponderous weight. Reality won again.

Holmes did fight for money. He also fought to prove that no one could beat him, but after the Cooney fight, money became most important. I heard him the following year, before he fought Scott Frank in Atlantic City, saying, "I've got seven million invested in Easton, and damn, I'll never get that back." Although Scott Frank was not the farthest thing from Holmes's mind, he was a poor second to the check. Easton, Pennsylvania, near and on the New Jersey border, was Holmes's adopted hometown. Holmes was a Georgian by birth. Frank had called Holmes one night in Easton and asked for a shot at the title, saying, "How about getting it on, Larry, since you're undefeated and I'm defeated?" Holmes laughed, thought about his bills, and decided maybe it wasn't so funny. On the night he fought Frank in Atlantic City, there were only four rooms blocked by reservation at Holmes's 150-room Commodore Inn in Easton.

After Frank was dispatched by knockout at 1:32 of the fifth round for Holmes's sixteenth successful title defense, the challenger said he'd been thumbed. Holmes said, "If I did it, I didn't mean to." Holmes gave Frank some dignity.

Holmes spied Joe and son Marvis Frazier in the interview area after the fight. "I see the Smokings are here," he said, referring to father Joe's famous nickname. Soon Holmes would add poor Marvis to his list of victims and go on fighting and ranting and not gently into anybody's good night. Holmes had bills to pay, mouths to feed, and he wanted respect. He was a busy man for seven years, as long as he was the champion of the world.

1985 was not a great year for my old acquaintance, the workman's champion. He lost for the first time in forty-nine fights, when his unsteady legs, spavined by age and relatively soft living, natural inadequacy, and ring wear, would not propel him around the ring after Michael Spinks, who became the first light heavyweight to move up and win the title.

After the fight, Holmes's wife, Diane, came up to him in the corner. Holmes said, "That's it, baby."

Diane said, "That's all right. I love you anyway."

Holmes had beaten the house no matter what else was said, and plenty was. Holmes was derided by the media after that fight, and all through his preparations for his next losing (said the judges) encounter with Spinks in early '86. Holmes was ostracized because he had said that Rocky Marciano, whose 48–0 record Holmes had attempted to break, "couldn't carry my jockstrap."

Here the code of conduct struck him down. Holmes had the nerve, the gall, to say what he thought and believed. In the way he thought of himself, he was the meanest one in the valley before and after fights. He had needed that attitude to go 47–0, for he was not the most physically gifted fighter, especially not coming in the wake of Ali. But Holmes was six-three, 225 pounds. It seemed perfectly logical, to me, for Holmes to feel that not only the five-ten, 189-pound Marciano but anybody else who asked could not carry his jockstrap. Holmes was the heavyweight champion and was trained to feel that way. Facile diplomacy had nothing to do with his line of work, and, if nothing else, Holmes honestly represented his work.

Holmes was supposed to say, "Aw, Rocky would've knocked my block off," or some other such deferential statement. He would have been canonized for his modesty. But it went against the grain of what he was. He was supposed to shed his killer instinct at will and say nothing but nice things outside the ring, which he did not or could not do. But the same people who ostracized him failed to realize that many times, inside the ring, Holmes had been truly civilized. He could have hurt people and chose not to. He could have killed Ali. But he said what he said in public and was therefore said to have no class. Ali had said he was the greatest of all time, let alone Marciano's superior, but Holmes made heads turn in a different direction.

But Holmes did have his relationship with Diane after all those years. He had avoided losing course to the women in the world who would be fascinated by the ultimate protector, the owner of the biggest pair of hands going. I didn't feel sorry for Holmes. He had what he needed, and so did the newspaper columnists, so everybody should've been happy. But Holmes left not quite content.

After Holmes dispatched Cooney in the summer of '82, I traveled to Martinsville, Virginia, hard by the North Carolina border, to visit with Earnie Shavers, one of Holmes's victims. Earnie's reality, his work, was of a different sort than Holmes's, or Ali's, or even Sylvester Stallone's, even though it had intersected with all three.

I had been assigned a feature story on the man Ali had nicknamed the Acorn because of his clean-shaven head. Shavers was an affable, uneducated man who spoke in a pleasant high tenor that would rise to falsetto giggling at the slightest provocation. He had four daughters and many debts, despite over fifty pro fights—including two unsuccessful shots at the title against Ali and Holmes.

Shavers owned one of the most powerful rights in the heavyweight division. He was a puncher who broke jaws and ribs and burst eardrums, so he was ducked by most sensible contenders until he aged. Then he was outboxed and survived by Ali, who was a codger himself by that time. Holmes outboxed Shavers as well, although Earnie had knocked Larry down—"I hit him harder than I ever hit anybody," said

Earnie. Now Earnie's eyes were going. He complained of seeing "black specks, all these black specks before my eyes." When
I told him it was too bad that he hadn't gotten to be champion
for a little while, he giggled and answered, "No, no need to
be sorry about it. It just wasn't meant to be. When I was
young I figured I could knock anybody out. Well, some guys
you just don't knock out. I happened to meet two of 'em."

Shavers lived in a lovely home which he didn't own. His
benefactor was a Martinsville businessman who said he had
grown to love Shavers while watching him fight. Earnie had
been set up with a janitorial supply business and was at-
tempting to interest everyone he met, including me, in some
magical elixir which would give one greater vitality or more
hair, I can't remember which. He had daughters and debts,
which was why he was in Martinsville in the first place, to
start again after being taken financially by equally desperate
men in his home state of Ohio. So Earnie was agreeable. He
could not afford to have the pride of a Larry Holmes.

What I remember most about this is Shavers, dressed in
shorts and a T-shirt, challenging two of his daughters to a
race in an open, grassy field. The girls were budding adoles-
cents, coming into their athletic prime. Their mother had once
been a track sprinter, and the girls were fast runners. They
ran with Earnie for a full fifty yards and leaned at my extended
arm, representing the finishing tape of the hundred-meter dash
at the Olympic Games of some far-off year. Earnie, breathing
hard, got the silver medal. They smiled and giggled together.
I wished the story I wrote had turned out better than it did,
but Earnie wrote me a nice note anyway and said that at least
it made him more welcome in Martinsville. A class act. But
what had it gotten him?

If Earnie Shavers had played Clubber Lang in the *Rocky
II* movie, it would have been much more true to reality—and
would have grossed one-tenth of what it made. Earnie au-
ditioned for the role at the behest of Stallone, but he didn't

get the job, despite his real-life credentials. Mr. T. had a much more threatening voice. Earnie sounded like a choirboy on helium.

Earnie had gone through some paces with Stallone in the ring, as the latter wanted to get a feel for the fight sequences he might want in the movie. Earnie had to pull punches dramatically to keep from hurting Stallone.

"He told me, 'Harder, Earnie, hit me harder!' I tol' him, 'I can't hit you harder, Mr. Stallone. I can't do that. You're a nice man.' He told me to hit him harder or it wouldn't look real. So I gave him a little one in the ribs, then another little one in the liver. He stopped the workout and the camera and went to the bathroom for a little while. When he came back, he tol' me he was sorry, but that they couldn't use me. But they paid my way out to California and they treated me great. Nice guy. Stallone was a nice guy. Only thing, people come up to me now, they know who I am, and they say, 'Hey Earnie, think you could beat Rocky?' "

The next time I saw Earnie, five years later in 1987, he had come to the Mike Tyson–Pinklon Thomas fight in Vegas. He looked at Tyson, giggled, and asked him for a shot at the title. Larry Holmes had already had his shot at Tyson. Sometimes a workman's compensation is retirement, and for those people who have enjoyed their work, like Earnie Shavers and Larry Holmes, retirement is the worst compensation of all. They'd rather have work. Unfortunately, fighters do not seem to age as well as other scientists.

6
Pandora's Box

I suppose it is common for people to question the lasting value of their chosen occupation. This should not be a difficult question for teachers, farmers, doctors, those in law enforcement, nurses, firemen, or researchers in the sciences, all of whom should be looking to preserve, prolong, or improve life, on the days they get out of bed right. They are supposed to help things along. But for lawyers, people who throw the switch for the electric chair, and sportswriters, the question of work value can be downright depressing. What good are you, except to show up where you're not particularly welcome or needed and to start arguments which almost always have no end?

One of the reasons I enjoyed boxing in the first place was the almost helpless public interest in the social phenomenon, not to mention my own instincts. Who would survive? The artist I wished was in me was absorbed in the means—the skill of the boxers—while my survival instinct, strongest of all, was absorbed only in the end. The knockout. Wars, car accidents, football games, and fights. Public interest in these forms of violence was practically assured. I knew why. It was more than merely life and death. It was facing life and death.

If someone did die, how could the full impact of that be relayed to those who had not seen it? When Ray Mancini fought and killed his relentless image, Duk Koo Kim, in Las Vegas, I was a war correspondent on a safe beachhead, watching the distant flash of fire from the front. I was a journalist. There were times I longed to be a writer (which is easier work than being a journalist, for a writer does not necessarily have to get people to talk to him when they don't want to) just as badly as my grandmother had once told me that people in hell long for ice water. After November 1982, it was quite hard for me to remain cynical about prizefights, as a journalist is usually cynical. I could not laugh off Kim and Mancini, completely separate myself from them. I had seen Kim's eyes dilate.

In rapid succession, I was shown more of the underside of boxing. It became Pandora's Box—no matter how or where I chose to open it, out jumped more misfortune, more bad luck, more horrors. My job was to record all this.

★

Sports Illustrated, November 22, 1982

Ray (Boom Boom) Mancini held his swollen left hand in front of him like a jewel and shaded his battered brow with his right. The bright lights were harsh and unwelcome. There were questions in Mancini's heart about what had just happened in the ring, though he didn't yet know the full horror. Was the WBA lightweight title he had just defended successfully against South Korea's Duk Koo Kim worth this? Was anything? "Why do I do it?" Mancini asked himself. "Why do I do this? I'm the one who has to wake up tomorrow and look at myself." He fingered the purple, misshapen area around his left eye. "A badge of honor," he said in a morbid tone.

Minutes earlier, a less reflective Mancini had scored a technical knockout off Kim nineteen seconds into the fourteenth round, and Kim had been carried from the outdoor ring at Caesar's Palace in Las Vegas on a stretcher. This was to have been an epilogue to the Aaron Pryor–Alexis Arguello WBA junior welterweight title fight the night before in Miami. It became a nightmare.

The twenty-three-year-old Kim, who rained an incredible number of blows on Mancini and in return was pounded by even more, was injured by two right hands his head could not bear. Kim was taking just four breaths per minute when he was transported from the ring to an ambulance that was destined for Desert Springs Hospital. Kim then underwent nearly three hours of brain surgery, performed by Dr. Lonnie Hammergren, a local neurosurgeon, who removed a 100-cc blood clot from the right side of Kim's brain. The clot, according to Dr. Hammergren, was the result of a broken blood vessel and was "due, in all probability, to one tremendous punch to the head." Had the punch been part of the thirty-nine-blow bombardment Mancini had delivered in the opening fifty seconds of the thirteenth round? Was it the first of the final two rights in the fourteenth? Or the second? Or could the damage have been done not by Mancini's fists but by Kim's head hitting the canvas after the final blow? Could Kim's brain have been damaged before the fight? "The hemorrhage was quite fresh," Dr. Hammergren said. "The trauma was caused by one punch."

Dr. Hammergren had previously performed two similar operations, one on a Japanese kick boxer, the other on another fighter. "Both men wound up normal, but this outcome will be much worse. Mr. Kim had a right subdural hematoma," said Dr. Hammergren, two hours after the surgery was completed. "He's very critical, with terminal brain damage. There is severe brain swelling. The pressure will go up and up, and that will be it. He'll die. His pupils have been fixed since he arrived. We have him on the respirator now. His body responds slightly to painful stimulus, and that is the only real sign of life we've had. They tell me he fought like a lion in the thirteenth round. Well, nobody could fight like that with a blood clot on his brain."

Kim had indeed fought like a lion. Through the thirty-nine minutes of the previous rounds and those final nineteen seconds, the crowd of 6,500 at Caesar's was sated with action, as was a CBS television audience. And everyone, especially co-promoter Bob Arum, seemed pleased when the fight was over. But later, at the hospital, Arum was somber. "Suspend boxing for a few months," he suggested, before calling for headgear for boxers and for more heavily padded gloves. "Get a blue-chip medical panel to investigate this thing first, and then suspend boxing," Arum said. "It's the height of irresponsibility to allow this to happen, and the old excuses are not working."

Back at Caesar's, Mancini learned of the severity of Kim's injuries and left his suite in the company of his parents and Father Tim O'Neill, the family priest, to seek refuge elsewhere.

Before the fight, Kim's training methods—which included hammering a tire with a sledgehammer two hundred times daily and ingesting large amounts of ginseng and garlic—and style had not impressed the boxing cognoscenti. His anonymity seemed to diminish his 17–1–1, eight-KO record and his No. 1 ranking by the WBA. But he became a haunting foe for Mancini, who now finds, eerily, that he may fight Kim forever.

Mancini is five-six, the same as Kim. Mancini fought low, Kim fought lower. Mancini is right-handed, Kim left-handed. There was a quarter-inch difference in reach, a half-pound in weight, little difference in power, and absolutely none in approach. "It was murderous," said Mancini's manager, Dave Wolf, immediately after the bout, unaware at the time that the comment would soon take on a macabre accuracy. "It was like Ray was fighting a mirror. I hope the people who said Kim was nothing are impressed now."

Mancini was left with several impressions by the fourteenth round. In the third, an infrequent Kim right lead—or perhaps it was the clash of heads—ripped open Mancini's left ear. Blood spouted, and only ice and pressure by cornerman Paul Percifield kept the wound closed. In that same round, one of Mancini's left hooks caught Kim's head too high and at a bad angle. The hand, badly bruised by the blow, began to swell, eventually to twice normal size. In the eighth, Mancini's left eye began to puff and discolor.

Kim's left hooks and slashing rights had exacted a toll, but Kim had been punished too, though he showed it less. When the fighters began the fourteenth, the mirror's image was still there. Mancini broke the pattern by stepping to his right as Kim's left whistled by. Mancini hooked his own wounded left ineffectually, but now Kim was off-center, exhausted and facing Mancini's corner. He never saw the punch. Mancini drove off his right foot and delivered the first of the final pair of rights on the point of the Korean's chin. A glancing left hook followed, then a crushing right which sent Kim to the canvas. Kim landed heavily on his back and head, rolled over in slow motion, grabbed a middle strand of the ropes, and stared blankly at the timekeeper. Kim's eyes dilated while the outdoor stadium rocked in celebration.

"He was desperate and I was hoping. My left hand was killing me," Mancini said. "But I felt that first right all the way up my arm."

Twice Kim failed to regain his footing but somehow he beat the count. Referee Richard Green looked at Kim's unfocused eyes and buckling legs and stopped the fight immediately. "He was not there and I wasn't going to let him go any further," said Green, who has officiated half a dozen world title fights, including Larry Holmes–Muhammad Ali.

Green was absolved of any blame for failing to stop the

fight earlier by the attending ringside physician, Dr. Donald Romeo, who worked to revive Kim. Kim's cornermen had offered no protest when the fight ended. "He just wouldn't go down," one of them said later. "He had great pride."

Perhaps Kim's pride had been too great. Wolf returned from the hospital eight hours after the fight, at 11:00 P.M., sobered. "Pol Tiglao"—Kim's American representative and translator and agent for a number of Oriental fighters—"told me that a couple of days before the fight, Kim had written 'Kill or be killed' on a lampshade in his room, in Korean. He was a warrior going to war," Wolf said. "Apparently he viewed this fight as a death match." Wolf then discounted Arum's suggestions. "I don't know what a blue-ribbon panel could do now," he said. "It was not a case of defective equipment, or a fighter being allowed to go too far, or any impropriety. It was one or two unfortunate punches. And those rights at the end were not nearly the best punches Ray had thrown during the fight."

The youngest of five children born to rice and ginseng farmers, Kim came from Kang Won-do province in Korea, one hundred kilometers east of Seoul. "He was the strongest of the family's three sons," said H. R. Lee, a Korean journalist with the *Hankook Ilbo*, who traveled to Las Vegas with Kim's small entourage and a larger group of Korean partisans. "He was not injured before the fight. He was in the best condition of his life."

Kim had been a bootblack, tour guide, and baker's assistant before starting a boxing career in 1976. His only hobby, according to Lee, was "music listening," but Tiglao said he also enjoyed reading. After a 29–4 amateur record, he turned professional in 1976, working with a hundred other fighters in Seoul's Tong-a Gymnasium. He was the best of the lot and won the Orient and Pacific Boxing Federation lightweight title in February 1982. He received $20,000 to fight Mancini.

Mancini had studied films of Kim and other southpaw

fighters for weeks. "We figured he'd come out kamikaze," Mancini said.

"After looking at film, I didn't care what anyone else said," Mancini's trainer, Murphy Griffith, declared. "I had Ray train as if it was the fight of his life."

Mancini started the first round with a booming left hook to the jaw, but Kim answered with two of his own, and the barrages from both sides continued for the first nine rounds, the only variation being target. When Mancini went to the liver or rib cage, Kim answered. Kim seemed to land the harder punches. At the end of the ninth, a left rocked Mancini back on his heels and Kim extended his arms upward in exultation. "He was getting lower than me," Mancini said. "I was supposed to be off him, but a lot of times when a guy is sitting in front of you like that, you want to move in and shoot. But he was getting his punches off first."

Said Griffith, "Ray had to adjust. We didn't know Kim would be *that* tough. He was skillful, smart. Ray couldn't get below him, where he likes to be. But Ray's physical conditioning determined the fight. By the thirteenth round, the guy was looking for the hook. I told Ray to go with the right."

In fact, that decision had been made some ten rounds earlier, when Mancini hurt his left hand. "Every time I hit him in the head, it killed me," Mancini said shortly after the battle, unaware of the terrible irony.

The constant pounding from Mancini began to tell on Kim in the tenth, when Green took a point from Kim for hitting-and-holding. Green was berated by Mancini's corner throughout the fight about that tactic, borderline low blows, hitting after the bell, and Kim's headfirst rushes. "He wasn't dirty," insisted Mancini, who appeared to win every round from the tenth on. "Rough and tough, not dirty. We both hit heads. We both hit low. He was just the worst type of guy to fight."

Said Wolf, "Already I can look back and see that [Green] did an excellent job."

By the eleventh, though his left eye was purple and hideously swollen, Mancini had taken control of the fight. He fired a left hook that buckled Kim's knees, and now he began to land three punches to Kim's one. At one point Kim went to one knee, but Green correctly ruled it a push. Mancini ended the twelfth scoring from a distance. He gave himself a clap and made an exaggerated nod at the end of the round. In the thirteenth, Mancini swarmed over Kim, starting the unanswered thirty-nine-punch sequence with a straight right hand. The right side of Kim's jaw ballooned and appeared to be broken, but he weathered that storm and even managed to punch out a weak combination. Then came the fourteenth, the sidestep, and Mancini's initial right, unseen by Kim. He reeled back, defenseless, and the second right landed point-blank on his jaw.

"Let all these guys who are screaming for a piece of Ray settle with Kim first," said Wolf at the conclusion of the bout. Later, after spending four hours at the hospital and being told that Kim didn't have long to live, Wolf said, "Ray is taking this pretty hard and his parents are pretty shook up also. I haven't given a single thought to how this may affect Ray as a fighter, and maybe that sounds silly, but that's the last concern right now. How it affects him as a person is what concerns me. I do think he's a very strong kid and sometime in the future he will be able to look at this, in the context of great pain, and see that once he stepped into that ring with Kim there was nothing else he could have done."

On Sunday morning, one hour before attending a mass conducted by Father O'Neill at the Tropicana Hotel, Mancini issued a statement on television. Dark glasses covering his closed left eye, his damaged hand resting on an arm of the couch in his suite, Mancini said, "I'm very saddened. I'm sorry it had to happen, and it hurts me bad that I was a part of it. I hope they realize that I didn't intentionally hurt him. I don't blame myself, but I can't alienate myself. I'm a Christian, and I've been praying that I'll get some answers to some questions that have been popping through my mind. I have to rely on my faith to help me get through this. It could easily have been me, and who is to say that it won't be me next time? I'm not saying I'll retire, but right now I'm not thinking of future fights. I have to see what happens to Mr. Kim. I need time to heal."

Emile Griffith fought eighty times after Benny (Kid) Paret died following their fight on March 24, 1962. Griffith was twenty-four at the time of the Paret bout, a career fighter comfortably lost in his craft. Was Mancini, still impressionable at twenty-one and a young man for whom "money is no god," different? "They're both sensitive individuals," said Gil Clancy, CBS boxing analyst and former trainer of Griffith, who happens to be the nephew of Mancini's trainer. "It took something out of Emile Griffith," said Clancy. "Griffith got hate mail, but he got encouragement too. Ray will have to deal with the same things."

Murphy Griffith said, "For a while it was doubtful that Emile would ever come back. He was a sensitive man. But time heals. He had to realize that what happened wasn't his will. People say it affected him until the end of his career. I think it did. Man, you don't forget. Some can handle it. Some can't. How it will happen in Ray's case, only time will tell. He's got a good head, but a human is a human."

Former heavyweight champion Max Baer never approached a fight with the same intensity following the death of Frankie Campbell soon after their fight in San Francisco on August 24, 1930. Jimmy Doyle died seventeen hours after fighting Sugar Ray Robinson for the welterweight crown in Cleveland on June 24, 1947. At a subsequent hearing Robinson was asked whether he knew he had Doyle in serious trouble. Robinson looked straight ahead and said, "Sir, they pay me to get them in trouble." Mancini's box-office appeal had had nearly everyone who could make the weight calling him to try to get a fight. Despite his 24–1, nineteen KO record,

Mancini inspired confidence in contenders. Says Hector Camacho, an undefeated junior lightweight from New York's Spanish Harlem, "You can't play Mancini cheap. He's the man right now. He's strong, he'll beat on you, but when the time comes he won't knock me out. He's the guy who will make me."

"Look, I know people either think I'm a bum or a superstar," Mancini had said before the fight. "I don't care. I know where I am. Somewhere in between." After the fight, just before he heard the news of Kim's condition, Mancini decided something. "This badge of honor," he said, studying his battered face in a mirror. "Well, ugly as it is, I'm proud of it." Then the nightmare came. Now there are only questions with no simple answers.

★

I met Mancini in Youngstown, Ohio, during the early summer of 1982. I flew into Cleveland, rented a car, and drove the Ohio countryside to the city of Youngstown. The long drive would give me more time to think of angles. Mancini had not yet killed in order to survive. He was just a fresh young kid with cheek who could box, the kind of kid every kid has known or been at some time.

The kid-fighting-for-his-father angle had been beaten into a straight line already. I was thinking of this when Mancini opened the door to his parents' home, a warm spot on a cold landscape. He was smiling. His world was wide open and growing past the economic impossibilities of his depressed hometown. Any consequences of this growth were positive or not worth considering.

I liked him and his parents, Lenny and Ellen. Lenny had been a contemporary of Lew Jenkins—in fact, many had said that Lenny, five-two and a 73–5–1 lightweight, would have taken the measure of old Lew. Somehow, I doubted it. Happily for them both, it was a question that had never been decided in the ring. Jenkins had died in Concord the previous year, 1981. Lenny seemed in robust shape, relatively, though it was hard to tell because he didn't have very much to say. But he must have been able to do some kind of talking, because Ellen Mancini was a bright, efficient, lovely woman.

Mancini honestly felt he was serving justice to his father, who had never won a world title. I made the rounds with him and his ever-present cadre of friends, former classmates of Mancini's at Cardinal Mooney High School, where Mancini had played basketball and football until the reality of his size drew him toward his father's occupation. Mancini's friends were also short. They ran in a group of five and looked like the cast from a teenage movie.

One of his friends seemed most aware of the fragility of this new, wonderful life-style. I was considered an interloper, perhaps even a bad omen, someone to take something from Ray or to take Ray from them—to change things back to the way they were before. Mancini would make the cover of *Sports Illustrated* after beating España. That was like being transported to Oz. Few could obtain the passport, and it was only one ride per customer. Fagin wanted to take the ride, but didn't want to risk the change which went with it.

"If Ray gets knocked out, will you still be his friend?" Fagin asked me.

I could only raise my eyebrows. Journalists are always intruders. There is little in the way of civility or decorum about the work, so I couldn't very well tell Fagin he was being rude. I was being rude just by being there. He had happened upon my Achilles' heel.

"Shuddup, Chuck," said Mancini. He was like a cat, the way he lashed out and then in a twinkling of an eye recovered his friendly, composed self.

I liked the little fighter even more. When he fought Arguello, he had been rushed—an underripe kid that Arguello methodically disassembled in the fourteenth round, in something of the manner Holmes took Cooney. But Mancini was different from Cooney. He went down swinging. He went down hating the fact he had gone down, railing against it. He was a fighter whose strengths, although not diversified, were not at all uncertain. He had a good punch with either hand, he was in tremendous shape, and he liked it hot in the kitchen. He was a pro by style.

Arriving in a local boys' club, we entered the stuffy gym. Mancini became even happier. His was a physical regimen which could break down even trained muscle. Hundreds of repetitions even so close to a fight. He performed them with ease. His condition was beyond dispute. Other Youngstown fighters, mostly black and Hispanic, worked out around him, but his fluid movements made it obvious he was the star of the gym. I could see why Sylvester Stallone had come to Youngstown this week to proposition Mancini about making a movie. This was the *Rocky* dream come true.

Mancini sweated mightily through the workout administered by Murphy Griffith. After a while, Mancini's head began to bow with weariness. He had a broad mouth, ample brow, and widely spaced eyes. A good target. All the while he worked out, Mancini chattered excitedly to me, his voice rising to a high tenor as he tried to make me understand the way he felt about things. He talked like a man on his way to someplace where he might not get the chance to talk again.

Stallone had arrived in the area and was ceremoniously walking the halls of a small chain hotel between Youngstown and Warren, where the fight would be held in a ring set up in a high school football stadium. Stallone wore a cream-colored suit and was accompanied by a would-be fighter named Lee Cantalito. As I left Mancini at the doors of the hotel, he apologized for having this other meeting. I wondered if he would let Stallone get a word in edgewise. "Remember," said Mancini in parting. "I ain't no Gerry Cooney."

There were three or four other fighters in America with

comparable skills at the weight, but he, Mancini, was white and therefore, it was said, more marketable. There was no reason for him to be blamed personally or to be somehow held accountable for that—but he wanted to distance himself from the thought of it. He knew he was legit. He fought to win and he fought to be paid, but more than money drove him. He fought with something to prove. Money was the reward a pro expected, but there came times when money alone could not drive a man past his limits—where Kim drove Mancini.

Before his friends and congregation, Mancini knocked out España in anticlimactic fashion. Stanley Christodoulou, the South African referee who worked in Bob Arum's shows, stopped the fight. Mancini excitedly chattered through the post-fight television interview in the ring, then ran to the home locker room, where he slammed his fists together like cymbals and yelled in true, solitary happiness. He paced like a good athlete who hadn't played long enough. He was so ecstatic he was unable to sustain our interview for more than one answer before more rapture would fill his head and tilt it back.

"Thanks for your help, Ray."

Our next meeting would come two months later, in Las Vegas, a few days before the Kim fight. I had rarely seen Vegas or Mancini in such a state of nonactivity. The demands made on both were lessened because most newspaper journalists were in Miami for Arguello–Aaron Pryor. Kim–Mancini was supposed to be a bit of a kiss-off.

In Miami, Pryor, his troubled soul making him an enraged fighter, punched spectacularly while his backers yelled, "Hawk Time!" Arguello, a more classic boxer, was beaten by (1) weight—Pryor was a natural 140, Arguello a natural 135—and (2) Arguello's infatuation with his own right hand. Arguello's right could not stop Pryor, who waded through those straight right hands to overwhelmingly knock out Arguello in the fourteenth round. Mancini watched the fight in his suite at Caesar's Palace. "I always wanted to be the one to do that to Alexis," Mancini said softly. "Don't get me wrong. I like Alexis. Nice guy. But I wanted him again." Pryor was another matter. "I preferred not to consider him . . . until now," Mancini said.

Only a few boxing journalists cared to fly all the way across country to Vegas from Miami for an afternoon fight the next day after the Pryor–Arguello deadlines, for a fight that would be televised. It wasn't a high roller's fight. Mancini was the prohibitive favorite among scant bettors. Kim had no visibility in the eyes of newspeople, either.

I had gone to see Kim in his suite at Caesar's on Saturday afternoon, the day of the Pryor–Arguello fight. The suite was darkened by drawn drapes. My eyes were slow to adjust as I moved deeper into the sweetened air of the rooms. In one corner of a bedroom sat Kim, his square face bathed in a swatch of daylight and the curling smoke of incense. He sat in a straight-backed chair by a window which faced away from the Strip, toward the open desert. The shades were parted just enough for him to see outside. Four of his countrymen sat with him, some smoking blunt, filterless cigarettes and chatting without animation, forming a semicircle a respectful distance away from Kim, apart but at hand in case he needed an ear for some exclamation or request. He seemed inclined toward neither.

Luckily for me, one of the men in the room was Mr. Lee of the *Hankook Ilbo* in Seoul. He seemed more pliable.

After brief formalities, I questioned Lee. Lee, in turn, and with crisp nods of respect punctuating his words, questioned Kim, who answered in monosyllables which seemed curt even to me. Finally, I asked Lee about Kim's ability to take a punch. Lee had trouble understanding my meaning. "Naturally he can take the punch, or he would not be boxing. Boxers must take the punch."

I inverted my wrist, grabbed my chin, and moved my jaw from side to side in order to translate my meaning. Seeing this, Kim's expression changed. I would like to say he smiled—but it was something else. Scorn. He gently touched his jaw with two fingers of his right hand, then without averting his gaze, he reached over and touched the marble windowsill with the same two fingers, just as gently. He turned to face the desert. The interview was over.

I have since studied the notes I took during the fight—notes which have the look of no others I have taken, and I've taken plenty. Even a cursory glance at your notepad during a round or between rounds of a good fight could be your undoing. So I kept my notes without looking down during rounds, and the size of the letters and the direction in which I put them down told me later of my initial reaction to the fight. The faster the action, the tighter, more manic the scribbling. The harder the punch, the larger the letters. If a line of letters slanted upward, this was a flurry that mounted in intensity, threatened a knockout. If a line of letters slanted downward, most of the punches had been partially blocked or absorbed without much effect. In this fight, there were large letters, huge letters, written in every single round. Not one line slanted downward. Normally, this imperfect blow-by-blow card would fill one page of legal-sized paper. I write small. This fight filled three.

Mancini, drawing on his deepest physical reserves, survived Kim, who, in one of the greatest physical feats I had ever witnessed, rose from the canvas in the fourteenth round while his brain was bleeding. He rose to all but die in the referee's arms.

I covered one more Mancini bout, this one some months later at Madison Square Garden. Mancini had been scheduled to fight Kenny (Bang Bang) Bogner in Sun City, Bopthuswana, South Africa. Arum had no compunction about staging fights in South Africa. It was business. By a thoughtful act of God,

Mancini suffered a stress fracture of the medial end of his clavicle and that fight was canceled. I could still respect him without reservation. He was still the champion and remained so after knocking out a Peruvian, Orlando Romero, at the Garden. Romero had gotten in some heavy shots before he succumbed to a well-placed Mancini left hook. I went with Mancini to Lenox Hill Hospital and watched as Dr. Jeffrey Schwartz stitched his eyebrows back together. "My poor face," Mancini said. He had just signed a contract with the William Morris Agency.

"Ray," I said, "do you remember when you said that money was no god to you?"

"Sure," he said, flinching as the syringe full of local anesthetic was shot gingerly into his face. "Jesus, Doc. You shooting me up?"

"Just a little, Ray."

"Oh, God."

"Why keep this up?" I said, too idly.

Mancini was too busy hurting to answer.

"Christ, Doc!"

"We have to clean it out," said the doctor. "We have to clean it before we can sew it."

"I don't wanna end up like Rocky Graziano," Mancini said softly. He looked jaundiced against the stark white background of the room. "I'm not a pretty boy, but I don't wanna end up like that. I don't like to feel this way. The pain. My face. I don't like this. Oh, God, my neck."

"Then what are you doing this shit for?"

In his next fight, Mancini would stop Bobby Chacon on a technical knockout, but Bobby took his pound of Mancini's flesh with him. Mancini lost twice to Livingstone Bramble. Ray and Hector Camacho didn't get around to seeing who would make whom great until the spring of 1989.

Bobby Chacon was thirty-two years old when he was stopped by Boom Boom Mancini. Chacon was a wife beater.

Other than that, he was a truly honest fighter, possibly the most honest I had ever met. Bobby was all smiles every time I saw him, despite the fact that he was a fighter who didn't have many fights left in him. He was an old lightweight, a contradiction in terms, and he had been a prizefighter since he was nineteen. But he was still cogent, a good talker, gracious—incredibly nice in the face of the vicious turns of his life.

Mancini and Chacon went to the Feast of San Gennaro parade the weekend after Ray stopped Orlando Romero in New York. Later, when Ray and Bobby fought, referee Richard Steele stepped between Mancini's fists and Chacon's bleeding face. Chacon lost by technical knockout. Bobby had been cut badly. Bobby always cut badly. "I figure I ain't fighting until you cut me," he would say, smiling. He and his cornermen offered a mild protest at Steele's just decision, but within a minute of the fight's end, Bobby caught Steele's eye and mouthed the words: "Thank you."

That was Bobby for you. He felt wronged whenever he was asked to stop fighting. But, deep in his heart, he was ready to stop.

The air is crisp and uncommonly clear in the rising plain between Sacramento and the high Sierras, where California is cut from the cord of a different kind of civilization. This is Pacific air, caught and cleansed by the grip of the Sierras and flung back in its own face. Rare air to the senses and system of a lifelong city dweller. Bobby Chacon chose to live here, where each breath was like a fresh start. Bobby had once lived to the far south and west, near the desert coast of Los Angeles. He'd been a San Fernando Valley tough, prowling the streets and alleys of Pacoima, looking hard for a good time. His smile was brightest when he drew blood or bruises with his fists or with the blackjack he carried in his lunchbox.

By the time he started traveling with the blackjack, he rarely needed it. He had become that good with his hands. Chacon was the world featherweight champion by the age of twenty-three, then, after a bloating orgy of good times, lost the title nine months later. After eleven long years among the Danny "Little Red" Lopezes, the Ruben Olivareses, and fifty-seven fights, Chacon still fought, long past knowing his youth had been misspent. He became champion again at the age of thirty-one. He still smiled a sweet, chilling smile at the sight of blood. It was his own blood he laughed at now.

He and his three children lived in a trailer that sat on blocks in a small stand of pines within eyeshot of the Sierras. I visited Bobby there in February 1983. In December 1982, a month after Kim and Mancini had fought, Bobby had struggled with Rafael "Bazooka" Limón and defeated him to win the WBC super featherweight title in Sacramento. On May 15, 1983, Chacon would be awarded a unanimous decision over Cornelius Boza-Edwards. Boza had knocked out Chacon in the thirteenth round two years before that (and nearly had knocked him out on May 15, 1983, for that matter).

In his early thirties now, Bobby still yearned for all the grisly truth the ring had to offer. The Chacon–Limón fight had been contested with so much fury that it was designated Fight of the Year 1982 by some periodicals, despite Mancini–Kim, Holmes–Cooney, and Pryor–Arguello. Bobby won barely, on a fifteenth-round TKO. They needed twenty stitches to close his face afterward. After the Boza–Edwards fight on May 15, 1983, Bobby would need forty more stitches.

On the way up to Oroville and Palermo, California, from San Francisco, I stopped over in Sacramento. It was the evening of February 1, a Tuesday evening, and I chanced to take on the evening's fights at the Sacramento Memorial Auditorium with Babe Griffin. Griffin was the promoter of the entire card. He lived near San Jose, in a town called Morgan Hill, some one hundred miles west by southwest of Sacramento.

He was often seen tooling about in his pastel-colored luxury car in the more northerly environs of the San Francisco Bay Area, where I had met him, mid-hoist, at Eddie Butler's Ringside Bar in Oakland. Every Tuesday and Thursday night, Babe drove to Sacramento to oversee the proceedings. He was eighty at the time. He'd been doing this sort of work for fifty years. He had promoted Chacon's most recent fights, up until the Limón title bout, when the TV money arrived, followed by a hungry school of promoters. Babe was not connected well enough and was circumvented as Chacon signed a more lucrative offer with men who had the ears of the network executives.

Babe shrugged his shoulders over it. At least he still had every Tuesday and Thursday night. He clucked a little over loyalties lost, but it was reflective, not vindictive, clucking. Babe had promoted and Bobby had stayed busy. What more could Babe say or ask? Griffin had promoted Chacon's three comeback fights, including one against a fighter called Ugalde at the Memorial Auditorium. Chacon's wife, Valorie, had committed suicide two nights before the fight.

Valorie had begged Bobby not to fight anymore—she had in fact been begging him for years. The day after her untimely death, Chacon fought Ugalde anyway. The attending physician, Dr. P. B. Montemayor, had said, "I can't say that Bobby's body is showing any grief. His blood pressure is normal. Fighting is the only thing on his mind." Chacon fought well with his father-in-law and brother-in-law in the corner, serving as his seconds. Bobby knocked out Ugalde in the third round with brutal definitiveness. After Chacon had dispatched Limón a few months later, the latter came by Chacon's dressing room, still woozy. "I'm sorry about your wife," Limón said in Spanish. "Take care of your children."

I sat with Babe in the third row from the ring in Sacramento while some of the local talent made bad moves and threw punches in front of us. The house was small. Six or seven hundred, at best. "Maybe a break-even night," said Babe, shoving the nosepiece of his black horn-rimmed glasses back on his face with a pudgy index finger.

Babe was a small man of regal bearing. Sitting under the auditorium's dull lighting, his presence refracted by chandeliers, he had an aura. The architecture of the old place was kind to him. The crowd, his crowd, had the same makeup as the fighters. Black, Latino, Anglo, all working hard to somehow stay working-class. Several apostates came by Babe's seat. They asked for his dispensation of their happiness. Would Babe grant them a payday, or even the promise of a payday? Babe answered with his eyes, acknowledging each, ignoring no one, all the while telling me what he knew about Bobby Chacon.

Griffin had worked with master boxer Eligio Sardines, aka Kid Chocolate, and later with Tony Canzoneri in the 1930s. Babe continued to make fights and fighters a half-century later. He had no illusions about the relative skills of his latest charges. "But," he said, "Bobby, in his day, could box and punch and move. And he had heart." For Babe to say that Chacon displayed these essentials was praise of the highest order, because Babe had had Kid Chocolate, you see. He'd had the best.

Babe's eyes were more experienced than all but a few others in the boxing world, yet he didn't cling rapturously to the past. He compared fighters as honestly as their different eras allowed, the only promoter or manager or trainer I ever knew to do so in public. Bobby had not taken Babe along for this latest ride on the gravy train, but that was already yesterday to Babe, who hadn't let being eighty go to his head any more than it did naturally. He was a great old man. He said, "I don't know that Bobby lacked for anything in the ring back then. And he's still a good little fighter. Just been beat on. Don't put a noncontender in there with him, though. Ugalde? Bobby walked out there and tried to kill the guy, which he damn near did. I don't think Bobby will fight much longer. But then again, as long as he's getting paid, he will."

Griffin said he remembered when he first met Chacon, more than a decade before. Joey Ponce had been Chacon's manager then, and he had told Griffin that the kid would be champion one day. Babe had told Ponce that he'd heard that shit for years.

"But then I saw him fight. Damn few really know what they're doing in there. Bobby knew."

One of the fighters and would-bes that came by Babe's throne that night in Sacramento was Pete Ranzany. Ranzany was very polite, an above-average hitter of the middleweights, thirtyish. He had been knocked out by the best of them. He knew his place and was not offended by it. "I was born and raised in Sacramento," he said. "I got a warehousing job over at Raley's. I'm looking for some kinda future here. Fighting's a chore now. I don't wanna lose my reputation. Guys like Yaqui and me, we were contenders. Real contenders. I'm proud of that. How many guys can say what we say, Yaqui and me? But Bobby—Bobby's a champion. You can't compare us to him. I'm a good fighter; Bobby a great fighter. That's just the truth of it."

I wondered if Ranzany had intentionally avoided saying whether Bobby was or is great, or if it just came out that way. To use a phrase without a verb to describe a fighter required a sense of tact only fighters could employ.

I drove Interstate 5 to Highway 70, then headed east toward the mountains. I took the Oro Dam exit and was directed to the Butte County Police Athletic League gymnasium, where Chacon was working against his shadow in the ring. He wore a T-shirt with "Bobby No Dice" emblazoned on the back. "An old reminder," Bobby said, smiling. "Don't masturbate."

Chacon was attended by two friends from different stages

in his life, Pedro Avedano and Bob Huskey. Nearby stood a bent, gaunt figure with a trainwreck of a yellowing smile, a local named Jack Hitchcock. Very appropriate name, I thought. Hitchcock wore crusted denim jeans. He got the first word in on me. "I break horses for a living," he said, not taking his eyes away from Chacon's slow-footed movements. "I'm seventy. At least seventy. Been around here forty-five years, breaking horses, or havin' 'em break me. This body here? This ain't no accident. Still break a horse or two, now and then. Now this man here"—he pointed toward Chacon— "he's my kind of champion. He fights like an old-timer. He don't move his hands to block the punches. And when he hits you, you feel it. Y'know, young feller, as far as you and I know, a schoolbook ain't nothing but a pack of lies. Ever think about that? But I seen for myself what he had to go through to come back. He's a champion. You tell 'em what an old cowboy has to say about this here Bobby Chacon."

Hitchcock cackled loudly, and Bobby looked down from the ring where he was working out alone and winked. From that moment until my departure on the evening of the next day, Bobby treated me like a long-lost friend. He began by explaining, without being asked, why he couldn't have contact work while training for a fight. "You see my eyes?" he asked. "I don't know what's holding 'em together."

Dr. Brevitar Creech's fine handiwork had done the trick so far. Dr. Creech's practice was in Chico, not far away. Creech had removed scar tissue, filed down what he couldn't remove, and cauterized, restitched, and revamped the area around Bobby's eyes after he had fought Limón. Dr. Creech's opinion had not been surprising. "He can't sustain too much more damage without affecting the eye itself," he said. "There's not much left to damage."

Having performed his ablutions, Chacon began to talk with hesitation as he drove us toward his trailer home in the woods. "I've always been a fighter," he said. "I figured that was my job in life. I was dedicated to it because I was off the streets. I didn't have nothing. Then I got comfortable. That's the worst thing a fighter can be. Comfortable. Then I fought to prove I could take a punch. To prove I was a man. Then, I didn't know why I fought. I was confused. Searching. Searching for nothing. Searching for what I already had."

Bob Huskey had told me this: "Valorie was just ready to go. I talked to her not thirty minutes before it happened. Bobby had been taking a lot of punishment in the ring. Valorie was feeling guilty because she had gotten him into fighting for money, and now she couldn't justify it in her mind." I brought up Valorie's name to Chacon with some trepidation, but Bobby expected it. His eyes didn't waver. They brightened. "Valorie," he said, "was my beloved. Fighting is like a wife. It can be good to you, if you treat it right. If you don't, then, like a wife it will know, because it's right there with you all the time."

Chacon had been what is commonly termed a good little athlete while at McClay Junior High School and San Fernando High. He was smaller than many of his male classmates, like Gary Matthews, the baseball player, and Anthony Davis, the football star. So instead of joining the athletic teams, Bobby joined gangs. The Group. The New Movement. Bobby was the eldest of four children, but he said he had to find his friends in the streets because he didn't adjust well to his stepfather, John Benegas. "Stepfathers—you know how that can be," he said. I told him that I did. "Seems like everywhere I went, I fought. Man. I was fifteen."

When he was sixteen, Chacon met Valorie Ginn and asked her to a party. Valorie was of Chinese-Irish-American extraction, with a Latin bloodline as well. Her beauty was undeniable, but not extraordinary. To see her, one would have thought of sweetness and peace instead of obsession. Chacon was transformed when he saw her. "There was a beauty about Valorie that only I could see," he said. "From that moment on, it was me and Valorie."

Concessions were still made to the gangs, and this made

Valorie uneasy. She sat with Chacon while he watched boxing from the Los Angeles Olympic Auditorium on television. Eventually she began to prod him. "You can do that, Bobby," she would say, touching him lightly with her fingertips. Valorie convinced Chacon to go to Johnny Flores's gym in Pacoima. Johnny told Bobby he'd have to pay $5 a month for a regular locker. Chacon didn't have $5. Johnny looked him over. Chacon wore his hair long back then. His jeans were torn. Johnny told him to come back the next day with a haircut and he'd see.

Chacon weighed 145 pounds then. After a few months at Johnny's, and in Rocky Lane's garage, the water and fat had been wrung from him and he was down to his fighting weight—125 pounds. By then he had said goodbye forever to San Fernando High and was working at the Lockheed plant. Valorie's parents, especially her mother, Mae, looked at Chacon with hard eyes. He was so unlike their Valorie, so volatile and prone to violence. But the more they suggested alternative boyfriends to Valorie, the tighter she clung to Bobby. In November 1971, she brought Chacon's lunch to the Lockheed plant in the usual brown paper bag. His professional boxing license was in it.

Bobby and I arrived at the fixed trailer in time to see his three children off to the dentist. Johna, the girl, was the oldest. She was twelve. Bobby Jr., also known as Chico, was ten. Jayme was seven. "The boys need to go to the dentist—they take after their father," said Chacon, flashing his crooked picket-fence smile, offset in his handsome, puffy face. "Johna has the strong teeth in the family—like her mother." Bobby brought out some old photo albums, and this helped him to remember. He sat with his back to a window with the late-afternoon sun, strained by the leaves of the trees, dappling one side of his face. "That's Valorie," he said, pointing to his favorite picture of his wife. She was at a distance and turned slightly to the side, some of her long black hair hiding one eye, the other eye peering out with mistrusting hope.

Chacon's amateur career had been very short. He had, in fact, left it behind long ago after his first few street battles in Pacoima. In his first two pro fights, he scored knockouts in less than two rounds. Valorie and Bobby were married while she was pregnant with Johna. He had turned pro and knocked out fourteen of the first fifteen men he faced. By June of 1973, he was 19–0, cocksure. In going the way he had chosen to take, he met the inevitable better man, Ruben Olivares. More skilled, more experienced, Olivares knocked out Chacon in the ninth round. "Ruben Olivares showed me what boxing was all about," Chacon said softly.

Now Chacon was truly a pro. Full circle. From those fights with the gangs, from his enjoyment of and proficiency in those fights, from his comfortable exhibition of his skill, to this. There is a false distinction between amateurs and professionals, not only in boxing, but in athletics in general. The notion is that professionalism has only to do with money and competence. It doesn't have to. Ideally, for the participants' sakes, it does involve money, but an athlete is not an amateur solely because he or she is not getting paid, and not a professional because he or she is getting paid. Does getting an allowance make you a professional child? An athlete begins to lose amateur status in an activity shortly after the third serious practice session. He or she either likes it and wants to do it or doesn't. Profession implies work done for compensation in society. Actually, it is work done for years, work done by rote, done by trial and error, done with a knowledge which runs deeper with each reenactment, and a final realization that one will never know all there is to know. Only then does the participant begin to realize his insignificance in relation to the work. The complete reality of a sport is found in its professionals—whether they are being paid or not. Olympic boxers are professionals by the time they get to the Olympics. Amateur status is not something that can be gained through a legislative body. You're either a novice or you're not. The athlete goes ahead and does the appointed work, does his best, does the learning, even after he realizes his limitations and the end-all of his efforts. That's a pro.

Chacon fought on, past knowing the limitations Olivares had shown him. Chacon won the featherweight championship in September 1974 against Alfredo Mercado and began to live high, to see other women beckoned by this fascinating skill of survival, his little torch of fame, his $50 bills. Chacon signed for another fight with Olivares while he was wrecking his body with what football coaches call dissipation. He was fourteen pounds overweight two weeks before the fight, in June 1975. Olivares destroyed him in less than two rounds. Valorie began to panic. Bobby was a professional. She had lost him.

After a February 1976 fight in which he had been battered into unconsciousness by a pug named David Sotelo, Valorie publicly begged Bobby to quit the ring. She had been begging him in private for months, and hoped the public embarrassment would make him stop. He did quit, but he came back.

"Valorie wanted me to sit down and love her. I fooled around. She left. I promised I'd give up playing around. I wanted her back. Val was always home with the babies. She never got the chance to develop her head."

After Chacon was knocked out by Alexis Arguello in 1979, Valorie insisted they move away from the Los Angeles–San Fernando Valley area to Palermo, where her brother, Alan, now lived. Alan had forty acres and sold twenty to Bobby. The Chacons moved into the mobile home in 1980. "Val thought that would do it, get me away from fighting, get me away from other women," Chacon said. In 1981, he fought five times. He was now an opponent for pay—and an unwitting accomplice. By Chacon's account, Valorie had turned to paranoia. "She made me buy her a gun—a .22 rifle," he said. "She'd say, 'Bobby, we've got to fence this place in.' Yeah, she knew how to use the rifle. I had taught her."

Evening had fallen. Bobby and I were alone in the trailer. He had made me comfortable in his company. He was quite serene. And somehow, he seemed a reasonable man. He spoke for the next hour, almost without interruption, pouring out what he believed—or had to believe—had happened to his life. It was like a recitation. The multiplication tables. This is what was. No changing it.

"In February of 1982," he said, "Val tried to kill herself when I was in Sacramento. I was fighting Renan Morata for Babe Griffin. Val and I needed the money. She begged me not to go. She was weak-looking. She had taken some sleeping pills. After I left, she told Johna, 'Now, I'm going to lock the bedroom door. Don't let anyone bother me.' Johna respected that. Alan came over and couldn't open the bedroom door. He knew something was wrong. He took the door off its hinges. Val got mad later, at the hospital, when she woke up and found out she wasn't dead. She ripped the tubes out of her arm and walked out. She disappeared. I suppose she thought I had something going on the side.

"She was missing for nearly a month. They found her wandering around the Sacramento airport. She was talking about guns. When I came to get her, she looked beautiful to me, like always. I never even thought about her seeing a psychiatrist. I would never think like that. Never. She had lost nearly twenty pounds. She wasn't a big girl to begin with. She just wanted me to get out of boxing. But I went back to Sacramento to fight Ugalde. We talked on the phone. We argued. Mae had come up to stay with Val for a while. Mae loved her daughter very much. Her father, James, came up later. Mae called me in the hotel in Sacramento and told me that Val was acting funny. Strange. A few minutes later, Mae called me back. It sounded like she was laughing. She was hysterical. She said, 'Bobby, Bobby. Val shot herself.'

"Val knew what she wanted to do. She told me she had

watched a movie called *The End* the night before on television. She told me that I wasn't going to fight anymore. I laughed her off. She said that we could move away. I asked her to where, where could we move away from it? She wanted me to stop. Stop fighting. Stop screwing around. And I wanted to stop. I did. I do now. I burned up the engine in a borrowed car getting back here. It happened here. Right here. I couldn't believe how much blood. So much blood. I turned her over. I saw the hole. Alan found her, taking her last breaths. She looked as beautiful as ever to me. All that foolishness I did. That killed Valorie.

"Sometimes the kids and me try to pretend she's not gone. Johna asked me if we were going to have a birthday party for Mommy. I told her, you bet. I feel Valorie is slowly leaving me still. Her father told me she'd come back to me in my dreams. She came back to him in his dreams. Then he died too. When she died—you have to try and understand me now—I still went back to Sacramento for Ugalde. And her father and brother were in my corner. And I tried to kill Ugalde.

"Oops, I forgot to put the roast in."

By then Melissa Mendonca, Bobby's live-in girlfriend, and the children had arrived back from the dentist's. I asked the kids what they thought of their father's fighting. Johna said, "It scares me." Bobby Jr. said, "I like it, 'cause my Dad's tough." Jayme said, "I'm hungry."

I left Palermo the next day carrying Chacon's best wishes with me. It is a matter of fact that Mendonca filed for a separation from Chacon within two years of our meeting, citing Bobby's infidelity and physical cruelty. Bobby had finished his career—no one was willing to pay Bobby anymore, so he had to stop fighting. After his split with Mendonca, Bobby slapped around another live-in girlfriend. He couldn't make the $50,000 bond when she pressed charges against him.

. . .

Now, I certainly didn't want to make these kinds of stories a life's work. I could have stayed on the night cophouse beat for this. But in boxing, this was all I was beginning to see. I guess I just stayed too long at the party. It was with resignation that I went again to Vegas, my old haunt, this time not for a fight but for a funeral. I went to see why Richard Green, the referee in the Kim–Mancini fight, had committed suicide, according to the reports of two Las Vegas police departments. Green had been shot in the heart with a pistol in his Las Vegas home.

On the plane to Nevada, I wrote the following in my notebook: *"Gun trace? Forced entry? Suicide? Contract hit? Premeditated murder? Revenge? Suspects? Robbery? Burglary? Forensics. Prints. Coroner? Drug traces? Single shot in heart? Powder burns? Koreans? Mob? Gambling? What?"*

I wasn't a detective and had never felt even the tiniest desire to try my luck in that role. I hadn't even read those comics and books when I was a boy. I had to admit the idea had charm early on, but even then I didn't have a trench coat. Here I was going to Las Vegas to find out about a presumed suicide that the family of the victim believed was a murder.

I went to the offices of the *Las Vegas Review-Journal* and the *Las Vegas Sun*. In searching the clip libraries at the newspapers, I found one two-inch story on Richard Green, who had spent the better part of ten years officiating fights about town. One two-inch story announcing the suicide and funeral service time was the complete file.

That piqued my interest, although it was not uncommon. I remembered when I learned this, with shock, in New York. I was traveling with the San Francisco Giants at the time, when I was working back in Oakland. The team was in town to play the Mets. Or the A's were in against the Yankees, I don't remember which. Minnie Riperton died. Minnie Riperton, if you don't know, had one of the most incredible voices in history. Yet history belittled her. She had a four-octave range sitting down. She sang like a bird. And I loved her for it. Her death merited a small, five-paragraph story tucked away in one spare column inside *The New York Times*. I think the headline was "Black Singer Dies," or some such. I was enraged, incensed, and then studious. When John Lennon died, you'd have thought he was Jesus Christ. But here was Minnie Riperton, just as wonderful to me. And she was buried, almost without a trace. Her talent was lost, insignificant compared to her basic adjective. "Black Singer Dies." So I understood two paragraphs on Green. It was expected. But it did pique my interest.

I called a Sergeant Rainey of the North Las Vegas police department to find out the official position. I figured suicide was always a possibility, considering the state of the world, but one most people considered far too limiting. There was no changing one's mind afterward. I knew next to nothing about Green, the referee, but enough to consider him an average person. And he had always been ready and willing with a quote in the wake of a fight he had worked.

He had officiated a couple of Holmes's title fights, including the kind dismantling of Ali. Green was big enough to stand in there and take the reverberations of the whacks of the heavyweight in-fighters. He had done a good job when Eddie Mustafa had lost to Mike Spinks. He had officiated two of Mancini's fights, including the death match. Roy Tennyson, executive secretary of the State Athletic Commission, told me, "He was better than a good referee. He was very good. This suicide thing shocked me out of my boots."

I never spent much time with referees. Why spend time with the gatekeepers when the princes are inside the palace? Once I had ridden a train from New York to Philadelphia with Larry Hazzard. Hazzard, now part of the New Jersey State Athletic Commission body, was at the time one of the two or three best referees working, if not *the* best. He moved as a technician would: he was precise and authoritative; he was in command of a fight. He told me he had no complaints about the job, other than what he considered the sad fact that he couldn't seem to get one of the major championship fights. "Other than that," he said, "I really don't want to be too obvious. I don't like any funny business."

I knew Rudy Ortega from the Bay Area, where we both had lived. I feared for his safety briefly in Pittsburgh when he stopped the Holmes–Snipes fight. Guards had to escort him backstage, and Rudy was sweating bullets, but doing what he had to do, as the crowd mooed angrily for his head.

Mills Lane. That name rang a bell. I knew him to be the sluggers' referee, the fans' referee. I didn't know if he or any other referee belonged to anyone else. We all belonged to somebody, or something. Mills stopped fights with a reluctance that bordered on palsy. He wouldn't let Cooney off the hook against Holmes in the thirteenth round. Valle had stopped that fight by strutting into the ring like a pigeon and telling Mills, "No more." Later, Mills would straighten up the head of a fairly unconscious Milt McCrory so that Donald Curry could hit poor Milton with an unobstructed left hook that sent McCrory's eyes into the top of his head like snapped windowshades.

Stanley Christodoulou's emotions got the better of him in the fights he officiated. An Arum man. He was from South Africa. He had handled Pryor–Arguello and nearly had Alexis's head handed to him on a plate with a radish garnish before he finally stepped in and stopped the fight. Alexis was fully occupied in taking unceasing punches to his head, which was already bowed. His hands weren't up. Stanley just stood there for a while. They had to carry Alexis out.

Most of all I remembered Bobby Chacon telling referee Richard Steele, "Thank you." But no referee, regardless of the situation, carried the blame for injury during a fight very far. Their defense was simple: How are civilized men supposed to control a barbaric event?

Sergeant Rainey had no answers for me about Richard Green. "It's still classified as a suicide," he said. "We've found nothing to cause us to list it otherwise. Ballistics did a chemical reaction test on his hands. Positive. There was no reason to suspect robbery. He did not have any drugs on him. We have no witnesses. No sign of struggle. His family is the only thing that says no to suicide. They'll criticize us, if you talk to them."

"I'm sure I will."

"Well . . . he had a girlfriend who wouldn't have anything to do with him anymore. He'd been married twice. The gun wasn't registered in his name, no. But I do believe he committed suicide."

"Why?"

"There was one shot through his heart and a powder burn on his shirt."

"Only one shot was fired?"

"I didn't say that."

"Oh?"

"We dug a slug out of the wall. One in a door, I believe. We figure he must have flinched a couple of times."

Of course, these extra bullets could explain any gun dregs on Green's hand. If he had been killed, the killer could have put Green's hand on the gun and squeezed off a couple of rounds. Silenced, of course. I didn't say this.

"He flinched?"

"Yeah. We figure maybe he chickened out once or twice and missed himself a couple of times."

"There was a bullet in the wall?"

"Yes, there was."

"Thank you."

"Anytime."

Now this was curious. The report of a gun, sans silencer, might be enough to convince even the most morose of would-be suicide victims to reconsider his position, at least temporarily. I talked to one of Green's daughters. Her name was Regina, and she was the child of Green and his first wife, Bertha.

"I don't go for any of it," Regina spat. "My father had too much to live for. Everybody liked him. He had no troubles. I was one of the first ones who found him. My uncle called me. Wendy—that's his second wife—she was there as soon as I was, and I live three minutes away from my father. First thing I asked her was, 'Who called you, Wendy?' Every door in his house was closed, including the bedroom door. I know he never closes those doors. I know my father's routine. And his car door was unlocked. I know if he never locks no other door, he locks that one. You know, I swear it's got something to do with boxing. It was a professional hit. That's what it was."

Professionals? Not them again.

"Clyde, my uncle, and Don Grove, my father's brother-in-law, found him. They said he was lying there with his arms up, like he was protesting. I started getting these calls later. Male voice saying, 'Yeah, your daddy killed himself.' Wendy said she got those kind of calls too. She worked as a security guard at the MGM Grand.

"The North Las Vegas Police, they didn't even seal the house. They ain't asked nobody nothing. Then they said they sent the ballistics report off to Washington. A policeman came to my house and demonstrated to me with his finger pointed at his chest. He said, 'This is what your daddy did. Bam.' They said the gun had been fired five times. Could he have clicked off all five? Something else happened. And I think the police know. They're hiding something."

Richard Green was from Tallulah, Louisiana. He had been a young man on his way to California, but he had found a foothold in Vegas and never made it any further, which was surprising, since black people seemed to be at odds' end in the town that crooked money built. Green did well enough for his family to follow him. After working for the local power company and climbing his way up into the refereeing circles, Green divorced Bertha and took up with Wendy Williams, and then later with a Jennifer Dixon. He had wanted to get back with Wendy, apparently, when the deed was done, at 6:04 A.M., on July 1, 1983.

Jane Broadfoot was a member of the State Athletic Commission and a timekeeper for some bouts. When I spoke to her, she said she had been friends with Green for years before his death. "He used to tell me, 'Jane, this town's been good to me.' The last time I saw Richard he was his usual capable self. I saw him the day before he died and there was nothing unusual in his manner. He told me, 'Well, Mama, I guess you're going to be happy. Me and Wendy are getting back together.' He was in an unusually good mood, in fact. Things were looking up for him. The only time I'd really seen him upset was after the Kim fight. Suicide is just not plausible to me. They'll never convince me of that."

Tennyson seemed no less convinced. "I went through his first divorce with him," he said. "I was one of his closest friends. He was not into gambling. He paid his bills. He was not really a carouser. His first ex-wife, Bertha, is a very nice woman. I can't stand people writing that this was a suicide. I will never believe it."

Bertha said she and Green had been married for twenty-five years and had three daughters, Sylvia, Annette, and Regina, before their divorce on August 19, 1981. "He did the divorcing," she said. "But he was a nice person. He remarried in December of 1981. Wendy. Basically, she was a nice person, too. Richard loved life. I just don't believe that he committed suicide. There was no note. Richard would have left a note."

The more people I talked to, the more improbable the suicide story became. Green. Journeyman lineman. Journeyman referee. Two wives and a girlfriend, yet no known enemies. Found with a gun that had been fired four or five times. Bullets in the door, wall, and ceiling. Arms up. Protesting. At least $270 found in his wallet, but certain items of jewelry missing—four diamond rings.

Clyde Green had found the body. "Everything was so neat and cleaned up," he told me. "Professionals clean up everything. I knew my brother fairly well, I would say. He didn't commit suicide. Mr. G. Sheldon Green, the assistant county coroner, never changed the report of a contact-wound gunshot to the heart. They said the toxicology reports would take from six to eight weeks to get back from Washington. We never heard anything. Hell, man, the whole of North Las Vegas is racist. Nothing new. There is something to hide here. That's what they've indicated to me by their actions. They kept his body for a week without even doing an autopsy."

When the autopsy was performed, it was done to an already embalmed body, according to Wendy Williams Green, whom I called on next. "They thought they had just another west side incident, just another black man gone," she said bitterly. "A common thing." I asked her if there were any reason why Green might consider suicide—or any reason why anyone would want to kill him. "I can tell you for sure that he never met a stranger," she said. "He was happy-go-lucky. We had gotten back together. He was elated."

I then spoke to Audrey Grove, Green's sister. Her refrain was familiar. "He loved living too well," she said. "It had to be somebody who knew him, who could get that close. He had brought that Jennifer Dixon by here a couple of times. He told me Jennifer was pressing him about moving in. I heard he had gotten into something with one of her boyfriends. For some reason, I think it had something to do either with that woman, or with boxing." She sighed heavily, and I felt sorrier for her than I had for Green's children. "It's just another black man gone," she said. "Why waste time trying to find out?"

Lieutenant Hal Miller had been with the Las Vegas police department for thirty years. He was now a watch commander. He was also involved with boxing. He had been one of Green's initial benefactors in Las Vegas and a pallbearer at his funeral. Miller had at one time been the president of the Golden Gloves of Nevada, and an amateur boxing promoter. Green had fought in the Golden Gloves briefly, and eventually began refereeing for Miller's shows. "Detective Gary Rainey handled the whole thing for the North Las Vegas department," Miller said. "As it is, it's called suicide, but to me it's an unsolved case."

Miller had been told by Sergeant Rainey that Green had been having arguments with both Wendy and Jennifer Dixon. "There are a lot of reasons to suspect, and no reason to suspect," Miller said. "What can I do? What can you do? Black people don't like the idea of suicide. No one does, I guess." I guessed not too.

"I checked everything out that I could. I'm not trying to discourage you. I hope you find something. I couldn't. Richard was the best-loved husband, the best-liked son, the best-loved father. He basked in all that. He loved life. He had a high opinion of himself. He was afraid of death—petrified of it. They found him with his fists balled up, arms up. I don't think they have any idea if the bullets all came from the gun they found. They never even swabbed his hands, as far as I know. The one thing he did—referee fights—he did well. I don't know. I don't feel he committed suicide because I knew him. But time has already passed. Things are getting fainter."

By now I was convinced Green had not committed suicide. Finding out who had murdered him was another fifteen rounds. And there were no guarantees. My talk with Lieutenant Miller discouraged me on all fronts. He had the entry, the means, and the methods to investigate, he knew the victim personally, the lay of the land, and he had come up with nothing. I did know that jealous boyfriends and scorned women did not often have the presence of mind to clean up behind their crimes of passion. But this crime was clean.

In less than a year's time, a fighter, a fighter's wife, and a referee had died violently, and these were the boxing stories I had pursued. Some time later, Kim's mother, who had come to America to see her son attached to a life-support system before giving the release for his disconnection, had taken poison in Korea. She died terribly too. Death enveloped this world of my choosing. I was sick of it. I left Vegas not with a story, but with a promise not to come back soon. And with a question. I hoped the universal balance, the great cycle of nonsense—you get back what you put out—would catch up to the murderer of Richard Green. I figured nothing else would. I looked through the thick window of the jet that bore me away from Las Vegas. And I let myself off the hook. I told myself:

Hey, I'm just out here.

But I was beginning to have my doubts.

7

Kronk

I never had to try to like Thomas "Hit Man" Hearns as a fighter. His style dictated my liking. He had the hot rod, the right hand. I cannot say I liked him otherwise, though I tried. Thomas was not to be liked. But I was awed by him when I saw him in his setting as warrior-king of the overheated, overcrowded, subterranean gym that lay beneath a red brick two-story building, the John F. Kronk Recreation Center on the corner of Junction and McGraw, on the west side of Detroit. I never liked Hearns, but he revivified me when I saw him at Kronk, in the Hall of the Undead King.

I had been awed by only one athlete before that, and never by any athletic setting. I was accustomed to them. I understood the heights and depths of physical competitions, therefore I was usually irreverent to them, the way everyone is irreverent, only to different deities. At the same time, I felt I was created to be at these places and to record these events. I agreed that after a certain age, there are no accidents. You name the athletic event and I'd stare at it fish-eyed, as if I were a tailor sizing it up for a suit. I was there to do a job. It was business. Nothing personal.

I had always considered this to be professional detachment. The largest part of me kept its distance from athletes, the better to see them accurately, perceive them as they actually were, as performers, without personal contacts or feelings which would influence my assessments. This, I figured, was a professional obligation. I supposed I had to be more professional than other sportswriters. This went back to the out-and-out warnings I'd always heard:

You'll have to be twice as good to go half as far.

So I could know athletes, but not like them personally or be bosom friends with them, for the most part. I never knew what I would have to write about them. And some of the things I wrote I wouldn't want to do to a friend. The truth hurts sometimes. So no, the boxers were not my friends. I neither liked nor disliked them. I knew them. My imagery would be based on cold, hard fact and observation, on un-impaired comparison. Nothing else. And so, in spite of my proximity to these athletes in the brotherhood of skill, I had been awed only by Muhammad Ali until I went to Kronk.

By the time I visited the Kronk Boxing Club, I couldn't afford to be awed. My job was to see things as they were, as best as I could manage it, so my recordings could be accepted at face value as accurate. Some media imagery had not taken the accomplishments of black people seriously, not given them proper history, even in athletics, where accomplishments were more difficult to ignore or water down than, say, at the patent office. When I met Emanuel Steward at Kronk, the first emotion he expressed was surprise that *Sports Illustrated* would send someone to do a story, and utter surprise that the person was me. "We can't get pub, we can't get deals made, we can't get much of anything," he said. "I know you know why. Because we're poor niggers from Detroit." I knew exactly what he was talking about.

.   .   .

I thought back on my brief history in Detroit. It was here, I knew, that Joe Barrow and Walker Smith—Joe Louis and Ray Robinson—had come from humble beds to gain world titles. This is where my uncle had briefly gotten off the ground as a middleweight. Where Aunt Helen and her progeny still lived, and where her husband, Robert, had died. Once one summer, when I was a boy visiting Detroit, I had been accosted by three boys while I was on the way back to Aunt Helen's from the A & P. They walked toward me, three abreast, five yards apart, their meaning obvious even to a country boy. I instinctively chose the weakest-looking boy and ran straight at him with my head down and my right fist up. His flinch gave him away, and I bowled past him, gaining a running start for the race, which had been my intention all along. But I had not yet started to run track, and I wasn't a fast boy until I did. I dared not drop Aunt Helen's precious Pepsi-Colas. So the would-be toughs caught up to me in the alley behind Aunt Helen's house—safer ground, but they now had me surrounded.

The other two made the boy I had faked out square me off. Figuring I was going to be beaten within an inch of my life anyway, I set the sodas on the other side of the fence and lit into the boy with all the strength of a panicked thirteen-year-old body. "You gon' let that chump kick your ass?" one of the other boys said. Something about that statement tired me and inspired my opponent. But he didn't hit hard. After less than a minute of fierce-looking but relatively harmless fisticuffs, we broke apart for air. I picked up the sack of sodas and backed up into Aunt Helen's yard. I was not pursued. The other two boys had forgotten me in their berating of their friend. "You gotta kick ass to run with us!" one said.

I ruminated on this as I went down into the bottom of the rundown bunker of a recreation center on an otherwise barren lot of the decayed inner city. And there I felt the unaccustomed awe. Something was at work here. Something bigger than images. This was a blacksmith's fire of heat. "I like to keep it at around a hundred," said Emanuel Steward, smiling. Emanuel was the trainer-manager of Thomas Hearns. Kronk was Emanuel's place; Hearns just ruled there. The center had been built as a haven of sorts for the children of Detroit. It had been named for a former city official.

Once inside the basement, you could sense the last desperate lunge for hope before hope was completely abandoned. The steel-plated steps led to a narrow threshold at the bottom, past which lay a concrete floor, sturdy host to an eighteen-foot boxing ring. There were wooden trays of sand and crushed glass in boxes in the corners. This combination on the bottom of the shoes provided more traction in the ring, so the fighters of Kronk could dig in with their toes. The better to punch.

The gym was packed. These were good-looking fighters. Quick. Whipcord-strong. Willful. Flawed, of course. Most of them were small, with thin arms and legs. Some were the products of the overdosed and the undernourished. The best-quality narcotics and the worst-quality produce made it to inner-city Detroit. And there were no accidents. But they all seemed to be on their way to being as good as their abilities and physiques would allow. If a boy was not up to the task at hand, the awesome heat in the hellhole would quickly make him swoon. The sparring sessions at Kronk were better than some of the feature matches I'd seen elsewhere. Boys with other prospects elsewhere in life would be driven out of the hot room by a long line of other boys, boys beyond boyhood, boys whose faces and hearts had been turned to stone and then only grew harder in the ring. They were just boys in the end, but they were boys who had uncaring, fully grown demons growling in their stomachs and whispering in the backs of their minds, assuring them that they would have to kick ass in order to survive. Well they knew it.

Hearns would be the former welterweight, junior middleweight, and light-heavyweight champion of the world. Kronk was his dominion. When he came there to train, even after making millions, the other charges deferred to his presence. These were young men who had deferred to no one, before they learned to box. Boxing taught them respect. The speed bag was Hearns's whenever he felt like it. He was the king of all the boxers at Kronk—and hence to all the quick, strong, willful, skinny, flawed, doomed boxers on the green earth. That, I suppose, was why I was awed by him there at Kronk.

The two greatest fighters of Hearns's generation, as a matter of historical fact, were Sugar Ray Leonard and Marvelous Marvin Hagler. Those two had made certain of their higher place in ring lore and on television commercials by knocking out Thomas Hearns. Hearns was the historical footnote with the pure knockout right, the hot rod, the Lew Jenkins Theory. In Hearns's case, I called it the Tommy. The Tommy was Hearns's unfortunate proclivity to forget he had everything else, including a brain. All he knew was right hand, and the fact that nobody was going to take his heart. He had none to take. He had only the will to fight. This did not make him a smart boxer, and that is probably why I never liked him. But Hearns was not to be liked. He was to be fought, or avoided. This was his greatness as a fighter—his best and only defense in the ring was his ability and utter willingness to trade with you, to try and knock you out. I called on him away from Kronk to see if the void held true.

Hearns was in casual training for his next challenger—Roberto Duran—in the basement of his sumptuous ranch house on a lane off Evergreen Road in Southfield, Michigan. It was late April 1984. He was then the WBC super welterweight champion. Hearns set his feet and lashed out with a right hand, snapping across a quick overhand shot. His opponent reacted too late and protested.

"Wasn't that a let, Tommy?" I asked.

"Ace," he said. "Let's do something else."

He switched off the power to his roomful of video games and fetched his yearling cougar from its glass-walled pen. Hearns had other guests: three Vanessa Williams clones, the Temptations, the actual Temptations, his mother, Doris, and his manager, Emanuel Steward. Hearns's first impulse had been to show everyone how well he handled a big cat.

Dinner was soon served by gracious help on fine tableware. Later, after most of the guests had gone, all the house's sounds were like softly pealing chimes. Hearns still paced his den. He was surrounded by comforts, but bored by them. He was unfulfilled with the gains of his dollars. They brought him no peace of mind. He wanted to prove he was the best man around. That had been a brutally tough fight. He had lost to Leonard. He couldn't believe it. He had lost to Leonard.

Owing to the Vanessa clones, I was in full hopes that no small degree of debauchery would be forthcoming that evening. Alas, it was not to be. Hearns retired early, shooing us away, all except the very prettiest girl.

The next afternoon Hearns entered the room in the bottom of the red brick building in search of a more serious workout. Steward greeted Hearns with a smile. Steward was and remains head trainer and captain of destinies at Kronk, just as he was when Hearns first came to the gym at the age of fourteen. Hearns came so he could survive any entanglements during the thousand walks he would have to take from his east-side home in the Brewster projects to Northeastern High, or to the corner store, or just to the bus stop. "I was made a fighter," Hearns said. "I wanted to keep my coats. I worked hard for them. I wanted to come and go as I pleased." He disappeared into the dressing room to shower and change.

The best young boxer at the Kronk gym when Hearns first arrived was a youngster named Bernard Mays. He was more than ready to teach Hearns everything he knew. The hard way. He broke Hearns's nose in training when they were both fifteen; Hearns's speech remains slightly nasal today because of it. Mays was "on the streets now, weighing a hundred and thirty pounds," said Steward. "The drugs got him."

Hearns went to the ring center, shadowboxing through vigorous, hard combinations. He worked three three-minute rounds at this, then three more on the speed bag. Then a medicine ball was dropped on his stomach while he lay on a table. He suffered through that. He made a joke that was laughed at too loudly by the handlers and boxers around him. Hearns got down and did some one-handed push-ups. He skipped some rope. He headed for the shower. His workout was short and brisk, for show. Less than a month remained before his fight with Duran, scheduled for June 15, 1984, at Caesar's.

Steward was wearing sparring mitts and was taking Duane Thomas through four- and five-punch combinations. Thomas was proficient enough to have a brief reign as the USBA Junior middleweight champion. A mere sparring partner for Tommy. Duane Thomas was then battered in a three-minute sparring session with 165-pound Ricky Womack. Womack had been quietly studying Hearns all through the latter's workout. He hadn't laughed at Hearns's jokes. Womack seemed to be watching Hearns for weakness.

In his own mind, Hearns had no weakness. "Leonard wouldn't fight me again," he said. "But I can do what Ray can't do." Hearns meant he could beat Hagler. Even though he was fighting Duran, Duran's face was not what Hearns wanted to see. He wanted to see Hagler. "Little short Duran?" he scoffed. "No contest."

Steward laughed at the insult. "Tommy would come in and pull Duran's cap down over his head when Duran was in Detroit training for Kirkland Laing," said Steward. "Duran would just leave the room. Back then, Duran called Tommy a jinx. If the fight were called off today, Duran wouldn't mind. No one looks forward to facing Tommy."

Once, perhaps. But Hearns had injured his right wrist in December 1982 while decisioning Wilfred Benitez. Hearns popped small wristbones through the set of linear muscles at the back of his right hand—the result of the force of his punches, the greater distance they traveled because of his longer reach, and the smaller, less even plane of the front of his fist. Hearns hit harder than his body could stand.

"And it's different taping Tommy's hands," said Steward. "Tommy always wants his thumb free, to grip tighter, to make a better, tighter fist. Even when he fought Leonard and had been hurt, all he wanted was his right glove to be tight. I told him if he was hurt, I'd have to stop the right. He told me, 'Pull the glove up tighter. Yeah, I'm hurt. But that mothafucka is gonna pay.' Say what you want, Tommy and Ray, that was the last great fight. They both could have retired after that fight with no shame."

Hearns disagreed. "People from Detroit told me they bet their houses on me," he said. "They showed me the betting slips. I didn't like that feeling of owing somebody."

Hearns was fighting Duran after a two-year malaise in which he didn't look good. He was beating people by decision, always mindful of the tender wrist, the brittle right. And, as Lew Jenkins had said, you can win a certain way and nobody cares. Hearns was to receive $2.5 million for the Duran fight. Life should have been good. But Tommy was troubled. Hearns had just made a guest appearance on the syndicated television show *Soul Train*. When the host, Don Cornelius, asked Hearns about his upcoming fight (with Duran), Tommy said, "Yes, against the one, the only, the unbeatable . . . Marvin Hagler."

Knocked off track a bit, Cornelius asked Hearns what had been his toughest fight. This was not the most probing question to a man whose record was 38–1. Hearns said, "Minchillo," meaning Luigi Minchillo, a luckless Italian Hearns had beaten by decision in Detroit earlier that year. A completely derailed Cornelius stumbled through a mention of the Leonard fight. Unruffled, Hearns said no. Minchillo had been a tougher fight. This was an interesting point of view.

On Saturday, May 13, 1984, Leonard was interviewed on ABC-TV tape. He was asked what had been his toughest fight. "I'd have to say Thomas Hearns," said Leonard. "His height, his reach, his talents . . . he was the toughest." So it must have been for Hearns against Leonard. But Tommy denied this. He would somehow try to get Leonard through Marvin Hagler. Duran, as great as he was in his time, at his weight, was little more than an afterthought to Hearns.

"Little short Duran and all Hagler was doing was eating right hands," Hearns said. "Marvin couldn't eat two of my rights. No. He couldn't even eat one. Duran? Duran can't avoid the right. There is nothing he can do."

"He just loves to fight," said Steward. "But how many more hard rights—bone-on-bone—can he land? Five thousand? Five hundred? Fifty? I don't want to leave them in the gym."

"You have to understand Thomas," said Dr. Frederick Lewerenz, who treated Hearns's broken wrist. "His whole value judgment is based on how hard he can hit. The man actually lives and exists mentally from the power of his right hand. It's his self-image."

Fighting was Hearns's single abiding interest. He bought a Young Chang grand piano and didn't learn to play a single note. He ordered the construction of an ornate bar in his home, but didn't drink. He built a glove-shaped pool, but didn't swim. He talked of becoming a businessman, while talk of business easily bored him. He said he wanted to be an actor, yet his expression never changed. A confirmed bachelor, he drove a gold 500 series Mercedes Benz. But he was not a carouser. He'd rather spar with you than speak to you. He'd get to know you better that way.

Later, Hearns leaned over his office desk at 19600 W. McNichols. "Fear," he said, "is something I see in other men.

I must get this Marvin Hagler," he says. "I want this superman everyone says is so good and has no fear. I think I can find it."

"Tommy can beat Duran with his left hand if he has to," said Steward. It didn't take a compass to chart a southerly direction for Duran.

"But whatever I do, Ray will seem greater," Hearns said absently. "Better. I learned a lot in there with Ray. What can Hagler show me? When I beat Duran, when I beat Hagler, great—but Ray—I wish—no—I can only see Ray in my dreams now."

I reminded Tommy that the only reason he had started boxing in the first place was so he could keep his coats and get home safe. He looked at me. "I don't worry about getting home anymore."

I liked Emanuel Steward, and I never even had to try. Steward's charges at Kronk numbered anywhere from sixty to ninety. The number fluctuated during any given month. He had saved many young men from fates worse than death, and from death itself. Sometimes he only postponed their fates. Addiction, crime, jail were his rivals. He had done his job well. I was surprised that not many people in boxing with whom I spoke recognized this. "I'm not surprised," said Emanuel when he met me at the airport for the last of my three visits to Detroit during spring 1984. "Remember. Poor niggers from Detroit."

Steward always said this lightly, with a smile. He lived happily, and happily performed a service for the society of Detroit and got himself paid in the process. He was not unlike an evangelist. And like any self-respecting evangelist, he expected reward for the bestowal of his earthly salvation. I had no problem with that. In fact, I was glad to see it. It was the American way.

Steward promoted and staged his own fights under the

aegis of Gold Circle Productions, which was a company fronted by a young chap of Polish-American extraction named Bill Kozerski. Kozerski had been a photographer who (like most people in Detroit) became prideful of the fighters of Kronk, especially Hearns. Kozerski now served Steward as a sort of front man with the boxing "Establishmess," an informal body of publicists, promoters, trainers, managers, state athletic commissions, and agents.

This group was not exactly the Supreme Court in terms of ethics. Yet, Steward's attempts to try to keep most of the money between him and the people who did the fighting won him no points with the Establishmess, or among the rival trainers, managers, and promoters, most of whom were doing the very same things Steward was doing, or trying to do. It goes without saying that this lack of points was an opinion held by much of the media, and that this opinion trickled down, as they say, to the general populace, despite the efforts of a few good men like Irving Rudd, who I considered the best of the boxing press agents.

One of my editors at *Sports Illustrated* had made cryptic comments about Steward all along. "He's not the kind of guy you'd really want to trust," he said.

"Oh? Why is that?"

"You'll find out."

"Oh."

"What kind of guy is Hearns?"

"A fighter. That kind of guy."

I trusted no one around boxing (or around journalism, for that matter)—not Angie Dundee, not Eddie Futch, not Bob Arum, not Don King, not Emanuel Steward, whom I liked. I was akin to my Uncle Charles on the matter of trust. He used to say, "Trust ye not a living soul . . . walk even carefully among the dead." Besides, this was not a question of trust. None of us were considering marriage to each other. The only question here was of news.

I admired Steward because he spoke to me conversationally rather than in oratorical tones. That was rare in the business. And he was being rewarded now for good work done for good work's sake. It was one thing to find out about a world-class fighting talent and then to agree to train that talent, as Angelo and Futch now did, or to agree to promote it, as Arum and King now did, or to recognize it as newsworthy, as I tried to do. It was quite another thing to go into an old recreation center to help some fourteen-year-olds survive better, to hone these pure novices into world-class fighters, make them world-class with your own knowledge and expertise, drive them to small club matches and competitions all over the Midwest and then not have anything bad to say about them after they lost the world titles that they never would have won without you in the first place. I admired Steward because he knew what he was doing and his ties to his inner circle of fighters— especially Hearns—were very strong, much more than mere ink on a contract.

The insatiable entrepreneurs of the boxing Establishmess were threatened by this. Emanuel threatened to make the money they were supposed to make. The nerve of the guy. So all was fair in love, war, and capitalism. Why was Emanuel so irksome to some people? The only answer I could come up with, outside of basic human nature, was what Emanuel had said with a smile. He was just a poor nigger from Detroit. *Twice as good. . . .*

Steward was from Kimball, West Virginia, born there in 1946 or 1947. Emanuel was eight years old when he, his two sisters, and his mother left West Virginia for Detroit in 1955. The move was expedient. Emanuel's mother felt nothing was left for her children in Kimball, least of all Emanuel's father, Manuel, a rolling stone of the first rank.

Manuel had prepared Emanuel for the vagaries of life and of his future vocation by teaching the boy the rudiments of boxing and entering him in illegal smokers. Little Emanuel fought against other boys for the entertainment of the residents of the hills around Kimball and the adjoining mountain valley communities. The mountain folk were starved for stimulating entertainment. There was church on Sunday, but beyond that, well, *I Love Lucy* only went so far. They knew a good fight when they saw one. Emanuel provided them with a rare gusto. He bloodied many a boy's nose in those days, and tasted the familiar trickle of his own as well. "I never minded fighting," he told me once. "I learned how. Then it was easy. It was not easy to do, but it was easy to *want* to do."

Emanuel got a charge out of whipping another boy. The adrenaline felt good, but it was more than that that put the smile on his face as he readied to box. Fighting spoke to the pleasure center in his brain. For some kids, pleasure comes from reading books, or hitting a ball, or telling lies, or dressing like grown-ups or the opposite sex, or any behavior that is learned and exhibited, in order to please parents, peers, and themselves, in a changing order.

For Emanuel, the great need of his young life was fighting. Fighting was its own reward. When his mother and father split, Emanuel told himself he'd miss his father more as a promoter than as a father. But Emanuel didn't miss fighting for very long. Not in Detroit. There he would find many peers. Without the unnerving bass commands of his father's voice to make him toe the line, Emanuel became his own little matchmaker. He did as he had been instructed to do. He fought raging battles in his west-side neighborhood and gained peer status. He became the leader of a punk gang because he was a good talker and the best fighter.

Once when another gang leader was baby-sitting a child, Emanuel stormed over to challenge the boy for some breach of gang conduct. Out of concern for the baby or fear of Steward, the boy kept the child in his arms. The baby was knocked to the ground in Steward's assault, shaken by the fall but otherwise unhurt. It landed Steward in jail. Had he been a few years older, the penitentiary would have been only a few ill-advised battles away. But he was a facile opportunist even then. He was young enough to fight Golden Gloves. He pointed this out to an Irish cop, who was kind enough to escort him to Brewster's Gym, and in two years, by 1963, Steward was the national Golden Gloves champion at 118 pounds. He fought under the name Sonny Boy. He was quick and hit hard. He led the Detroit team to the national Golden Gloves title. The bout for the gold medal at 118 pounds, which Steward won on points, was his last fight. Even if he was crazy enough to keep fighting for nothing, he had met a girl who was too smart to let him. Marie Steele was her name.

Eventually, Steward became a lineman for Detroit Edison. He soured on that vocation during one vicious winter storm, a storm such as only the Great Lakes can whip up and deliver. The night wind lashed into him atop a utility pole, in subzero temperature. "Freeze to death or be electrocuted," Steward told himself. "Gotta be another way to go."

Somehow, the most obvious choice of a life's work can be the most difficult to find. It wasn't until after the riots in 1968 that Steward began to see boxing with more than a nostalgic or lustful eye. He quit the lineman's job and invested in a doomed cosmetics venture. The company failed and Steward was stuck with bootlegging electrical work and selling health insurance to make ends meet for Marie and his baby daughter.

Then there was another unexpected mouth to feed. Manuel Steward had sent Emanuel's half brother, James, to Detroit. James was fourteen and didn't give a damn. He was belligerent, full of himself, quite like Emanuel at fourteen. Emanuel elected to send James to the Kronk gym, as he was too busy trying to figure ways to bring ends to within hailing distance of each other. When Detroit Edison turned off the power to his house, Steward was seen by neighbors turning the lights back on by tampering with the equipment. His neighbors laughed at him.

"What about them Gold Gloves now?"

After a few weeks of sending James to Kronk, Emanuel asked his brother to show what he had learned.

"He showed me nothing," Steward recalled. Dissatisfied with James's progress and hoping to keep a bridle on the boy, and because he had nothing better to do, Steward began accompanying his brother to the Kronk gym. "It was like a bell went off in my head, once I was standing in the corner with somebody I had shown what to do. I could tell them what I knew. It just hit me. I got along with people. I could communicate. I could show these boys how to box."

This was not some old trainer set in his ways working with some journeyman fighter whose bad habits were entrenched. This was a fairly recent amateur champion with a gift of gab and fidelity who was helping his little brother get along better. Steward had the gift, and he had the clay. Within a year, James won the Detroit Golden Gloves at his weight class. More ragged boys who didn't give a damn began to come to Kronk, asking for "Man-yul."

Ten years later, just watching Steward train the Kronk boys was a lesson in the art of instruction. These boys were beyond attentive. They were captivated. And the more intensely they listened, the more intimately Emanuel talked to them, with an inflection both kind and unsparing.

Steward usually demonstrated as he spoke to the fighters. His little exemplary punches traveled in short arcs. His feet ended in perfect position. He talked a great fight. He was a little Merlin, able to transmute these youths into skilled fighters—with the agreeable help of the upper-echelon boys waiting to spar in the ring. Within a year of that initial Golden Gloves title he had coached out of his brother James in 1970, seven other Kronk fighters had won Golden Gloves titles. It was at that point that heads began to turn, and business came to town. Steward welcomed it. He took the eleven-, twelve-, fourteen-year-olds and won with them, even when Kronk was closed for two years for "renovations," beginning in 1973.

They trained for a while at a church on 14th Street. The place was called King Solomon's. Apt, somehow.

The little troupe moved back into Kronk in late 1974. Steward kept bus schedules on the walls for his fighters. One of those was a new boy named Hearns, a skeletal face with hollow eyes, who only wanted to learn enough to keep the bullies off him at the time. And this is how Steward saw Hearns at first. Not as a champion, but as a threatened boy. Lois Hearns, Tommy's mother, had to call and beg Emanuel to take Tommy in. Emanuel had suggested the Brewster Gym to Hearns, as it was closer to the boy's home in the projects. Hearns said he'd just as soon catch the bus.

Steward had not liked Hearns. Not as a fighter. Too many holes. Not enough boy. But Steward threw Hearns into the Kronk ring to spar with his betters, expecting him to eventually tire of the whippings. Hearns took his lumps, then refused to go home and stay there. One day in Columbus, Ohio, early in 1975, a kid from Columbus had Hearns on the ropes, belting him with glee during a club fight. Suddenly, the right flashed out. The boy from Columbus was knocked cold. It took nearly five minutes to revive him completely.

From then on, Kronk was more than just the good turn Emanuel was doing for a few kids. Perhaps Emanuel had known it would come to this all along. He just had no idea that Tommy would be the meal ticket. With that right, Steward knew Hearns could be a champion—holes or not. On November 2, 1977, Kronk staged a professional show in Detroit for the first time, at the Olympia, just a few tough corners from the gym. Hearns knocked out Jerome Hill in two rounds. Less than three years later, he won a world welterweight title.

Was Steward wrong because he helped Hearns become champion and then took a cut? I thought not. By the time I got to Detroit in 1984, good times had already been there and left a bestowal on Hearns and Steward. They worked out

of the ESCOT offices, a two-story building at 19600 W.
McNichols. The building was upscale in decor, with new
fixtures, large windows, and a wide spiral staircase. Metal-
framed photographs and blowups dominated the walls; pictures of the history-makers at Kronk and their good company.
Leonard was displayed with Hearns in one. They were smiling. They looked like good-natured friends. But we all knew
better than that by now.

Laudatory proclamations sat framed on desks. A secretary
tended busy phones. Steward had his own office, large, stuffed
with trophies, bric-a-brac, memorabilia, and billowing
sheaths of papers. Hearns had an office too, very spartan,
devoid of character or activity. In the back room there was
a large boxing ring, seemingly in better repair than the one
at Kronk. I watched Hearns work out at ESCOT a couple of
times. His efforts were halfhearted. He worked harder at
Kronk to keep up appearances in his domain, but in all of
his workouts he didn't appear to be a man who feared losing
anything to anybody.

Hearns was feral. He seemed to absorb all attempts at
good humor into an inner vacuum, although we went clubbing
one night and he did enjoy himself. On the other hand, Steward was congenial to the point of irresistibility. He *always*
had a good humor and a swell time.

"Yeah, Tommy brought us to where we are," Steward said
from behind his desk. "I'm in no hurry to see him fight Hagler.
Tommy's hand is fragile, and fighting Hagler is like fighting
a bowling ball." Steward was prophetic. Pragmatic.

At this time, early in 1984, Steward was working with
Mark Breland, the skinny welterweight from Brooklyn. Some
other 1984 Olympic boxers-to-be, such as Frank Tate and
Steve McCrory, both of whom won gold medals, were already
Kronkites. Steve's brother Milton was testimony to Steward's
abilities as a trainer-manager. Strictly speaking, Milton was
a flawed boxer, with the classic Kronk body—the Tommy

body. But he had nothing resembling Hearns's fearsome punching power or presence. Yet, under the tutelage of Steward, McCrory held the WBC version of the welterweight title for more than two years before surrendering it via knockout to the left hook of Donald Curry of Forth Worth, Texas, in 1985.

This was ironic, because if there was another Kronk gym and another Emanuel Steward, it was Gorman's Super Pro Gym, headed by Dave Gorman. Gorman's Gym started out as a tattered heavy bag hung up in the Gorman's barn, where Dave, an old brawler and amateur, and his wife, Loretta, saw to it that their sons had boxing lessons. More kids came to see the Gormans there, until one day Gorman moved his operation to a small space he leased in one corner of a tortilla factory in Fort Worth. He trained Curry and Stevie Cruz, who would become the featherweight world champion for a while, and Gene Hatcher, who gained the notoriety of being knocked out quicker than any welterweight in history when Britain's Lloyd Honeygan decked him in forty seconds of the first round in 1987. Honeygan had also burst Curry's bubble via knockout. Donald was not as adamant about his craft as Tommy, although he might have been a better boxer once upon a time—not because he was ever more skilled, but because Tommy was Tommy.

Gorman was just a guy who knew boxing and had a way with kids he had taken through the amateurs, like Steward. And, like Steward, he felt unwanted and abused by the boxing Establishmess. But Gorman, in his central Texas drawl, would say, "I'm just a poor chicken farmer from Texas." Fate had carried them in the same direction, in completely different surroundings—but in the same America.

Emanuel's suggestion that he was thought of and portrayed as the poor nigger from Detroit would manifest itself at the coming Olympic games. Steward had three boxers from his charge entered. All three would win the Olympic gold medal, including the media-beloved Breland from Brooklyn, the soft-spoken, likable, very talented Tate, and the scrappy McCrory. Yet Steward was denied a position at or near ringside and generated controversy by even working off-site with the fighters he had trained. This led to a running feud with the U.S. Olympic Committee and its boxing coach, Pat Nappi.

Regulations being what they are, this was not strange to me until the television light was placed on the Olympic gymnastics competition. Bela Karolyi, an immigrant from Romania, had coached Nadia Comaneci in the 1976 games and now was living in Houston and responsible for the training of the U.S. women's favorite, Mary Lou Retton. Despite not being the official Olympic gymnastics coach, Karolyi was omnipresent during the competition at Pauley Pavilion on the UCLA campus in Westwood. Plenty of media airplay was given to his connection to Retton. Her dependence on his advice and desire for his approval were displayed after her performances. It is safe to say Karolyi got more mileage out of all this than the official U.S. gymnastics coach, whose name escapes me. I do recall he was not pleased with Karolyi's presence. But Karolyi, a new immigrant, was not portrayed as some guy butting in, as was Steward, the poor nigger from Detroit.

All this was months away, and even after the slight occurred, it did not throw Emanuel. He was ready for it. But then, nothing seemed to bother him. He had serenity. During my three visits to Detroit to visit Kronk, Emanuel's most pressing problem always seemed to be whether or not he would let his teenage daughters borrow the car, or rather, which car he would let them borrow. Steward reveled in this "problem" as he did in just about everything else.

Emanuel lived with his wife and daughters a few blocks from the ESCOT offices in a nice, airy ranch-style house with a small half-moon driveway in front. Steward's basement contained video games for his children—his children by Marie and by Kronk—and a pool table. We had long talks about boxing while we shot short games of eight ball. He always won.

"You know," he told me, "after Thomas beat Cuevas, Jesse Jackson came into the room and asked us for a hundred thousand dollars, for Operation PUSH, his campaign or whatever. I like Jesse, but I had to tell him we didn't need a write-off that big."

Steward is a very compact man, usually clean-shaven, with naturally downturned eyes and mouth. He spent a career begging Hearns to shave off his goatee. Hearns would not. Emanuel didn't lose sleep over it. He had the look of one who understood suffering or stubbornness and could comfort both. He had a receptive ear for a joke and the enviable talent of telling stories of misfortune and making them funny. Even if the joke was on him, it was no less funny.

Steward put me up in a two-story house he owned a few doors down from him. The house was nicely furnished and clean, kept ready in case a Breland or another out-of-towner interested in training with Steward at Kronk came to Detroit. I spent several nights there, with the complete run of the place. I spent some time with the expressionless Hearns and a good deal more time with the lively Emanuel, who took me to a number of restaurants and clubs. Local businessmen recognized Emanuel at once, with unfeigned happiness, and he introduced me to them. One, in his cups, began a tale of how well the races got along in Detroit, which up until that moment had been self-evident in Emanuel's circles. But now I was lectured on it.

"It got to the point that some white people were leaving because they didn't want to do business with black people," said the man. "I mean, real business. I stayed. Money has no color. I told them, 'Listen, the only thing you're really going to have to deal with is seeing black and white together.' You know, men and women. Some of my friends said, 'Well, I don't know if I can deal with that.' I say hey, how many wives can you have?''

By now little of Steward's time was being devoted to actual instruction at Kronk, much to the dismay of another visitor Steward had at the time, one Michael Nenad Matijasevic, who was originally from Yugoslavia and at that time retained Spanish citizenship. Michael was a former amateur boxer himself, a tall, well-built fellow with a great Slavic face who was close to a contender named Slobodan Kacar. Michael had come to Detroit in hopes of procuring some young talent from Emanuel to take to Europe, as I understood it. While ingratiating himself to Steward, Michael was making some rather strange comments like "Breland? Why, Breland is a hundred times better than Leonard at the same stage of his career."

Steward would laugh and wink. Mike never did get any fighters out of Emanuel, but we all had a famous time dreaming what could be. The Yugoslavian and I drove to Cobo Hall during my first visit to see Hearns's final workout before the Minchillo fight. In the car, Mike turned to me and said, "You know, the black man is just naturally superior in the ring."

I couldn't let that go. I knew the unspoken clause. "No," I said, "don't kid yourself, Mike. It's the greater will that wins in the ring, in the end. No man is naturally superior to another man when it comes to will."

Mike looked at me as though I had just vomited all over the front seat. I changed the subject and he was back to telling his intense stories by the time we arrived in downtown Detroit.

Kronk had been transplanted into the riverfront dining-room facility of the hall for the convenience of the media and other out-of-towners. There were twenty fighters working out around the large upper-level room that looked out over the Detroit River. The room was so large that the eighteen-foot ring looked much smaller. I went over to where Steward was preparing to tape Hearns's hands. Next to one wall stood the "amateurs," including Breland, Tate, McCrory, and Ricky Womack. All had aspirations, but I wanted to speak to Breland, specifically about sparring with Hearns, which he had done before down underneath at Kronk.

Breland was thin—naturally, irrevocably thin, yet he had fair power in his punches. Only fair, though. Nothing like the Tommy. He was about to spar with an older Kronkite, a trial horse named Reggie Holmes, no relation to Larry by blood or ability. I went over and asked Breland about sparring with Hearns. "He's fast," said Breland. "Faster than I thought. Much faster. And I thought he was to begin with. Slick. So many feints. Hands, head, feet, shoulder."

Womack was outfitting himself three feet away from us. "Hey, Breland," he said malevolently. "What the hell is he doing over here?" One of Steward's seconds had told me about Womack. "He's one of them kind you'd have to shoot to stop. He just don't care."

Steward had high hopes for Womack at the time. I had no intention of disturbing him. I was not protected by pad and pen. I had come up to Breland and just started talking. "Am I in your way, Womack?" I asked.

Womack looked surprised. There was a break in his concentration. I had known his name. What did this mean? Who was I? Womack's insistence became less sure. "Naw, you ain't in my way. You over there. I'm over here."

"Well, Womack, I guess we'd better keep it that way. You outweigh me. I don't want you to have to kick my ass."

Womack gave me a curious look and began brisk shadowboxing. He was strong and tough, but the breaks in his manner would keep him out of the Olympics as he wound up second-best to a fighter named Evander Holyfield.

Breland sparred easily with Reggie Holmes. At times, he would merely turn his head away to avoid punches, his eyes never leaving the opponent. He was already a fighter of great cunning. Steward removed his mouthpiece almost lovingly between rounds while Reggie explained to those near his corner why Breland seemed difficult to hit. "He's just awkward, man," said Reggie. "He don't hit hard enough. He's just awkward. The motherfucker's awkward."

Breland landed eight uppercuts on Holmes in the next two minutes, then left the ring to lie on a table and have a medicine ball dropped on his nearly emaciated body. Then he spent three minutes punching hard into the mittens held by an older second of Steward's, listening politely as the older man made suggestions.

Double left jab, right cross, double jab, left hook off the jab. "That's a beautiful combination," said the old man, whose name was Dave Collins. He had worked for thirty-four years at the Chrysler plant. He seemed to be near tears, and I couldn't tell if it was because his hands hurt or because Breland's combinations had been so beautiful. I asked Collins if his hands hurt.

He laughed. "At night, when I have to turn over, I have to get completely up and lie down again. They'll hurt too bad for me to roll over on them."

I was more impressed by Breland, but still felt he didn't hit hard enough to be as proficient as Tommy. He was too thin not to hit hard. Being quick—and awkward—was not enough professional firepower.

The champion, Hearns, occupied the center of the room. He sat on a platform as Steward began to tape his hands, a hypnotizing act which sends the mind elsewhere. Steward began with three thin strips of tape anchored in the deep ridges of Hearns's protruding knuckles. Now gauze was wrapped around the wrist and across the top and around the palm and around the base of the thumb. I thought of how far Hearns's punches traveled because of his long arms, the speed of those punches, the impact of his natural power. Physics, not bad taping, broke up Hearns's hands. He had a seventy-nine-inch reach, which ended in a small twelve-inch fist held in place by a thin 7½-inch wrist. The bony knuckles did nothing to aid dispersion of the impact. Hearns threw this mace without quarter. If it landed on something hard . . . Steward wound the remainder of the gauze and lightly folded it back and forth across the knuckles. Now half-inch tape was applied.

I thought of how Steward was derided in boxing circles because he didn't have the stool out in the ring waiting for Hearns at the close of a few rounds against Leonard. The stool wasn't out there within a second of the bell's ringing, so Steward was suspect. Hearns damaged his right time and time again, so Steward's taping was suspect. It was almost like saying he couldn't bake because he had no apron. I thought about how I'd never seen a trace of dope or of anyone who looked as if he was on it around Steward or his tough young men, a miracle unto itself. I thought about how dope didn't grow in inner-city Detroit. Somebody brought it there. I thought about six liquor stores within a block of the house I grew up in. I thought about how Emanuel had overcome long odds, and helped his young men overcome long odds, just to be strong and functional. I thought of how ordered they looked in their red-and-gold Kronk jackets. I thought of the ease of Steward's company. I had to like him.

The tape went low on Hearns's wrist now, perhaps two inches below the bone, then rolled up across the road already traveled by the gauze, then twice over the knuckles, then two figure-eights around the thumb. A complete roll of tape was gone. "There," said Steward. "Flex."

Hearns moved his right hand. It looked like a huge black widow spider. "Right. Good." He smacked his fist into his palm.

Later that day, I told Emanuel that I had to leave for the

airport. He insisted that I couldn't. Not just yet. "I want to take you to the airport," he said. "That's the least I could do. You came all this way."

"But I've got a flight."

"Oh, you can book another one. I know a guy. What is it, New York Air? Besides, Marie baked a pie. She likes you. Maybe you've got more questions. We can get in another game of eight ball." I couldn't tell him no.

After the Olympics of 1984, Breland and Tate moved on to other gyms, other trainers, other management. Yet Kronk stayed the same, because the King of the Undead would not die. Hearns destroyed Duran in one round. Roberto was never one to stay around where he had no chance. Then in April 1985, Hagler destroyed Hearns when the flawed right met the bowling ball and shattered, while splitting Hagler's face open between the eyes. Hagler ran Hearns out of the ring after that. I'm sure that somewhere, people blamed it all on Emanuel Steward and not on Marvelous Marvin Hagler, where all the blame belonged. In March 1986, Hearns was back in Vegas on the same card with Hagler, who knocked out John "the Beast" Mugabi in the eleventh round.

I was not surprised to see Hearns again, or ever. Not in the ring. The ring was where he belonged. It was his home away from Kronk. He hit the NABF middleweight champion with a left hook to the body to open him up, a move Hearns had learned to appreciate from Leonard. Then with a single, compelling right hand, Hearns stopped James Shuler, a 160-pound Philadelphian who was 22–0 at the time. Shuler was knocked cold while the sounding of the bell for the end of round one still hung in the air.

A week after his fight with the Motor City Nosferatu, Shuler died in a motorcycle accident in Philadelphia. Thomas "Hit Man" Hearns came to Philly and gave Shuler's mother the NABF middleweight championship belt. He told Shuler's mother, "Your son had this longer than I did. It belongs to you now."

Emanuel Steward, Tommy Hearns, and all the minions of the Kronk gym were not to be liked. They were to be dealt with, and respected. They would not go home and stay there.

8
Tyson

Dear Cole,
You were conceived and born in the era of Larry Holmes and grew up in the time of Mike Tyson. You cut your teeth on iron. You will shake up the world, no doubt. Just be yourself. For that, for anything, you need background.

Boxing affected you even before you were born. It happened like this. I met your mother with no idea that she was going to be your mother. I met her with the idea that she was somebody's daughter, and I thought somebody had done a good job raising her. She had what the people that raised me called "home training." She was a very nice girl. Very easy on the eyes. She worked for the phone company. Her smile was genuine. Words spilled from her mouth in clear, bubbling streams. She talked more than I did, which I considered no small feat at the time. I picked her up outside the shopping mall in Oakland. She walked slowly toward my car. Maybe she was restricted by her Calvin Klein jeans. As she walked toward me, I must admit, you and boxing were not the first things on my mind. I'd seen fine girls in my time, but, frankly,

Calvin Klein should have paid your mother to wear his jeans. She had gorgeous legs all over the place. She had better legs than Ali.

About a month later, I suggested we take a weekend outing to Las Vegas. This was the second weekend in April 1981, back when Larry Holmes defended the heavyweight championship against Leroy Jones.

"Berbick. It was Berbick."

That was your mother. She claims not to know or care anything about it, but she remembers boxing opponents better than I do. She was right. It was Berbick. Trevor Berbick. I had to look it up. Holmes decisioned Berbick, hit him with everything but the Bible, but Holmes, who had knocked out eight opponents in a row, couldn't KO Berbick. Your mother scored the only knockout of that weekend that I recall, though my memory of the events is not to be trusted. I had become a victim of brain damage. Some call it love.

"It was definitely Berbick." Your mother and I walked up and down the Las Vegas Strip the day before the fight, and I should have known then that this might be a woman worth having around, even should I not solve the riddle of the Calvins. She laughed uproariously at my smallest jokes, laughing so heartily she nearly choked on one of her ever-present Pepsi-Colas. As I pounded her back and cleaned the cola off her chin, I thought, Surely this is a woman of perception and great character.

Later, in a corner of Caesar's Palace even darker than the rest of the joint, we sat on a fake barge which stood in a vat of stagnant water. This vat was supposed to represent the Upper Nile, and the fake barge was labeled as Cleopatra's. Your mother was the only original around. The next day, I wondered why Holmes didn't have the common decency to knock out—Berbick, was it?

You were always kind of a distant sparring partner with Larry Holmes. Rather, you two were the champions and I

177

was the sparring partner. A little more than a year later, when your mother was great with you, we had moved to New Jersey. We wanted you to be born in New York City. Nothing against New Jersey, but we didn't want you stigmatized because I hadn't been able to afford the space we needed in Manhattan. We wanted a two-bedroom apartment with a living room and a view of something besides dirty bricks and discarded bottles and syringes. Sky would be nice. So would a tree. The last apartment of that description in Manhattan had been rented around 1936. We decided to live in Jersey. Such is parental sacrifice. It was a fifty-mile drive, one-way, from our apartment to Albert Einstein Hospital in the Bronx.

I got an assignment to go to Dallas for the WBC featherweight championship fight between Salvador Sanchez and Rocky Garcia. This also meant an audience with Holmes.

"If you go to that fight, it means I'll go into labor," your mother said.

This was but my third assignment for *Sports Illustrated*, and I was in the throes of neophyte fever. "Nonsense," I said. "I have to go. He'll wait until I get back. He knows we took those stupid classes. He wouldn't show me up."

"We'll see," she said. Sure enough, Friday, May 6, 1982, dawned, and as I puttered about in Dallas unearthing facts that meant little to a few people and nothing to most, you announced your arrival. Your mother was good enough to call.

"My water broke."

I do not really remember what I said to her. I'm glad because I doubt it was worth remembering. Your grandmother had come in from Pennsylvania. I told her I'd be there immediately, and not to let anything happen without me. I got no reply, as your grandmother is a well-mannered woman. I do remember buying a ticket and flying in a jet to La Guardia Airport. And I remember thinking that a jet never flew so slow.

Once at the airport, I commissioned a cab and offered to double the fare if the cabbie could get me to the hospital before you were born. The cabbie drove moderately, watching me warily in the rearview mirror. My hands were shaking by the time I arrived at the hospital just after midnight. You beat me by a good half hour. They said you let everybody know you were upset with my absence, right off. Great lungs. Holly's mother was waiting for me when I hit the hospital doors.

"You have a son," she said.

Your mother was radiant. "Did you see him? He's beautiful!"

She was right. The blood from three continents flowed nimbly through your veins. I stayed at the window looking at you until they ran me out of the hallway. The next day I caught the jet back to Dallas, where Sanchez dispatched Garcia and Holmes glowered. I felt bad about missing your grand entrance into the Great Ring for such ordinary matters as fights. But I did miss it, and that's something that I can't change. Those are the only things you're not supposed to worry about, the ones you can't change. Of course those are the things you remember.

I'll give you an example. I had been invited to Philadelphia by a friend of mine to watch Tommy Hearns and Marvin Hagler fight poor James Shuler and John "Beast" Mugabi in March 1986, along with nine of his friends. It was fun being in their company, although I had only the one friend. I watched the card on closed-circuit television at the Spectrum, a large auditorium where sporting events were staged and televised. Outside the Spectrum stands a statue of the actor Sylvester Stallone as the fighter Rocky Balboa. Never trust a statue, son, or the people who build them, for that matter. Idols should be alive so you can see they have flaws. You see, son, you can change history, especially if you're an actor and know a good sculptor.

It was fun being in the company of my friend's friends. We were in our thirties and their interplay reminded me of my own college days, when your friends know you right down to the color of your toothbrush and are more fondly remembered than the friends you meet later in life. Time gilds. The old days seem better because they're gone. Reunions are a nice place to visit, but you wouldn't want to live there.

One of this group of men had earned the title of court jester in their long-ago school days, and he was razzed with accurate barbs as Hearns and Hagler scored their respective knockouts. The beer flowed in our box. Suddenly, the court jester was standing in front of me, and I got the feeling. I can't explain it, but you'll know when a fight is available to you, son. You will learn. He was right in front of me, taunting me, the outsider. I don't know if he wanted to prove something to his buddies or what.

For a long second I stood there, trying to think of him the way I had thought of Merv in college a long time ago, when I had tried to knock his ass to Ithaca merely because we were playing football and he had knocked me down. I stood there, looking at this new Merv's chemically treated hair. I saw the driving head butt, or the right hand feint and the left dug up through the body. The right forearm. It was all there.

Then I just let it pass. I no longer wore a helmet. I had on a necktie. I had plenty of reasons not to fight. But part of me, until this day, says, "Number 80, you should've just smoked him. You punked out. Fuck that brother shit." Another part of me refuses to allow myself to be pitted against other men for less than a great reason. But what was a great reason? We all are always either little boys or ancient men with territories and honors and rights to defend. I had reasons not to hit him, but I still gnash my teeth because I didn't. Sometimes it's better to hit just so you'll sleep well.

. . .

I was assigned a story on Mike Tyson on your fourth birthday.
By now you were ranked No. 1 in our household, begging
for a shot at the title. But your mother wouldn't give you a
shot, because you had a lot to learn. So you sparred with me
and Tyson.

I met Tyson on May 6, 1986, in Glens Falls, New York,
the day before he was to fight James "Quick" Tillis. A press
conference was called at a local hotel. Mike came in and was
surrounded. I had to convince myself this was a nineteen-
year-old. He looked like two nineteen-year-olds. His legs were
thick pillars of muscle, slabs merely hinged by knees. His neck
size had been reported at 19¼ inches, and after standing next
to him, I considered this a low estimate. It would take a Liston
or a Foreman or a baseball bat to hurt this kid. His chin was
a long, even horizon. His jawline ridged out from his neck.
He had puncher's hands—his fingers were short and thick,
his palm immense. I looked him in the eye. He nodded with
interest.

I caught him later in the hotel hallway, after he had done
a five-minute sit-down television interview. He was agreeable
and courteous. I was as impressed with his bearing and his
way of expressing himself as with his battleship physique. He
was skilled at talking with the media, honest while he was
playing their game. He was no politician.

"You handle yourself pretty well, Mike. It's all up front
with you. And I haven't even seen you fight yet."

"Oh," he said, in that impossibly light voice, "you'll like
me in there. I go about my business."

I asked him to make a fist. He did. It looked like he already
had a glove on. He had nearly a flat plane on the knuckle
side, the business end of his hand. He was about 5 foot 10½,
I'd say. He weighed 215 pounds. He bulged all over the place,
and where he didn't bulge, he was hard and even and flat.

And he just had this look: this Geech look; this Lew Jenkins look; this Tommy look. The look of iron. The lisping voice only barely made him seem less ominous.

George Plimpton once wrote that he had thought being knocked out by Archie Moore in the ring would not be unlike "being tucked in by a Haitian mammy." As I stood there nose to nose with this nineteen-year-old engine of destruction, I thought that being knocked out by Iron Mike Tyson would be like being tucked in by God. Tyson's presence was completely suited to his business, more so than that of any fighter I had seen since Duran—more so than Duran's, more so than Hearns's, far more so than a Leonard's or Ali's or Hagler's. Tyson seemed just as pitiless as Duran or Hearns, and Tyson weighed 215.

Yet he could be a sweet kid. He happened to grow up tough, in the bloodhole bowels of Brooklyn, and just happened to hit harder than winter at the South Pole. He was living in the Catskills. It was driving him crazy, socially, which is why he had looked at me with interest at the press conference. We were the only black men there. His solitude was all for the best for his fighting at this point. He was at the stage where it was not a question of succeeding. It was a question of avoiding failure.

"I've been trying to get next to some girls," he said.

"You owe it to yourself, Mike. Just be careful. You can beat anybody, but you have to be careful."

"Maybe in a year I could beat anybody," he said. "I don't know if I could beat anybody now."

As we stood talking, I spread my feet apart in order to meet him eye to eye better, as I was a couple of inches taller. I don't know, maybe this was some ritualistic stance from the streets of New York, something of which I knew nothing about, like the hand in the jacket pocket of my youthful days. Tyson, laughing, said, "Lookit you. What you wanna do? You wanna do something? You stand there like that against me? Where you from, the Bronx?"

He squared off, smiling. I laughed and said "No" as many times as I could in ten seconds. I was not from the Bronx, as was Mitchell Green, Tyson's intended opponent after Tillis. "So, Mike, you'll square anybody off, right?"

"Right. But people started squaring me off first. I got beat up a few times. I didn't like it."

Tyson could have used a father or an uncle or someone else to be a confidant, not merely on boxing but on all matters pertaining to manhood. His manager was Jimmy Jacobs, whom I respected because of his vast knowledge of the sport. But Tyson needed a friend, a mentor, not as Cus D'Amato had been or as Jacobs was. In the end, he was a meal ticket to them. Nobody understood this better than Tyson. "I fight whoever my manager wants me to fight. I'm just a fighter."

It seemed odd to me that a fighter like Tyson, who would have to be close to do damage, would be asked to tie up his greatest protection—the power of his punches—by inverting his hands and holding them in front of his face *à la* Floyd Patterson, in D'Amato's desired peekaboo stance. This might have been fine for Patterson in 1961. But Tyson was a different kind of fighter entirely. His success depended on hitting the other guy harder than the other guy could hit him. His dimensions were those of a great fighter, not a classic boxer, a defender. Perhaps he could become a great boxer, one day. But he was already a great fighter in 1986.

Saturday was the day of the fight. As the crowd began to assemble at the Glens Falls Civic Arena for the fight, a half-naked Tyson came out of his dressing room to take a look at the house. He wore his trademark black trunks and black shoes without socks. An adoring public immediately piled in around him, asking for recognition in the form of autographs. *Do something with your hands for me, Mike.* Tyson signed, then moved back toward the dressing room. His companion, a young white man, said to him, "Do you believe the nerve of white people?" Tyson laughed at this double-talk.

A few minutes later, the nineteen-year-old manchild snorted in disgust and stepped back to compose himself. This was an unusual posture for Tyson. He had never taken a backward step in a pro boxing ring before, but now he did. He had moved up in fighting class, and it showed. Sooner or later, boys will be boys. Even if they are undefeated.

Tillis had befuddled Tyson by tying up his insistent hammers for the better part of four rounds. This sudden indecision on Tyson's part was Tillis's best chance to shake up the boxing world. He threw caution to the winds and launched his best left hook, intending to circle Tyson's peekaboo defense. Tillis's left hook missed. Tyson, finally presented with the bull's-eye, fired a short left hook in return. It was not his best punch—not even close—but it landed cleanly on Tillis's jaw. Tillis's eyes rolled up in his head as he went sprawling toward the canvas, a victim of Tyson's Complaint with thirteen seconds left in round four.

Tillis wasn't saved by the bell, but he was grateful for it. Once the bell stopped ringing in his head, he'd get back where he belonged. On his bicycle. He'd teach this ferocious kid how to survive in the ring. Let somebody else suffer the consequences of trading haymakers with Mike Tyson. "I've heard of baby-sitting," Tillis would say later, "but this is ridiculous."

Tillis's manager, Beau Williford, had said, "It's tough to hit shadows," just before the fight, and with that knockdown as warning, Quick went back to ducking Tyson's bombs and occasionally punching out smart combinations. At times Tillis made Tyson look young, unfinished, but mainly, Tillis merely survived. He lost a ten-round unanimous decision as Tyson won his twentieth straight pro fight. The bloodied Tillis was the first man to go the distance with the manchild. Maybe that would be worth an asterisk one day.

"He punched harder than the Acorn, Earnie Shavers," Tillis said while Tyson entered the interview area. Tillis then said, "Boy, you punch harder than a muthafucka."

Tyson accepted the sincere compliment with a knitted brow. He was not in a particularly good mood, though he'd handled a twenty-seven-year-old contender with relative ease. The trouble with being Mike Tyson will always be that he can never knock his opponents out soon enough. The crowd always wants more of that. The world looked at his 215 sculpted pounds, his ominous glower, his wrecking-ball punches, and said, "That's *my* champion. Show 'em, Mike."

Boxing is not that easy. "Some people want to rush Mike," Jimmy Jacobs said. "The object isn't for him to fight for the heavyweight championship. The object is for him to *win* the world championship."

After Tyson had won his last fight, a third-round knock-out over Steve Zouski, in Uniondale, New York, on March 10, he had felt he had to apologize to everybody for not dispatching Zouski in a more expeditious fashion. "I'm having personal problems," Tyson said achingly. Tyson was still a nineteen-year-old, and as such, yearned for the joys of youth, joys which are usually denied a working heavyweight contender. "Girlfriend problems" was how his comanager Bill Cayton portrayed Tyson's lament. It seems Tyson, ever honest, did go a little stir-crazy up in the Catskills, with nobody around to keep him company other than trainer Kevin Rooney, "stepmother" Camille Ewald, a few pet pigeons (where that idea came from, I never knew, but I wrote it off to Budd Schulberg and *On the Waterfront*), and some unfortunate sparring partners. "Hey, I was running around looking for girls," Tyson had said. "But I had to decide, did I want to hang out at night, did I want to be a playboy? I didn't."

That, of course, was on a day-to-day basis, and never written in stone. Tyson suffered an ear injury when he fell while trying to capture a rogue pigeon. His left ear swelled to three times normal size after the fight with Zouski. Treatment at Mount Sinai hospital brought him back to New York, where you never knew how people might be standing. Rooney, in the Catskills, became frantic. Cayton insisted both he and Jacobs knew about the trip. There was also a little ruckus at the Crossgates Mall in Albany. One of Mike's friends threw some sweaters around. Ordinary stuff, until the next champion is involved. Tyson was at the Tryon School for Boys at the age of thirteen. To think he would reach thirty without any kind of newsworthy public behavior was ludicrous. If Mike Tyson had acted like Sean Penn in public, four or five people would have been dead by then.

Tyson took his frustrations out on the sparring partners before the Tillis fight. Tyson hit one with what Rooney described as "the perfect uppercut," loosening four of the poor man's bottom teeth. Another sparring partner was knocked down on his first two days at the job. "I told Mike to stop hittin' him after a while," said Rooney. "I ain't no butcher." Another sparring partner, looking to mix it up, was knocked cold. Tyson wore eighteen-ounce gloves during all these sessions. Even pillows couldn't muffle the thunder.

"Sooner or later, somebody has to try hitting Mike on the chin," said heavyweight James Broad, who attended the Tillis fight and saw Tillis try it. Back to the drawing board. His best right hands bounced harmlessly off Tyson's jaw.

"Tillis ran, just like we knew he would," said Tyson. "And anybody can look good running. But nobody will beat me by running. Nobody." With that, Tyson rose to leave, and nobody had to ask where he was headed.

I'll tell you this right now, Cole, always take the boxer over the puncher, everything else being equal. With Mike Tyson, everything else was not equal. As he continued to fight he amassed all the heavyweight titles, and he also proved to be a difficult riddle to fight. It was amazing how quickly he warmed to the more subtle skills of the professional fighter. He slipped punches with aplomb and had no problems with some of the less than decorous behaviors of in-fighting. Good old Trevor Berbick, our old friend, was stripped of his WBA crown when Tyson knocked him down three times with one punch. One of those you'd have to see to believe. Then Mike dispatched big Pinklon Thomas in Las Vegas. I caught that one live.

Mike was twenty-one by that summer of 1987. He wore a three-day growth of beard before the Thomas fight. He was anxious to get it done and get on with the good stuff about being the champ. I sat down with him at the podium in the Vegas Hilton, and he had no trouble remembering me.

"Yo, main, whatup? How come you couldn't get me on the cover last time?"

"You didn't hurt anybody bad enough, Mike."

"You here with a fighter?"

I looked out over the audience of perhaps two hundred. I saw Earnie Shavers out there, his bald head gleaming magnificently, looking at Mike and smiling.

"I'm here with you, big guy."

"Good selection."

I always enjoyed hearing Tyson describe his fights in that elfin voice. "I threw punches with bad intentions . . . . I was trying to hit him behind his ear . . . in a vital area . . . . It was a clean, devastating shot . . . . I'm the baddest man on the planet." After he knocked out Pinklon, "Did you see that hook? Ooo, that was nice. That took all the fight right out him." This kind of elocution made Tyson unique. He dissected himself and what he was doing in a cold, almost clinical fashion. He could say what he wanted to do to you. He knew why.

This was chilling to some people who considered the harmless patter of Muhammad Ali threatening. Ali was having fun most of the time, warming to the lights of the stage, making love to the camera, or merely defending himself. Tyson knew he was no television personality. What he could do was the thing. He could hit you harder than you could hit him. There was no doubt that he was more intelligent than Ali, to me. Ali had been quick with repartee, witty in his way, but Tyson seemed to me to be much more reflective, much more volatile. He knew what was happening to him. He just didn't have enough experience to make sense of it, but he knew, even as it all happened. He reminded me of my old friend, the Geechie.

Before the Thomas fight, I visited Pinklon's suite, where the contender, former heroin addict and part-time singer, was busy trying to develop a keen distaste for Tyson.

"He told me to *suck his dick*!" Pink said incredulously.

This was an insult which left Pink with no alternative but to fight as he had never fought before. If the guy in Philadelphia had told me that, we'd still be there today. So Tyson had tried to make it easier for Pink to stand there and fight him! Some people were casting aspersions on Tyson's sexuality. Fighters usually called each other homosexual, *maricón*. Everyday Joes said this about Mike. One sportswriter for a Los Angeles–area newspaper, Rick Talley, said, "Boxing has come to this. One guy's named Pink and the other one's a fag," just before the bell rang for the Thomas–Tyson bout.

Nobody said this to Tyson's face, you can be sure. Tyson would hug and kiss his foes after he had blasted them to the deck and they had been revived. He'd kiss Rooney on the mouth in the corner between rounds from time to time. Far from making him suspect, I figured this only made Tyson all the more secure. He'd kiss whoever he felt like kissing. Word was going around that Tyson was taking girls out of clubs three at a time, now that they were readily available to him. Tyson was always aware of the manner in which he was perceived. He seemed well able to dismiss it, telling one television interviewer, "Look, so I'm supposed to be homosexual, or I'm supposed to be taking all these women out of nightclubs." Then he merely shrugged, as if to say, "Make of it what you will."

Before Pink was KO'd, one of his manager-backers said to me, "I think it's gonna take an Ali type to beat this Tyson guy. That's what I think. This guy hits like nobody else."

Hardly. Tyson hit rather like Sonny Liston, rather like George Foreman. In fact, in fights involving the three of them, I rather thought George might have the edge in punching power. While it was true that Ali had taken the measure of Liston and Foreman, there were no more Alis. Ali was not a type. If the world had to wait for an Ali type to beat Mike Tyson, the world would be waiting awhile.

After dispatching Pinklon, Tyson was charged with assault and battery with deadly weapons in Los Angeles after taking a parking attendant to task with but the heel of his palm after Mike had ogled and asked for a kiss from a female parking attendant. This is a good lesson, son. Never stand between the heavyweight champion and his chosen. Tyson ran around after Tony Tucker, who was 35–0 and a boxer type. He hit Tyson in the first round with a great left uppercut that (physically) lifted Tyson up and knocked him back six inches. The point here, though, was that the punch didn't even daze Tyson. It had no effect on his clarity of thought, even though it knocked him back. Tyson had something unique—that buttressing neck. That neck and chin combined as an impregnable defense. "After he hit me, it was history," Tyson said. "It just went away."

Tyson hit hard, but no harder than Liston or Foreman or Joe Louis. The most devastating quality was the speed of his punches. He got off quicker than any heavyweight since Louis, as far as the power punchers go. At times he seemed to be as quick as Ali. Some people tried to compare Tyson to Joe Frazier, but there was no comparison to be made. Tyson was far superior to Frazier. The only person even close to the image of an Ali type during this time was Michael Spinks, who had held up well. Michael had all the experience Tyson lacked. Spinks had fought against

Mustafa, against Indian Yaqui, against Holmes, thirty rounds' worth. And in taking the title from Holmes, Spinks could lay claim to the heavyweight title—only until he met Tyson. Always take the boxer over the puncher, son, everything else being equal. With Tyson and Spinks, it would not be equal. Spinks had the experience to make it interesting, to lead on points briefly, perhaps. But he was flatly outgunned, out-weighed, overmatched. When Ali had beaten Liston and Foreman, he had backed them up, knocked them out. He was as big as they were. Unless Spinks could do that to Tyson, he would have no chance. But it might be worth the price of admission.

It was this linkage to the puncher, to Liston and Foreman and Frazier and Marciano and Louis and Dempsey and John-son, that gave Tyson his mystique and his great advantage in these Ali-less years. This is what made old George Foreman mount a comeback in 1987—the thought of Tyson. This is what brought Earnie Shavers to Las Vegas. Tyson spoke a language they understood. They *knew* Tyson. They *were* Tyson. Tyson walked past Earnie in the Hilton ballroom. Earnie giggled and asked for a shot. Mike clapped him on his shoulder. Hard. Just so Earnie would know that he was not to be played with. And Earnie understood him. *Everybody* understood him, somehow. It was as Lew Jenkins had said. You can win a certain way and nobody cares. But that hot rod!

After Tyson manhandled Pinklon, he strode through the Las Vegas Hilton with a security guard on each side of him. The guards were window dressing, superfluous. The lobby of the Hilton was crammed full of people. They parted before Tyson, fell back in awe as he strode through, rolling his shoul-ders, walking as if he owned the joint, which he surely did. I walked behind him in his wake, watching the faces of hu-manity as their prizefighting champion came within arm's length of them. Everybody understood Mike Tyson.

But for every bull there is a matador. It's a matter of putting the right two together. So, all things equal, always take the boxer over the puncher—unless the puncher was Mike Tyson when you were a little boy.

Tyson had no idea of how to properly court Robin Givens. He just waded in throwing. He visited her apartment in the wee hours of the morning just to ask her to be his girlfriend, and the first time he tried to kiss her, she ran. As a tactician, if indeed these were tactics, Robin Givens was Leonardesque. Tyson only knew he had been smitten by her. He found himself outside her apartment ringing her doorbell, not taking her initial no for an answer. No was not an answer suitable for the heavyweight champion of the world.

Givens and Tyson had a whirlwind courtship which ended in marriage in February 1988, one month before Jimmy Jacobs died and four months before Tyson was to meet Michael Spinks in the largest-grossing athletic event of all time, to be held at the Atlantic City convention hall in June 1988.

Tyson's take was to be between $21 and $22 million for this fight. But he was managed in the old, pre-Ali style. He was giving up 33 percent to Bill Cayton and Jimmy Jacobs's widow. Robin Givens had already surmised this after demanding a full accounting when there was a delay when she and Tyson decided to buy a $4.5 million house in New Jersey shortly after their wedding. Entertainers are accustomed to their agents' getting anywhere from 3 to 5 percent, and 10 percent is around normal for other professionals. Robin Givens could count. She had dated Eddie Murphy and Michael Jordan before she met Tyson, and those who think that Tyson's pre-Spinks net value in the neighborhood of $50 million had something to do with her interest in him are not being naive. Of course it did. Probably no one knew this better than Tyson. He was too smart not to know.

But the spell of the heavyweight champion of the world is quite enough to woo most women, no matter how much hard business is involved. After Tyson performed the inevitable knockout of Spinks, Robin sat on Tyson's right, holding his right hand—the same right that had just dispatched Spinks—while Tyson addressed the media. Robin rubbed his hand against her cheek and closed her eyes. A relationship between a man and woman is based as much on security as on love, and Robin Givens knew in her soul that for all Tyson was not, he in fact made her the most secure woman in the world. She was rich, and she had the ultimate protector. I believed this was more than even she had bargained for.

Shortly after this, Tyson took on the real estate magnate Donald Trump as an adviser, and sued for separation from Cayton. Jack Dempsey had done almost precisely the same thing sixty years earlier, marrying a Hollywood starlet, fighting in Atlantic City, separating himself from his managers at his wife's insistence. Yet Tyson was castigated from pillar to post in the media, and, of course, this was racist at its core.

Of his $21 million purse for Spinks, Cayton's cut was $7 million. Even Rooney, a mere trainer, got $2.1 million, 10 percent. Then all expenses. All this before the Internal Revenue Service came to call. Of course, this was ridiculous to Robin Givens. It would be ridiculous to anyone not used to the involuntary servitude of black people. Cayton was just a wallet. Tyson was just a fighter. Other words were pressed into service in the media, like "caring," "loyalty," "disbelief," "ingratitude," and plenty of gossip about Robin Givens. Tyson was said to have beaten her. She appeared constantly and was always unmarked. And it would have been worse, but the bottom line was that Robin Givens was Tyson's *wife*.

One writer in a New York newspaper went so far as to write an open letter to Tyson, saying in it, "I don't care about

your wife." Between the lines was, "I care about Bill Cayton."
But with Robin Givens in the equation, the issue could not
be so cut-and-dried. *Sharecropper getting uppity* wouldn't fly
in the face of the holy institution of matrimony. Marriage
meant turning over that institution, superseding it for the
invisible institution of racism. It had to die down, or at least
become more subtle. Soon after the fight, Cayton settled out
of court for something like 16 percent—still quite a chunk
of change for what had been maybe a $100,000 investment,
total, in the beginning. Robin Givens had performed her service for Tyson. And he had performed his service for her. It
was a fair exchange for the time being.

In August 1988, the undefeated heavyweight champion of the
world got into a street fight with Mitchell Green, whom Tyson
had already decisioned in the ring more than a year earlier.
Green was a former street-gang leader who hadn't had a ring
fight since Tyson had whipped him. The only reasons he had
survived then were a pair of good legs and an ability to cover
up. I don't know, perhaps the fact that he had gone the distance with Tyson gave him a kind of honor. "I fought Mike
Tyson, and he didn't knock me out."

So Mitchell Green and Mike Tyson took it to the street.
They were on the one-two-five, 125th Street in Harlem, in
front of Dapper Dan's, a haberdashery and house of games
with a bit of a reputation for nefarious late-night activities.
Above the haberdashery was a window painted with the
words DOCTOR OFFICE. There were two versions of the story
about that night. Green said Tyson started it. Tyson said
Green started it. In any event, Tyson ended it. Green did admit he called Tyson a sissy. If he did this to Tyson's face, I
have no doubt who started it.

Green was a big man, well over six feet, around 240
pounds at the time of this smoker. Tyson only hit him once,

with a right to the face. Tyson's hand was not in a glove, but his fist was so solid and thick it still would take tremendous pressure for him to break his hand, which he did—a hairline fracture of the third metacarpal. Green was not so lucky. He needed five stitches in his nose and suffered a black eye.

Walter Berry, a professional basketball player, and a relative of Berry's, Thomas Smalls, were in Tyson's company that night. Tyson could afford better company, but he chose not to do so. Who knows if this was guilt, or desire for a kind of acceptance he would never know downtown? Tyson likes the word "pure." On the streets, the admiration for what he could do, who he was, was pure. He was a bad motherfucker there. Not a meal ticket, or husband, or criminal element of an underclass. In the street he was pure, the "baddest man on the planet," in his words. The streets were his mother's milk. No man wants to give that up, no matter what he grows to be.

Shortly after the set-to with Green, Tyson suffered a head injury, was in fact knocked out for nearly an hour and suffered resulting amnesia, after spinning a BMW into a tree by the driveway of Camille Ewald in Catskill, New York. So that's what it would take to knock him out. A car wreck. Doctors reported neurological damage, and Tyson's scheduled fight with a now greatly relieved black man from Britain named Frank Bruno was temporarily canceled.

One story had it that Tyson had attempted suicide this way, in order to get the attention of Robin Givens. Poppycock. If Tyson wanted to commit suicide, all he needed to do was drop his hands in the ring while fighting. Briefly I wondered if Tyson, once recovered, would regard this wreck as a kind of sign. He must have been backing out of that driveway at a high speed to have been so injured. He had been in a hurry to move, for some reason. Perhaps this accident was some fate telling him to slow down, to be more careful, to take his time, to be more serene.

If nothing else, the accident proved to him that he could be knocked out. I have always been of the opinion that a fighter does not truly know the totality of fighting until he has been knocked out, technically or otherwise. Now Tyson knew how it felt, and in so knowing would probably take pains to see that it didn't happen again soon.

There was no doubt that he was the most fascinating heavyweight champion since Ali. Perhaps Tyson would be the last of the great heavyweight champions before he was through. First, though, he must find peace of mind. The only certainty was that someday he would be through. There were many fights to be fought in the meantime, and only a few of them would occur in the ring. Only time would tell, and time is a bad motherfucker.

The other silver slipper finally dropped on Friday, October 7, 1988, at approximately 11 A.M., when palimony attorney Marvin Mitchelson filed a petition for divorce in the name of Robin Simone Givens, with declarations by Givens, her mother, Ruth Roper, and a family employee, Olga Rosario, in the Los Angeles Superior Court. Included in this action was a temporary restraining order against Tyson. Tyson then retained Howard Weitzman, formerly the legal counsel for ex-automobile tycoon and accused cocaine trafficker John DeLorean, to defend him against Givens' claim of community property under California law. Community property would mean a hailstorm of silver slippers. To her credit, Robin Givens always did say she came in a package deal.

So in the end it was Givens who proved to the world that Tyson could be whipped after all. Seven days before the petition was filed, Givens held an astonishing interview with Barbara Walters on the September 30 edition of ABC-TV's 20-20, declaring that "Michael is a manic depressive," and that their life together had been "pure hell." Givens outlined an amazing scenario of her fears of Tyson, while Tyson, amazingly self-contained for such an alleged brute, sat and rubbed her back. Later, Tyson admitted he was on drugs at the time, drugs prescribed by doctors Givens had hired. The drugs included some combination of lithium, ativan, desipramine, and thorazine.

Walters: "There was no prenuptial agreement?"

Givens: "No. And why should there be? We got married to be together, not to plan for divorce . . . I want to live with Mike for the rest of my life, and I want to have little Tysons . . . That can't happen if Michael doesn't get help."

Tyson: "If you're going to marry somebody, you trust them. My wife just has to ask for it and she has everything I have. If she wants to right now, take—she can leave right now, take everything I have and just leave."

Givens: "Just recently I've become afraid, I mean very much afraid . . . Michael is a manic depressive. He is . . ."

Hardly. Tyson was diagnosed by one Dr. Henry McCurtis as a manic depressive shortly after Tyson crashed his BMW into a tree outside the home of Camille Ewald. He was taking lithium, ativan, and desipramine by the time he accompanied Givens and Roper and a female "former employee" of Givens to Moscow, along with Rosario, where Givens was filming a segment of the television show, *Head of the Class*.

According to the declarations of Givens, Roper, and Rosario, Tyson drank heavily while in Moscow, then broke champagne bottles and threatened and chased Ruth and Robin around the hotel. The one certainty was that Tyson never felt he needed to take drugs. He was trying to please his wife, but something was wrong and he knew it instinctively. A Dr. Abraham Halpern, who was hired by Bill Cayton, claimed Tyson was not a manic depressive after an hour-long consultation with Tyson at Cayton's office. "I don't know the details of his sexual life," said Dr. Halpern, "but there's no doubt that that's part of the problem here."

Givens: "When he's in a depressive state he doesn't sleep.

He has enormous amounts of energy. So your sleeping agitates him. He gets you up. There's an argument. I mean, of course you want to sleep."

"I saw nothing that would support a diagnosis of manic depression or psychosis," said Dr. Halpern. The seven symptoms of manic depression are as follows: inflated self-esteem, decreased need for sleep, more talkative than usual, flights of ideas, distractibility, increase in goal-directed activity, and excessive involvement with pleasurable activities. By those criteria, half the people in New York City could be diagnosed manic depressive. In fact, those symptoms and others that Tyson had manifested—threats, call after call to Givens when they were apart, fits of jealousy and name-calling, then cow-eyed acceptance of even the most ridiculous of Givens's orders and pronouncements—these were symptomatic of another illness: lovesickness. There is no drug to control that.

On Sunday, October 1, according to the declarations of Rosario, Roper, and Givens, Tyson drank heavily, called Rosario in particular "whore" and "slut," and beat Robin Givens about the face and body at their Bernardsville, New Jersey, mansion on fifteen acres. Givens claimed Tyson hit her with a drinking glass. Just before the local police arrived, Tyson threw an andiron through a foyer window and drove away in his BMW. Givens filed no complaint with the police. "That's not unusual," said Bernardsville police chief Thomas J. Sciaretta. Sciaretta had met Tyson before. "He was always quite calm, and very polite to me. We never had any complaints from neighbors, none at all. I think he thought he could move to Bernardsville and be left alone. It didn't happen for him. It's been like a siege at that house. The man could not come out of his own door without people with microphones and cameras around. I personally ran some of them out. I think that's what happened when he threw a radio at a film crew when he was out running one morning last week. And do you know what? I don't blame him."

Tyson was obsessed with his wife. There was historical precedent. Dempsey left his manager at the behest of a Hollywood wife. Louis was obsessed with Lena Horne after what was only to have been a tryst of mutual admiration. Tyson had never been in league with a woman like Givens before. She introduced him to another world. Many go through this, especially around their early twenties. As it happened, Givens broke Tyson's heart, but at least now he knew he had one. Anything else that got broken was purely optional. Givens made an error in going for the quick knockout. Mitchelson, it turned out, was being represented by Weitzman in an action filed by two of Mitchelson's former clients, who were alleging sexual assault and rape. Givens would immediately drop Mitchelson and hire a New York attorney, Raoul Felder, who said he merely hoped to reach an out-of-court settlement. With all the skeletons rattling around in Givens's closet, and considering the estimable talents of Weitzman, it was no wonder. "Clearly, the personalities involved are interesting," Weitzman said. "There's something here that's not right. I spoke to Mike and his interest is to make sure the proceedings be conducted in a gentlemanly manner. My impression from the get-go is, why was this petition filed in California, and not in New Jersey. My impression is that this is a great relief to Michael. He's disappointed, but his mind is clear." Soon after this, Tyson announced, "Sometimes you have to go beyond love. Sometimes you can love someone who doesn't love you in return." Soon after this, he said, "There's no more turmoil." Tyson was a quick study, keenly intelligent even in the throes of love. In his own brave words, he was "a conscious black man!" And he was still heavyweight champion.

I want to pass along a few other things to you, son. You are descended from great peoples. Don't let anyone fool you about that. You are a New World man. You stand on your own dirt. People will throw color at you from time to time. Everybody's blood is the same color, and the dirt you stand on was fertilized by that same blood. Never give up on your dirt. All this used to be wilderness. A path was cut for you, because your ancestors felt you'd know what to do with it. This is a short version of how it came to pass.

About four hundred years ago, some of your (and Mike Tyson's) European ancestors brought some of your (and Mike Tyson's) African ancestors to the New World of North America as slaves. Some two hundred years ago, the people of the New World of North America decided against taxation without representation, as they were being taxed at the time by a European country, England. Around one hundred years ago, after the slave trade was stopped, the Europeans went to Africa and decided to tax the people there instead of making them slaves. Nearly all the countries in Europe put a tax on nearly all the people of Africa.

The people of Africa could not well resist this taxation without representation because they had no guns, and guns were used against them. So many, many people died. The others planted and grew "cash" crops like rubber and cocoa, and mined precious minerals like gold and diamonds, and set tables in all manner for the Europeans, in order to gain the European versions of money to pay these taxes. There is great suffering and drought in Africa today because of this. The cash crops, by largest measure, were not food staples. So now people in Africa starve. The cash crops raped the land as well, so now the deserts encroach where for thousands and thousands of years Africans had grown food to feed themselves. So a continent starves because of taxation without representation.

In addition, there is this disease called AIDS. They say this disease comes from Africa, and I have no doubt that that is where it was first cultivated. That's usually how it works. Try it out on Africans. See if it'll fly.

Whenever someone tries to tax you without representation here in the New World of America within North America, don't go along with it. If you can, call up a Mike Tyson. Or a Robin Givens. Get them on your side. The line of people fighting taxation without representation should be a long one, but if not, get in it anyway. Africa is the prime example of what will happen if you don't fight—to the death, if necessary—taxation without representation.

What follows is secondhand advice you might get anywhere, but I'll save you the time and trouble. This is what fathers are for. When in doubt, read. Find out as much as you can about all that you can. Don't worry if some things remain a mystery to you. No one has ever learned everything, and if anyone did, he didn't live long enough to put what he learned into practice. Life usually lasts a long time, and you have to live all your life with the decisions you make along the way. Don't be rash. Well, not after you're twenty-one. Have fun. Be yourself. Laugh.

If push comes to shove, watch the other guy. If you can see what he's doing to you, he can't hurt you—just as Charlie Boy said. Teach yourself, stand up for yourself, know yourself, respect yourself, defend yourself, and be yourself, and if you make your bed hard, roll over.

You are my greatest champion, even greater than Ali. Trust your ability. You have it. It's up to you to find it, develop it. Happiness, son, is not built for the long haul, for the full fifteen rounds. It comes and it goes. Better to have serenity, the inner peace which comes from doing something well enough to understand it.

It may be that your best ability is to love, or to fight. It may be your best ability is less complicated. It may be the ability to sing, or play music, or work with numbers, or to find out where AIDS *really* got started. Whatever it is, serve your ability and it will serve you. No one can take it away from you. It will bring you peace of mind. Serenity. And ability

plus serenity will bring you progress. Progress toward what?
I would not hazard a guess. Progress is to be desired merely
because it is progress. Men who stand still are lost. That's
the best notion I can give you, other than:

I love you,
Dad

9
Serenity

One night, like a shot out of the dark, my old friend Roy called me. I knew this had to signal something momentous, for Roy and I rarely talked anymore, even though we had been roommates for three years in college. Roy was a cop in Memphis, and I was a guy who went around watching ball games and fights. But a good friendship is always there, like an old book of photographs. Open it and it's there. I figured his call meant bad news on some front.

"Wiley. Geech is dead."

I could say nothing.

"Shot in the neck and head. DOA."

Robert, Roy, and I had known this was coming, sooner or later. Robert Aldridge, the first name on the roll of the gifted and talented class, the infamous Geechie of the streets, had been killed. Robert had never hesitated in that long second of deciding whether he had more to lose by fighting or not fighting. The streets would be safer with him gone, yet Robert was also the boy who got me out for the track team in the ninth grade. I was going to play baseball, and play it miser-

202

ably, if any of my initial efforts were to be taken seriously. But after a day of butchering the game at the Hanley baseball diamond, I went to a track meet at the old stadium to drown my sorrow in anonymity.

There was Robert, about to run the hundred-yard dash. He was in a maroon sweat suit with gold block lettering. Some girl's kerchief was pinned to his leg. Robert looked then about as dashing as he ever would look. And I knew I had to run track then, because every boy in ninth grade who's worth his salt wants to look dashing and have a girl give him a memento of her affection.

When I came out for the track team the next day, the coaches looked at me, held their chins and said, "Hmm." I found that maroon warmups with gold block lettering and a girl's kerchief were not always to be had merely for the asking. Work was involved. The coaches ran me a bit (until I puked, actually) and then suggested that I concentrate on running the two-mile, or possibly the hurdles. Or maybe I'd better just confine myself to the jumping pits in the field and stay out of everybody's way on the track so I wouldn't get run over. I was disheartened, but willing to accept my fate. Robert would hear none of it.

"Don't you want to sprint?" he asked. Of course I did. What kid does not? The one great tragedy of track is that you are usually placed in the running distance just above those you actually wish to run. No one wants to run long distances. Runners only tell themselves that after they are told by coaches that they will never sprint.

"Look," Robert had said unequivocally, "if you run with the sprinters, you're going to get fast."

So I ran with Robert and Roy and these sprinters, every spring day for the next three years, picking their cinders out of my eyes as they ran on into glory and the agate type of the *Memphis Press-Scimitar*. Miraculously, during my senior year, I became fast. The cinder diet paid off. The sophomores and juniors, and even Roy and Robert, depending on the day, ate my cinders. Roy, Robert, and I became the first three legs of the 440-yard relay, and we were a good team. We won medals that took two whole years to turn green. We were as fast as any team in the state, but the handoff between Robert and me was not good, for some reason. I always waited too long in the exchange zone.

In later years, when I wanted to take my mind off something, I would think of those 330s, 220s, and 110s we would run in practice, barreling out of the final turn on that old cinder track, moving through the air as fast as we could, not touching the ground much at all. Nothing was better than being three abreast, flying down that final straightaway on good, young legs. Sometimes winning, sometimes losing, but always flying. I never again felt as invulnerable as I did then. It was as close to being Superman as I ever got, and for that I could thank Robert.

After high school, Robert had been enrolled in at least two small colleges. Roy told me that he had gotten a prelaw degree. The last time I had seen Robert was in 1978, on a trip back to Memphis. He was working for an elderly Jewish lawyer downtown. I gave him a lift to the offices and met the old man. Later, Robert asked me to stop the car as we drove by the two-story housing projects on Lamar Ave.

"Right here."

"You live here? I can take you where you want to go."

"Here is fine, Ralph. See ya."

Robert got out and disappeared into the maze of brick, and that was the last time I saw him. The old lawyer died not long after, and his partners had never understood his relationship with the ugly, thuggish, unkempt ne'er-do-well from the streets. Maybe Robert never understood it either. Eventually he wound up back on the streets full-time, taking what was available to him in small-time drug dealing. He went back to where he was intended to go. As a street fighter, his reputation never suffered. He was a legend by the time he reached the end of his life.

"They tell me that Geechie was something like fifteen-and-zero on the high corner over the last few months," Roy said. "Must have been another generation of people who didn't know any better. Anyway, last weekend some twenty-four-year-old punk named Griffith or Griffin got into a fight with Geechie over some kind of drug thing. And you know what happened. Geechie cleaned up the corner with him. Whipped him real bad. But then he pulled a gun on the kid and told him that the next time he saw him, he'd kill him. Now you and I know that Geechie knew better than that. You never know who's gonna take it to heart. I don't know why he pulled a gun on the guy without using it. I think maybe he was trying to go, trying to get outta here. Trying to die. I don't know. A week later, this Griffin or Griffith comes up behind Geech, who's sitting in a car at the corner of Grand and Select. He shoots Geech twice. Head, neck . . . DOA."

Roy told me he was going to the small funeral service and would say a few words. Roy had been our senior class president and was once good at such things. "He was our friend, Wiley," Roy said. "Sometimes I was scared of him. We ended up on different sides. But he was our friend."

I decided to call up Uncle Charles to see how he was getting along. I thought I finally understood the great secret of his serenity. As a child, I thought it had to do with his boxing, with his ability to defend himself from the first act of violence from another man. Maybe it wasn't the boxing, but the *ability* to box that gave Uncle Charles his serenity. Then again, it might have been his ability to run the buffer. I didn't know.

"Hiya, Charlie Boy."

"Is this Butchie Daytime?"

"You got me."

By now, Uncle Charles and Aunt Izetta were living in a

trailer in Ringgold, a small township in northern Louisiana. Aunt Izetta had wanted to go home. I asked Uncle Charles if he was still running the buffer and he said that he was, at a local elementary school. I asked him if he still watched the fights, and he laughed and said, "Always."

"Have you seen this Mike Tyson?"

"I caught him."

"He looks like he's got the goods."

"Got sledgehammers, all right. But that ain't no new thing. If he trains, keeps his mind on his business, he'll be the champ a long time. If he don't, he won't."

"That's what I see, too."

"You always did have the real good eyes."

"So. I feel good, Unc. Strong."

"That's good. I'm all right, too. Had a little health problem, but it's coming around. Had a little problem with one of the school officials. Wants to look down on me. The kids like to talk to me, 'cause I've been a lot of places, you know. But the man doesn't think I'm a good example. Hell, I keep the school clean, but I'm not a good example."

"How's life down there?"

"All right. I miss California from time to time. Every now and then people start acting simple. You know the white man. But nobody bothers me. I've got firepower. You still working for that magazine?"

"Yep."

"Well, you know we're all proud of that."

"I'm just working like everybody else. I'd like to write for film. Movies. Hardly anybody reads anymore, they say."

"I always knew I was ahead of my time. Well, you know I'm one who believes you can do whatever you think you can do with the Lord's help. Just remember, you can't make any mistakes. One mistake, and you're gone."

"I know. Say, who is Arnold Cream?"

"Arnold Cream? Jersey Joe Walcott. Arnold Raymond

206

Cream. December 5, 1947, they robbed him. That was the night he beat Joe Louis in fifteen rounds, but they robbed him. They're still robbing people today. They robbed Holmes."

"It's a tough hustle."

"You better believe it is."

"Hagler's a tough guy."

"As long as he don't hesitate."

"Will Leonard make him hesitate?"

"Shouldn't . . . but he might. Leonard better leave Hearns alone, though."

"You think so?"

"He better leave Hearns alone."

"Ray could probably take Tommy again."

This was even before Leonard came out of retirement to beat Hagler. Leonard was well retired, and Hearns had been knocked out by Hagler and would be knocked out later by Iran Barkley. It should have dawned on Tommy by now that he had a glass jaw and that if he didn't use the hot rod early and often, he would be knocked out. Still, he had taken Ray's eye, split Marvin's forehead open, and cut Iran Barkley to pieces before he went down. After Leonard had beaten Hagler, he said Hearns must have been sick while watching, because he should have fought the same way. Charlie Boy and I knew they had to fight again, inevitably.

"He better leave Hearns alone," Charlie Boy said.

"Tell me something, Charlie Boy. How did you always manage to seem so contented and peaceful? Did the boxing do that for you?"

There was a long pause.

"That was part of it, I guess. You just learn to accept, that's all. You do what you can do. You accept the rest. Life made me that way. All you can do is the best you can do. You better come away feeling like that's enough."

"Hey, Unc."

"Yeah?"
"Thanks."

To be a great champion you must believe you are the best. If you're not, pretend you are.

—Muhammad Ali

In the fall of 1986, Sugar Ray Leonard signed to fight Marvelous Marvin Hagler. Soon after, a question arose about Leonard. People are civilized now, for the most part, and asked, "Why is he doing it?" Not "Can he win?" but "Why would he risk it?" Was it the money, a guaranteed $11 million? Was it an irrepressible urge that goes with having been a champion? Was it merely ego, a grab for a higher place in boxing history?

No one thought to ask the uncivilized people. Men have lived warmed by the fire of civilization for so long they have forgotten what it takes to survive with nothing but their wits and bare hands to fend off the jackals that stalk them. So the men who had forgotten this, or had convinced themselves they had, continued to ask, "Why?" I went to see a man who knows why. He wasn't too hard to find.

"Ray."
No answer.
"Ray."
"Nnnnn."
"Ray."
"Nn?"
"Can Sugar Ray Leonard beat Marvin Hagler?"

Sugar Ray Robinson didn't answer. It might have been that he couldn't answer. That would seem most likely. There was the advancing Alzheimer's disease to consider, and the medication he was regularly given. He also had diabetes and hypertension. Beyond all this, there were the terrible lessons that 201 fights over twenty-five years had etched on his mind.

Finally, there was Millie, his wife of twenty-two years. Any or all of these could have been reasons why Robinson didn't answer. But it also could have been that he chose not to answer. The one incontrovertible truth is that Sugar Ray Robinson had earned his silence the hard way. He didn't have to say anything. He left all the answers in the ring.

The sixty-five-year-old former nonpareil welterweight and five-time middleweight champion smiled, then looked toward his lap. He was watched by Millie Robinson, who sat nearby in the modest offices of the Sugar Ray Robinson Youth Foundation, on Crenshaw Boulevard in the mid-Wilshire section of Los Angeles. It was November 1986. The board of directors of the foundation was meeting. Ray sat at the head of the table, his paper plate laden with meat and exotic fruit. He had not taken a bite. He had no appetite. Business was discussed by six other board members, the officers of his legacy. Robinson was oblivious. He was in his own world.

"Ray will still talk, sometimes, a little bit," Sid Lockitch had said earlier at his office in Century City. Lockitch, an accountant, had been Robinson's business manager for more than twenty years and was the treasurer of the foundation. "When Millie's not around, he'll say a word or two. But even years ago, Ray was always a gentleman. He would never have said that Marvin Hagler is going to beat the crap out of Sugar Ray Leonard. He would have said luck to them both."

The telephone rang at the foundation office. For Millie.

"Ray, can Leonard beat Hagler?"

Robinson's smile became even broader, even more vacant. Then he leaned close. "Is he sweeter than me?" he asked, cloaking that once satiny voice in a whisper.

"No, Ray."

In the spring of 1987, on Monday, April 6, Ray Leonard (33–1), the former welterweight and junior middleweight champion, fought middleweight champion Marvelous Marvin

Hagler (62–2–2) in Las Vegas. Leonard, thirty-one, came into the ring after a layoff of more than a thousand days and with a surgically repaired left eye. The question still hung in the air: *Why?* Leonard was already known as the greatest welterweight since Robinson. Leonard could never be considered greater than Robinson. Not unless he fought, say, a hundred more times. Certainly not unless he somehow beat Hagler. "I care nothing for history," Leonard said on the Friday before the fight. So saying, he did the improbable— he beat the bigger, stronger man, just as Muhammad Ali had done, more impressively, against Sonny Liston and George Foreman.

"Ali absolutely worshiped Ray," Sid Lockitch says. "Still does. Usually, the greatest fall from grace is by fighters. People tend to avoid ex-fighters. They feel they took one too many. Randy Turpin once asked Ray, 'What's worse, being a has-been or a never-was?' Then Randy committed suicide. But the people never forgot Ray. He felt God had made him a boxer for that reason. So he would not be forgotten. So he could help."

It is eerie, the similarity in technique between the three of them—first Robinson, then Ali, now Leonard. It was Robinson who was the original, the paradigm, the handsome master boxer with matchless hand speed, charisma, and the fine legs of a figure skater. It was Robinson who went 123–1–2 to *begin* his career and became the welterweight champion, and it was Robinson who went on to win the middleweight title those incredible five times. Yet it was also Robinson who *lost* six times while fighting for the middleweight title. He won the national Golden Gloves featherweight title in 1939 at age seventeen, when Joe Louis was heavyweight champion of the world. He lost his final fight at forty-four, to the No. 1 contender, one Joey Archer, in 1965, when Ali was champ. In the years from 1945 to the middle of 1951, Robinson, at 147 pounds, was unbeatable and irresistible. To the men of that era, and to some of their many sons and daughters, Leonard can only be a Sugar substitute.

"I like Ray Leonard," says Irving Rudd, a veteran boxing publicist with Top Rank, Inc., promoters of the Leonard–Hagler fight. "I think a lot of him as a fighter. That's why I say that, at his very fittest, he might have gone five rounds before Ray Robinson knocked him out. Five rounds, I say. Tops."

"He was the greatest. A distance fighter. A half-distance fighter. An in-fighter. Scientific. He was wonderful to see." Max Schmeling once said that of Robinson.

"The greatest fighter ever to step into the ring." Joe Louis once said that.

"The greatest . . . pound for pound," wrote the late columnnist Jimmy Cannon, who, it is said, was impressed by hardly anyone—except Sugar Ray. When Ali was champ, the acerbic Cannon told him to enjoy it while he could, because the jackals would come for him one day.

In February 1964, when he was still known as Cassius Clay, a long shot who was about to fight Liston for the heavyweight title, Ali had invoked the name of Robinson, who was in Miami for the bout: "You tell Sonny Liston I'm here with Sugar Ray!" In a weigh-in performance that almost assuredly convinced Liston that Ali was a madman, Ali screamed to the press at the top of his lungs, "Sugar Ray and I are two pretty dancers. We can't be beat." After Ali had stopped Liston, he began again, with Robinson by his side at the pressroom podium. "Oh, I'm pretty . . . " said Ali as Robinson, with a smile, tried to cover his mouth.

"Ray was the pro's pro," says Rudd. "When they told him he had a fight, Ray never asked who the opponent was or where the fight was going to be. Ray asked, 'How much?' "

A general reaction of the middle-aged and older American public to Sugar Ray Robinson could best be summed up by a reminiscence of the late Red Smith. Smith was reminded of

Robinson while visiting the zoo one day. When the columnist stood transfixed at the cage where the black jaguar paced back and forth, he gazed at this superbly muscled predator who had no known natural enemies—except man—and said, "Good morning, Ray. You're looking good, Ray."

Ray isn't looking so good anymore. "It's very painful to see him like this. The situation is not going to get better," Lockitch says. Lockitch speaks of Ray's health, but another officer of the foundation adds, "It's like Ray's in prison. Millie treats him like a child. She lets him go nowhere with no one. Not even his own son."

Robinson's son, Ray II, says, "My father is virtually being held captive."

I had only wanted to go with Sugar Ray to the barber shop and ask him if Leonard could beat Hagler, and how. That's all. I knew Robinson still went to the barber shop at least once a week, sometimes more often. So I asked Millie about it and she said, "I take care of Uncle Wright. He's eighty-seven. I take care of Ray. He's my husband. I love him. I've been what I've been to him for all these years. I could hire help, but I don't mind doing it. I don't need help. I have tears in my eyes, I'm trying so hard. Ray's going to get better. He's not better now. He's not going to the barber shop with you because I'm by his side every minute. He goes to five different barber shops. Only I know which ones. My husband is not a yo-yo for people to jerk around as they please. I'm in charge now. I take care of Ray. I'm the one in control.

"Now . . . " Millie fixes me with a defiant gaze. She doesn't ask who. She doesn't ask where. She asks . . .

"How much?"

It might seem odd, wanting to watch Sugar Ray Robinson get his hair cut. But, being one of the younger baby boomers, I am not old enough to remember what it was like to see the Sugar fight in his prime, much less to anticipate his fights, to go through the sweet agony of not knowing and then to be so utterly convinced by his skill in the heat of battle. I had missed the pleasure of that tension. I had only seen the old films. The fights had long been decided, the participants' places in history secured.

I first learned of the emotion stirred by Sugar Ray when, as a boy, I went to the barber shop, that sanctuary of masculinity and tonic with the striped pole outside. Cokes cost a dime there. Razor straps were used for their intended purpose. It was a place that buzzed. Great lies and great truths were tossed about like glances. The barber shop was a place where men gathered, and wherever men gathered they talked either about women or going to war.

When I was a boy in the barber shop, one name came up louder than the rest. It was Cassius Clay. There would be a great deal of murmuring assent—and an occasional derisive sneer that a *real* tough guy would eventually show the kid what for. Probably Liston. Then someone would say: "Liston won't see what hit him. And neither will you." But there was at least one barber—he almost always seemed to be the one holding a pair of scissors perilously close to my ear—who would become physically agitated and say, "Hold on. Let's get it straight in here. The boy is good. He's *good*. But he ain't Ray Robinson. Ain't but one Sugar—and sugar give you diabetes *quick*."

After Ali had gone through the best part of his career and had endured a three-year layoff because of his refusal of the draft, he signed to fight Oscar Bonavena on December 7, 1970. That was to be a warmup before his epic loss to Joe Frazier in Madison Square Garden in March 1971. At the weigh-in with Bonavena, the Argentinian attempted to get Ali's goat. He succeeded, to his later sorrow. "Clay? Clay?" Bonavena mocked. He spoke little English. "Clay . . . why you no go in ahrrmy? You cheeken? Peep-peep-peep . . . peep-peep-peep."

A look came over Ali's face that I had not seen there before—true anger. Usually, Ali was like Ray, and Ray held his temper, in his own way. "Don't get mad," Robinson liked to say. "Get even."

Ali grimly asked Bonavena what seemed to be a curious question: "Did you cut your hair?"

"Whaat?" replied Bonavena.

"Did you cut your hair?"

"Whaat?"

"I'll cut your hair," said a deadpan Ali, who would knock out Bonavena in the fifteenth round. So this thing with the hair-cutting was always there for me. Perhaps it went back even further, to the stories in Bible school about Samson and Delilah. Robinson, for his part, had a nickname for his youngest son. From the time Ray II was a child, his father has always called him Trimmer.

"Oh sure, Ray loves to get his hair cut. Loves it," Lockitch had said. "He's still vain that way. He wouldn't dream of going anywhere without going to the barber shop. Whenever he'd go to New York, that's the first thing he'd do." Before he became the fighter's business manager, before he became involved with the foundation, Lockitch was one of the men for whom Robinson was the Sugar. Lockitch became Ray's friend when Ray and Millie moved to Los Angeles, back in '65, right after they were married in Vegas. Lockitch was there when the foundation idea was proposed in 1969, in Millie Robinson's kitchen in the lime-green duplex on the corner of West Adams Boulevard and Tenth Avenue. The house is owned by eighty-seven-year-old Wright Fillmore.

Millie and Ray still live on the second floor, "Uncle" Wright on the first. Fillmore, who was a close friend of Millie's parents, is president of the foundation and has been a benefactor of Ray's since 1965. Over the years, he has been the owner of a lot of property on West Adams Boulevard.

"Ray used to say he knew every man," says Lockitch. "Ask

him if he knew the chairman of the board for Standard Oil and Ray would say, 'Sure.' What Ray meant was that the guy knew *him*. All he had to do was call and say, 'This is Sugar Ray Robinson,' and the guy would know who he was and do whatever he could to help Ray out."

It was men Ray Robinson championed. Women were different, except for his mother, Leila Smith. Women were to be won. They were part of the spoils of war. Even Ray's mother could not completely displace Ray from his male constituency. After young Walker Smith, fighting under the assumed name Ray Robinson, emerged from the anonymity of the underclass in 1939 by boxing like a dream and being nicknamed Sugar because he fought so sweetly, he was visited by his father, Walker Sr., whom the newly minted Sugar Ray Robinson had not seen in eight years. Robinson happily shelled out some bucks to his pop. When Ray later told his mother what had happened, she was indignant. After what Walker Smith had done to her. To them. Said Robinson to his mother, "That's your business."

Still, she was his mother and his biggest fan. "Didn't matter what weight they were, he was the best," says Leila Smith. It is a cold day in January 1987, and she is sitting in the apartment she shares with her daughter, Evelyn Nelson, on University Avenue in the South Bronx. For a woman of eighty-nine years, Leila Smith is full of wit and vitality. Her memory is uncommonly sharp.

"That Maxim fight. That was the one Ray shouldn't have had. The only one," she says.

During his career, Robinson had twenty or more fights like the one Leonard undertook with Hagler. After overwhelming the welterweights of his day, Robinson moved up to middleweight in 1950 and was involved in stirring battles and rivalries with the likes of Jake LaMotta, Randy Turpin, Carmen Basilio, Gene Fullmer, Bob Olson, and Paul Pender. He was not the same fighter at the heavier weight of 160 pounds. He was still a great fighter, but he was not the unbeatable Sugar. This long uncertain demise began on June 25, 1952, when he was thirty-one, when Robinson climbed into a ring that had been set up in Yankee Stadium to fight Joey Maxim for the *light-heavyweight* title.

"It was a hundred and four degrees that night. It was a hundred and thirty degrees ringside, that's what they said. I was there. It felt like it," says Leila Smith. "Whatever you call 'great' nowadays, I guess Ray was that then. I went to his fights. I wasn't superstitious. When Ray sat between rounds that night, I dropped my head. People said, 'Why do you drop your head? You crying?' I was praying."

Robinson wore black that night. His mother wore white. Ray had already won the middleweight title from LaMotta, lost it to Turpin, then regained it from Turpin; then he defended it by decisioning Olson and by knocking out Rocky Graziano with one perfect right in the third round in Chicago. The right was so devastating that Graziano lay stretched out, holding one of the ropes, his right leg twitching. The world seemed to be Ray's oyster, and the Maxim fight would showcase him in his backyard. Robinson was the pride of Harlem, but admiration of his abilities was not restricted to people of his race. Black heavyweight champions like Jack Johnson and Louis had to beat heavy sociological burdens whether they liked it or not. Ray straightened his hair and he was the Sugar to everybody. "Color means nothing to him," Lockitch had said.

It seemed that Ray had many friends when he stepped into the ring to fight Maxim in the sweltering early-summer heat and under a battery of hot lights. "I had won welter and middle, beaten most of the people in my class," Ray said once. "People wanted to see me fight Maxim."

Maxim's given name was Giuseppe Antonio Berardinelli. He was born in Cleveland. He was strong for a six-one 175-pounder, and he was an earnest campaigner. He had fought ninety-nine times before he met Robinson. He had won seventy-eight times, drawn four. He had been knocked out only once and was better than any light heavyweight in the world except Ezzard Charles, to whom he lost five times, and Jersey Joe Walcott, who beat him twice. As a boxer, Maxim was not in Robinson's class, but he was still an excellent fighter—and *two* classes above Ray in natural weight. Maxim was thirty years old and the light-heavy champ almost by default, since Charles and Walcott had moved up to heavyweight to meet their fates at the hands of each other and Rocky Marciano. Maxim himself had fought for the heavyweight title, losing to Charles in 1951. At the end of the tenth round, the referee, on the verge of collapse, had to quit and a substitute took over. "The world swam before my eyes," says Leila Smith. And it swam before Robinson's. He had used his brilliant moves and blinding hand speed to hit Maxim with every punch in his repertoire. In the seventh, he nailed Maxim with the perfect right—similar to the one that had left Graziano twitching. Maxim was turned sideways by the force of the punch but did not go down. The light heavy was too big. Robinson could not hurt him. At the end of the thirteenth, Robinson, well ahead on all cards, was done in by the heat. He staggered across the ring into the arms of his cornermen. He could not answer the bell for the fourteenth round. If the fight had gone twelve rounds, he would've won. Robinson retired that December.

"Ray had promised me back in 1940 that I would never have to work again," says Leila Smith. "And I never had to. My son always took care of me."

Upon retirement, Robinson set out for Europe, ostensibly to begin a second career as a tap-dancing troubadour and to enjoy the spoils of war. He had been married on May 29, 1944, to Edna-Mae Holly, a beautiful show girl who, in 1949, bore him Ray II. Edna-Mae would later have four miscarriages. Robinson was a man of extravagant tastes, appetites, and generosity. He could eat a dozen doughnuts and wash them down with a pitcher of sweet tea. He ordered fuchsia Cadillacs, first-class staterooms, and the finest of champagnes for his valets, golf pros, chauffeurs, secretaries, and, of course, barbers. "He wanted to buy me a Cadillac," says Leila Smith. "But I only saw hard men and rough women in those cars. So he bought me a Buick."

Robinson was back in the ring within two years. "Sure, I could use a buck as well as the next guy," he said. "But this was not the reason. I just had the feeling. I got the urge. People wanted to see me fight."

Robinson's career would continue for another eleven years and twice more he would hold the middleweight title, but he was never again a god. In 1960, in the twilight of his boxing days, he married Millie Bruce and moved to L.A.

"Now, for four or five years, I don't get nothing. I don't hear nothing," says Leila Smith. "And I don't ask why. Ray had been sick only one day in his life. Pneumonia. Maybe food poisoning. It was before a fight. I had to go to Philadelphia because he wouldn't go to the hospital. He called the hospital a good place to die. He didn't ride elevators either. Ray was not a man to be trapped."

Five years before, Robinson had fallen ill but wouldn't allow Millie to hospitalize him. So Millie sent for Leila Smith. Millie had suffered at Ray's hand physically and she had temporarily moved out. Frank Sinatra called Robinson and told him that Millie would come back to the house if Ray agreed to be hospitalized. But it took Ray's mother to finally convince him to put himself in doctors' hands.

"The doctor who examined him at the house said his blood sugar was very high," recalls Mrs. Smith. "He wouldn't go to the hospital for nobody but me. He seemed to be delirious. He got upset whenever she [Millie] came near. It was her. Just her. I could go and talk to him. But her—she had gone away, and Ray was waiting for her on the porch. She said Ray had knocked her down before. I told her,

'You better do something or Ray will hurt you.' Sugar is dangerous, you know. She didn't seem to know what was wrong with him.

"That was the last time I saw him. I used to talk to him on the phone. Sometimes he'd repeat himself. Sometimes he'd say, 'Ma, I didn't mean it.' "

Leila Smith took this to mean Jimmy Doyle. On June 23, 1947, the night before Robinson fought Doyle in Cleveland, Ray dreamed he killed Doyle with a single left hook. The next morning, a shaken Sugar told his manager, George Gainford, and the fight promoters that he couldn't go into the ring against Doyle, but the promoters brought in a Catholic priest and a lay minister and they assured Robinson that his fears were unfounded. The fight must go on. That night, in the eighth round, Sugar hit Doyle with a textbook left hook. Doyle was taken out of the ring on a stretcher. He died the next day without regaining consciousness.

"He meant Doyle. I know my son. But . . . I can't be sure," says Leila Smith. "Ray used to take care of me. I used to know him. To me, Millie is a Johnny-come-lately. I don't know much about this last marriage."

Mildred Bruce, several years Ray's senior, had two sons and a daughter by a previous marriage. Her younger son died at an early age. The other son, Herman, is now called Butch Robinson. He helps run the activities program for the foundation. "She got her son named Robinson," says Leila Smith. "But when little Ray (Ray II) went out there, he was pushed to the back. Just like Leonard. Just took Ray's glory. Millie doesn't care who doesn't like what. She keeps Ray shut away because somebody would see how bad off he is. Evelyn says it's bad. My chances of ever seeing Ray again are poor. If I didn't have Jesus, I would lose my mind. It would hurt me not to be able to even talk to Ray. It brings tears to my eyes just to think about him. I want to do what's right, but what is right, these days?"

Later I talked to Millie. She was upset, which was not

good because she too suffered from hypertension. "So, you went ahead and talked to Ray's mother behind my back," she said.

"No, Mrs. Robinson. Not behind your back. Mrs. Smith is Ray's mother. She was very kind."

"Well, I'm his wife."

Leila Smith had mentioned that she was a little bit tired. On Monday morning, February 9, 1987, just after midnight, she suffered gastric distress. She was quickly hospitalized and underwent emergency surgery for an intestinal blockage. She was not strong enough to survive the trauma. Before morning light, the mother of the greatest boxer pound-for-pound that ever lived died in a small room at Montefiore Medical Center in the Bronx.

"Ray."

"*Nnn?*"

"Do you miss New York?"

". . . Well, sure."

A chill wind whips over the burial grounds of Ferncliff Cemetery in Hartsdale, New York, causing the small gathering of mourners to huddle closer together and pull their winter coats tighter. It is a cold Valentine's Day. Edna-Mae Robinson holds her hand over her mouth and leans toward her son, Ray II, as the minister says simple words over the casket bearing the remains of Leila Smith.

A large wreath of white carnations stands at the head of the open grave. The banner bears script: *Your Son, Sugar Ray.* Blood-red boxing gloves are pinned to the center of the arrangement. Once the minister has finished and the mourners have moved reluctantly away, the gloves are removed by the boldest of the male relatives. Some carnations are plucked as melancholy souvenirs. A letter from Ray to his mother was read at the funeral service. Ray was not present. Millie has to help him when he goes to the bathroom, so a transcontinental trip seemed out of the question.

"Oh, I'm real clear on what kind of person Millie is," says Ray II. "I guess she doesn't want him in these surroundings anymore, or out from under the influence of his medication. My father is virtually in prison, yes, but it's a strange kind of prison. He can be pumped up to go to a party at Frank Sinatra's house, but he can't come to his own mother's funeral." Actually, Ray Robinson had been hospitalized the day before his mother's funeral. He had become agitated and his blood sugar had risen.

Seven years ago Ray II moved to Venice, California, to work for the foundation and spend time with his father. He never got that time—and he never got that job. "My dad had written me an amazing letter. I was thrilled at the chance to get to know him. My father had always been a . . . businessman. His business kept him away. But he wrote and said he wanted me to work with him. When I got there, I was shocked. He weighed two hundred and fifteen pounds. For six and one-half years, I lived not more than twenty minutes from them. I've been in their house no more than ten times— most times uninvited."

"I don't want any problems with Millie," says Edna-Mae. "I don't want anything, really. I used to be the first lady. But she is now. When I found out that Ray was sick, I sent out literature on high blood pressure and diabetes and Alzheimer's, and she became very upset with me."

Sugar Ray remained fit for ten years after he retired in 1965. He worked out nearly every day, either on the road or with the bags. Lockitch tried to introduce him to health clubs, but Robinson went into one, looked around, and said, "This ain't a gym. It's got to look like a gym. It's got to smell like a gym." And so he went off to find a real gym, and he continued working out until 1975, when he finally let it go. But he couldn't let it go. After all, he was still the Sugar. That could never change.

"It hurt me when they started calling this new young man Sugar Ray," says Edna-Mae. "It must have hurt Ray." If it did, he never showed it. Robinson posed for a few photographs with Leonard and never said an unkind word about his fistic namesake and heir.

For a time, Robinson was fanatical about the Dodgers. He became a friend of Dodger manager Tommy Lasorda. All it took was an introduction. One day at Dodger Stadium, Sylvester Stallone showed up. A fan asked to shake his hand. Stallone's bodyguard intervened, saying, "Mr. Stallone doesn't like to be touched." Then Stallone spotted Sugar Ray. His bodyguard asked Robinson if they could meet. Ray sent a message over. "Mr. Robinson doesn't like to be touched." Ray had enjoyed that.

But baseball and simple one-upmanship could not satisfy Robinson's soul. He remained a womanizer until the diabetes, hypertension, and Alzheimer's began to take their toll. Millie was no fool. Neither was Edna-Mae. When Gainford died in 1981, Ray made a trip to New York, unaccompanied by Millie, but with a bodyguard. After the funeral service, Ray met Edna-Mae and suggested they go to his hotel together. "I told him we couldn't do that. He got very upset. I had to tell his bodyguard to please take him away because I didn't want to get hurt." Robinson returned to California and Millie.

"I could never understand Millie's attitude," says Edna-Mae. "At first I thought it was just because she was afraid she might not get power of attorney. But she has that. She's his wife. But Ray is his son. Leila was his mother. They should have been allowed in his life. That letter they read at the funeral—Ray didn't write that. It was signed, but he didn't sign it either. In my seventeen years with him, when I think of all the thousands of pictures that I signed 'Good luck, Sugar Ray'. . . . So I know. That letter wasn't from him. I don't know what Millie is doing. I suppose she's trying to keep alive the myth of Ray's competence."

"Ray."
"*Nnnn.*"

Katy Riney is the program administrator of the Sugar Ray Robinson Youth Foundation. It was Riney who helped bestow the honors on Ray's mother on the day of her funeral, drafting the letter, helping with the sending of the flowers. These were merely two of her many duties as the foundation's most indispensable employee. And if the foundation were Robinson's only legacy, it would be a good legacy, the very best. Since the organization became active in 1969, thousands of inner-city children have had constructive activities to fill their idle weekends—from volleyball and flag football to pageants and talent shows. The foundation sponsors no boxing programs.

On one Saturday morning, a hundred girls are playing volleyball in the gymnasium at Bethune Junior High in south-central Los Angeles. It is some weeks before the Leonard–Hagler fight. Riney referees and takes the girls through their paces, team by team. Outside 150 boys under the supervision of Butch Robinson play flag football. There are six community directors present at Bethune. Most have been with the foundation for ten years or more. One of them is forty-year-old Reniell Beard.

"I've got all Ray's fights on tape," says Beard. "I had four older brothers. Ray was like a god to them. They stopped me from watching *Amos 'n' Andy* and made me watch Sugar Ray's fights. I guess that's why I do this. It's like repaying a debt. It's nice to do something for the kids, although most of them have no idea who Sugar Ray Robinson is." One look at the kids at play, keeping amused and interested amid some of the most depressing urban blight to be found in America—in south-central Los Angeles some apartment houses have their street numbers painted on the roofs, the better for police helicopter pilots to identify the buildings—is enough to create genuine admiration for this tangible part of Robinson's legacy.

Michael Dear, thirteen, has been involved with various foundation programs for one year. I ask him if he knows Sugar Ray Robinson. "Yeah," he says. "He's fightin' in April." No, that's Sugar Ray *Leonard*. Sugar Ray *Robinson*.

"They're not the same guy?"

Jattea Johnson, sixteen, has been in the program for four years and is now in high school. She still comes by on weekends. It is a good habit she doesn't want to break. "I know Sugar Ray Robinson is an ex-boxer," she says. "All I know is that one Sugar Ray is older than the other one."

"That's okay," says Beard. "And as far as the fight goes, the referee will call it before nine. Leonard is in there with a warmonger."

The Sugar Ray Robinson Youth Foundation must pass the scrutiny of the California state legislature every year and satisfy the state auditors. It won its funding in the first place because former governor Edmund (Pat) Brown was a great fan of Ray Robinson. "Dollar for dollar, we're the best bargain they have," Lockitch says.

The foundation receives approximately $488,000 a year from the state and $50,000 from Los Angeles County, and this year it got $71,000 from the Olympic Games surplus funds. Some of the money goes for the buses that transport the children to the activities and pageants. Robinson, as the titular head of the foundation, receives a salary of $37,000. Riney points out that Ray and Millie can use that stipend, but they are not hurting that badly. There's a lot of property on West Adams Boulevard owned by Wright Fillmore, who isn't getting any younger. And he and Millie Robinson have always been very close indeed.

So money is why Millie asked, "How much?" Not that she is to be blamed—no more than Robinson was to be blamed for being paid to fight. You use what you have. Butch received money from a gossip tabloid for "revealing" that Ray had Alzheimer's. Evelyn Nelson's son, Kenneth, asked Millie for permission to use Sugar Ray's name for an Urban Coalition fundraiser, in conjunction with a showing of the Leonard–Hagler fight at the Apollo Theater in Harlem. Millie said yes, then changed her mind and informed the Urban Coalition that she was withdrawing her permission. It was decided that the event would have to be canceled. Millie's position was that she didn't want to intrude on Leonard's night, Leonard's glory.

When Robinson became ill after his mother's death, he was admitted to the Cedars-Sinai Medical Center in Los Angeles. He remained hospitalized for a week. A few days after he was released, Robinson sat in their yellow Cadillac while Millie went into the foundation offices. Ray no longer wore the vacant smile. I came over and spoke to him. "Ray, *how* can Ray beat Marvin Hagler?" He didn't respond.

"I don't expect the fight to last long," Ray II had said. "My father did it, but he always had tune-up fights. And he's my father. There was no one else like him. He was Sugar Ray."

But Leonard did win. He defeated Hagler, in twelve artful rounds. Leonard is the Sugar now.

Leonard is not to be asked why he fought Hagler. "Why?" is a nervy question to ask a prizefighter. As Robinson often said, "Because it's what people want to see." Leonard fights for us as much as he fights for himself. Like Robinson, like a lot of other people, he can't separate who he is from what he does best. What Robinson did best was fight. Like Leonard,

225

he was not to be asked why. He did indeed leave all the answers in the ring. Ray II had one thing exactly right. While his father may no longer be *the* Sugar, there was—and is— no one else like him. He was pound for pound the greatest fighter ever to step into the ring. The Ultimate Warrior. Even he wound up a victim of the spoils of war.

Epilogue

Boxing is an art of self-defense. In order to refine and exhibit this art, one must fend off attack. The more powerful the attack, the more resourceful the boxer must be to overcome it. Often the best defense is a good offense. At times, in fact quite frequently, the attack is so relentless that a boxer is knocked down, out, or dead.

Over a twenty-year span, the body and head of Muhammad Ali were laid siege to by such plunderers as Sonny Liston, George Foreman, Ken Norton, Earnie Shavers, and the remorseless Joe Frazier. Ali spent some 102 three-minute rounds, some five solid hours, fending off these men, buffeted by what amounted to a seventy-three-inch fist.

After seeing Ali endure this and much more, did we really need an anonymous British neurologist to tell us that the champion has suffered brain damage?

This is better than *The Emperor's New Clothes*.

Damage, specifically brain damage, is what boxing is all about. Boxing is assault and battery with deadly weapons called the fists of man. Ali's brain could not possibly be the same as before he entered the ring, and Ali was a pitcher.

Think of the catchers, the guys who took three to give one, the crowd pleasers, the club fighters, the meat, the stiff, the tomato cans, the ham-and-eggers. Boxing is full of brain damage. Ali seemed untouchable. But he has urinated blood after a fight, had his jaw broken, felt his face tighten as it swelled to twice normal size, been knocked on his can, battered his hands beyond repair, and suffered several concussions. After fighting Frazier for fourteen rounds in Manila in 1975, he said, "It's the closest thing to death that I know of." Maybe people have deluded themselves. Maybe they think boxers beat each other for fifteen rounds and come out ready for a set of doubles or a movie premiere.

Have you ever wondered at the miracle of a cauliflower ear or a nose warped in three directions? Do you know what a smashed Adam's apple feels like? How long it takes for a shattered cheekbone to heal? Do you know what it's like not being able to wait for that cheek to heal properly before getting in the ring again? How it feels to have a ruptured sinus cavity drain into that cheek? Think this is some kind of game? Ever hear of Frankie Campbell, Jimmy Doyle, Benny Paret, Cleveland Denny, Willie Classen, or Duk Koo Kim?

What would you think if you couldn't get out of bed in the morning because of a traumatized liver? Can you imagine having your jaw broken and not going immediately to the hospital, but instead fighting for ten more rounds? Can you imagine hearing the man in front of you being exhorted to blast you on that jaw? Can you imagine not being able to reason with him, other than with your fists? Can you imagine thousands of your fellow humans screaming for your blood? Can you imagine the look on your mother's face while all this is happening? Brain damage, indeed.

Muhammad Ali's mother could tell you he's not the same man without consulting Great Britain about it. So could his longtime camp followers, only they might not admit it, even to themselves, because they'd rather see him as he was than as he is. This is no indictment of the system, the participants, or the viewers. This is just an expression of amazement at the world's naive and detached view of a prizefighter's eventual lot. If you fight for twenty years, you're lucky if all you end up with is slurred consonants and a memory that blinks. Yes, Muhammad Ali has suffered brain damage. But not 1 percent of the brain damage he has dished out. You see, none of them ever really wins.

The last time I saw Muhammad Ali was in the spring of 1987, after I left Ray Robinson for the last time. He was in the United Airlines terminal at the Los Angeles International Airport, sitting on a long seat of plastic cushions, near the windows, in the sun. He was alone and not sad about it. I did a double take. I had never seen him alone before. His traveling companions had probably gone to make sure of some arrangements. Ali sat there in dark glasses, unbothered, looking straight ahead. Serene.

I made his acquaintance again.

"Hello, Champ. You're looking good."

He smiled and said, "Thankyou, thankyou," and offered his right for an even handshake. I bent over to accept, moved as ever. As we shook, the jacket I was carrying slipped off my shoulder.

"Whoops"—But I hardly had time to get it out of my mouth. Quicker than I can describe it, Ali's right released my hand and caught the jacket well before it reached my waist. He even smoothed it out for me. Reflexes. "Thanks, Champ."

Ali is an immense man, and nothing is more imposing than that great, handsome lion's head. I thought about the news of the day and the day before. Ali going to the other board members at K mart, wanting answers because the store wouldn't stock his shoe polish. Kinshasa. The Ali car. I'd never seen one. Manila. And, soon, the brain surgery Ali would consider, and later, other treatments. One doctor thought it might be exposure to pesticides that left Ali's tongue less supple, his brain less sharp. *"I shook up the world!"* The Parkinson's disease. *"I am the greatest!"* The numbing. *"I'm a baad man!"* He was only forty-five. He was not old enough to be my father.

I stood there next to him, saying nothing. I thought about asking him if Sugar Ray Leonard could beat Marvin Hagler. But then I knew what he would say to that. *Ali KOs Liston. Ali KOs Foreman. . . . Float like a butterfly, sting like a bee. . . . Rumble, young man, rumble. . . .* I knew. So I held myself back. We had nothing but time. I told him, "You're one of the five greatest men to draw breath in my lifetime." He didn't say anything to that. He merely kept on smiling. So I smiled back and gained strength from the peaceful moment. Then I went on about my business.